Mr Unavailable and the Fallback Girl

This book is for my girls.

Naughty Girl Media

First published in 2008 as an ebook. This 2011 version is the first print edition but it's a completely updated and reworked book.

Natalie Lue asserts the moral right to be identified as the author of this work.

Book design by Lula Creative

www.lulacreative.co.uk

Copyright © Natalie Lue

Contents

MY STORY

Once upon a time, I was an eight-year-old girl living next door to a hot boy who was two years older. I wistfully watched him over the wall each day and hoped that he'd fancy me back one day. He wasn't interested in me, but that didn't stop his smiles or our conversations from lighting up my world. Fast forward a few years, and I was 13, at summer camp and blindly in love with an aloof, miserable-looking character called David. I actually don't recall if we ever had a conversation and I have no idea *what* I was interested in. Camp finished after two weeks but my feelings stretched out for a year.

Fortunately, I learned not to go for the miserable, self-absorbed, barely-say-a-word ones any more, but my interests turned to boys, and then men, who would pursue me relentlessly, then toy with my emotions until I didn't know my arse from my elbow. I had a string of relationships lasting from months to years, so I assumed that I loved being in relationships – it was just a shame that they were never with the right guy! My love life, and my penchant for show-stopping breakups, men that blew hot and cold, and the shift in my persona that I felt around these life-sappers became entertainment fodder for my friends and family, and eventually for my blog readers. As far as I was concerned, the issue wasn't with me and I was just damn unlucky in love.

Even when I was struck down with the autoimmune disease sarcoidosis in the year that I both got engaged and broke it off, I couldn't connect with the notion that I might have needed to look within myself for the answers. I left him because our relationship was a catastrophic mistake and I wanted to be true to myself and live life on my own terms, but, a couple of months later, I took up the starring role of the Other Woman to a guy with a girlfriend. I thought I was a smart, sophisticated, single woman-about-town who was in control of this no-frills arrangement, but I rapidly slid into *When Exactly Do You Intend On Leaving Her?*

1

mode, and even issued a few ultimatums where the deadline passed and I was still there.

During this period, my health seriously deteriorated. As I struggled with my vision, being able to breathe, move around, and the lumps that riddled my body, I wondered if I'd ever lead a normal, healthy, happy life, but seemed to be stuck in a vicious cycle of pain and a dangerous, co-dependent relationship. When my mother said, *"You need to love yourself and reconnect with your spirit,"* I felt offended that she would suggest that what was happening to me had anything to do with a lack of self-love.

It took 18 months of drama and broken promises before I managed to extricate myself from the affair. There were so many times that I should have walked, but none more so than after a terrible panic attack. He'd been whining about other men being interested in me and pressuring me about our 'situation', and suddenly I couldn't breathe and was sitting in a doorway in the middle of London trying to pull myself together. It was one of the most devastating things that ever happened to me and his way to deal with it was to escort me to the Tube, and go home to his girlfriend as he was too afraid to make sure I got home in one piece.

Afterwards, shell-shocked, my worth hit an all-time low. My primary thought was, *"I am such an unlovable person that he put me on a packed Tube on a Friday night in the midst of a panic attack. If I were a lovable person, he would never have treated me that way."* It took three weeks to recover and I realised that I had to find a way for things to end, because I didn't think I could *bear* a repeat. He apologised profusely and made every excuse under the sun, but the damage was irreparable. It was hard to let go but what kept me focused was putting myself first. He put himself first and then his girlfriend and if I couldn't prioritise myself, who would?

Like an apparent breath of fresh air, another Mr Unavailable entered into my life a short while later. He seemed so nice and normal, and he chased me until he had my full attention. He'd broken up with a long-term girlfriend a few months before and still shared a home with her. Because *he'd* pursued, I assumed that not only was he interested, but that he must be ready to move on. After five months, in which the relationship barely got out of the gate, he finally admitted that he wasn't ready for another relationship.

The frustrations I experienced with him, and what I wrote about on my blog after ending it, were the beginning of a self-defining, life-changing period in my life. While I'd learned some painful lessons, I recognised that I'd have to go through some self-discovery to extricate myself from this unhealthy pattern. Waking up at the age of twenty-eight and acknowledging that I seemed to have a penchant for emotionally unavailable men (Mr Unavailables) was terrifying.

Confronted with the truth of my relationship history, I had to accept that I'm the only recurring character in the soap opera called my life.

I am, of course, the common denominator in every single relationship I've ever had and, if I've found myself in a pattern, I created it. I'd spent years chalking up my experiences and patterns to bad luck and laughing it off, either for my own sanity or for the benefit of others, but, with the past ten years playing out in my head and my health in tatters, it was time to stop using humour as an avoidance prop and get serious.

When I began writing about Mr Unavailables and sharing my insights with readers around the world, I was basically thinking out loud and organising my thoughts and past experiences to do some self-evaluation. Initially, I genuinely thought it was just me, but as soon as I declared my penchant for Mr Unavailables, I heard from many others who seemed to be living my life. At the outset, I thought recognising it was enough, but I went on to date two more Mr Unavailables (albeit briefly) and attracted plenty more. It became clear that my relationships up to this point were about avoiding commitment and intimacy, only I was discovering that pseudo-relationships were no longer enough, because my self-worth was improving.

When I admitted that being involved with these men meant that I couldn't possibly have been that happy within myself, others joined me in liberating themselves from the pretence. There was an undeniable sense of relief. I realised that many women numb themselves to the pain of what's happening in their lives because they don't think they're supposed to admit how difficult it is to balance your self-esteem with your quest for a relationship and all of the attendant external pressures. I'd buried so much of what was bothering me that it seemed to have manifested itself by throwing out my mystery illness.

3

I used to wonder why I was the girl that these guys thought would be ideal for a pseudo-relationship.

Why did they think they could disappear and then call me up and just expect to pick up from where we left off? What happened to all the promise I saw at the beginning? Why did I always seem to draw in men with girlfriends, wives, or an ever-present mother in the background with long apron strings attached? Why did I keep apologising for being me? Why did I always have to change myself in order for things to 'work'? There were so many questions.

Literally at the same time that I experienced my epiphanies about my relationships with Mr Unavailables, my illness returned full force. Terrified of the prospect of a life on steroids, I started kinesiology, a type of complementary therapy that works with your muscles and the Meridian System, used in acupuncture, to redress imbalances and underlying causes of health issues that may be linked to allergies, emotional or physical issues, etc., and found myself inadvertently having to confront many things that I'd buried. I was being tested for food allergies, but found myself discovering a lot of unresolved hurt eating away at me.

My health dramatically improved and a sense of inner peace that I'd never felt before began to descend on me. Sometimes I wept with grief over the emotions and memories that I pulled out and inspected, but as I laid things to rest and began to understand my own contribution towards my relationships, I felt a sense of relief, because I no longer felt that my future and the possibility of happiness in a relationship was going to be down to 'luck'. I had to make my own.

Around the time that I dated the last Mr Unavailable, I started acupuncture and the recovery process from my illness sped up, and so did my self-esteem. When I told him to beat it, I did so because I acknowledged that when a woman feels happier about herself and her life *without* the man in her life, there doesn't seem to be any point in being with him. I accepted that I might be single for a long time now that Mr Unavailables were no longer attractive, but less than a week later I met the most wonderful man and I didn't chase him away because he was nice or tar him with the ex brush. If we'd become involved any sooner than we did, it's unlikely that I'd have appreciated him or not created a boatload of drama. As it is, we're still together now and we have two daughters.

I'm in no way suggesting that my 'ending' is your ending. In fact, it's not even an ending, but more a 'new beginning'. It takes willpower, courage, and consistently doing things differently to change this destructive pattern. You need to believe in yourself more than you believe in them.

YOU'RE NOT ALONE

Every single day, through my website, Baggage Reclaim (www.baggagereclaim.com), I come across thousands of women (and men) who are 'stuck' in an unavailable relationship. Some of them know they're involved with someone who's emotionally, physically and spiritually unavailable, making their partners limited in their capacity to have a relationship and commit, never mind love. For many others, they have *no* clue what they are involved in. They think that their situation is 'unique', that they said or did something to provoke their partner into 'changing', that they can do something to change their partner via fixing, healing and helping them or changing themselves, or even that they're losing their minds. They think that they've misunderstood something or their eyes are deceiving them. Often, they think that they know better.

When people discover my site it's often because they went in search of information to help diagnose their 'problem' and discover a solution. When they embark on the search, while they may be looking for some support, they're also hoping that the solution will ideally involve 1) a magic move or strategy that will help them 'win' over the object of their affections, 2) tactics for helping 'fix' their partners into a committed relationship, or 3) confirmation that the problem is all the fault of the other party. Generally, they're hoping that the solution doesn't involve admitting that they're in a relationship that cannot work and that is highly likely to involve them opting out.

They're often shocked when they discover that their story has been told many times over, often with some readers asking, "Are you sure you're not going out with *my* guy?". You could be fooled into believing that these men have all been reading the same playbook and learning the same moves, because they all follow a well-honed pattern of behaviour. Hell, you'd almost think they were all part of a secret society, following some unspoken code between unavailable men, because you can take one woman out of her story and put you into it to make yours. All this time, you've been thinking that your situation is unique or that they're 'unpredictable' and it turns out that most of the stuff these guys do is about as predictable as the surety that the sun is going to come up tomorrow.

Following my epiphany in the summer of 2005, I've been documenting my experiences and observations about dating, relationships, and self-esteem on Baggage Reclaim. Recognising that I'd been OK with substandard relationships, the question **"Why do I want someone who doesn't want me or only wants to be with me in a limited capacity?"** needed to be answered.

Mr Unavailable and the Fallback Girl not only tells you how to spot the signs and recognise an unavailable relationship, but also explains why they don't work, why you wanted to be in this relationship in the first place, and how to cut the ties, move on, and start building your self-esteem. It's very easy to focus on his problems, his excuses, his actions, his everything, but, ultimately, when you start to understand why some relationships don't work, you can take the focus off him and bring it back to you and recognise that these relationships are symbolic of the fact that you need to treat yourself better and have some boundaries in your life.

It's very easy to be hijacked by your imagination and need for validation when you don't believe you're good enough, when you actually know no better because unavailability is what you've been around all your life, and when you truly do believe that *this* man – emotionally unavailable with a limited, if not outright defunct, capacity for a mutually fulfilling healthy relationship – is the key to your happiness. Learning about the common types of relationship behaviours these men exhibit means you can stop making problems that existed long before you came along your responsibility.

It's not about you.

While you will learn that there are behaviours and thinking on your part that are helping you to slot in with his behaviours, ultimately creating an unhealthy dynamic, it's important to realise you're enabling already existing behaviour, not *making* an unavailable man. When you stop seeing Mr Unavailables through a lens that says their behaviours are directly linked to your worth as a person, you start to see in them an independent, individual entity that more often than not has form for this behaviour, often with a track record that would have you falling off your seat in shock. Even when their unavailability comes down to the fact that they're still getting over a previous relationship, in *Mr Unavailable and the Fallback Girl,* you will also learn that it's not your *job* to run around catching men as they fall out of their relationships. Nor is it your job to let them default to or 'fall back' on you repeatedly, let them enjoy the fringe benefits without the commitment, or to let them keep you as an option in their back pocket.

While I've educated many thousands of people on the perils of unavailable relationships and helped them to see what healthy, committed relationships look like, this is also a journey in recognising that if you can't date with your self-esteem in tow, you need to *stop* dating until you *can*. *Mr Unavailable and the Fallback Girl* will help you to stop being a passenger in shady, depleting relationships and to stop treating these broken men like they're messiahs, while you're someone who has to clamour around them for crumbs of attention, affection, and hints of commitment. These crumbs don't become loaves and will leave you hungry for a real relationship. I want you to read this book and recognise that you need the loaf, the whole loaf, and nothing but the loaf.

UNDERSTANDING UNAVAILABLE RELATIONSHIPS

It's not unusual to assume that when we're involved with someone who wants attention, sex, a shoulder to lean on, an ego stroke, money and any other fringe benefits we can enjoy in a relationship, that they're actually available and want a relationship. After all, surely if they're not available and aren't 'around', they'll either use us for a shag and then disappear, or straight up say that they're not interested, right? We'd like to think that they'd be honest and let us make up our own minds about whether we want to be involved and they certainly wouldn't keep coming back, hanging around, overpromising and underdelivering.

We think that 'unavailable' means not available at all and that it removes them from the dating equation. We don't think of unavailable as 'limited availability'. They'll treat us 'badly' and it'll be obvious that it's a 'bad' relationship; after all, we all know what a 'bad', or even not-so-good, relationship looks like, don't we, and surely we'd walk away?

We imagine that if *we* weren't ready for a relationship or only half interested in someone, that we'd simply opt out or be upfront...which actually isn't as true as we think, but we'll come back to that later.

Surely someone who isn't available won't take such a keen interest in your life, cry when you tell them to beat it, give you amazing sex, share many of your interests, and seem so right on? Wrong. We'd also like to think that there's no way in hell that they'd cheat on their wives or girlfriends and refuse to get lost if they weren't serious about being with us one day.

And if someone knows they're not over their ex or not ready for a relationship, we're sure they won't go through the rigamarole of starting something new and messing with our emotions, after all *we* wouldn't, would we? What about when we've been together for a gazillion years and stuck with them through thick and thin and we've given them more time because they insist that it *is* us that they want to be with and ultimately want to settle down and marry? We can't believe that they've overestimated their level of interest and capacity to commit! It's scary that they may actually be afraid of letting us go for fear of changing their mind, getting it wrong, or not having us as an option.

We keep asking ourselves "Why are we still here?" and that's simple: because it's 'love'. Surely we wouldn't be with unavailable men because we're unavailable ourselves? Welcome to the world of unavailable relationships.

Meet **Mr Unavailable**, the emotionally, physically, and spiritually unavailable man who enjoys the fringe benefits of a relationship such as a shag, an ego stroke or a shoulder to lean on, without truly committing to you. You know him well: ambiguous, tricky to read, blows hot and cold, backs off when you come too close, chases you when you cut him off, has a list of excuses as long as his arm, and his actions rarely match his words. He's probably the most popular man to date as he tends to straddle the fence between 'nice guy' and 'bad boy'. Only doing things on his terms, he's mastered the art of getting all the trappings of a relationship, often by creating the illusion of a promised loaf and chucking you crumbs of attention and affection instead. Put on a pedestal by every woman he becomes involved with, he throws out *just* enough promise to have you betting on potential but he perpetually disappoints. He's the man who doesn't commit – to you, to action, to his emotions – and, as a result, he's a limited man, with a limited capacity for commitment, creating limited relationships.

Emotionally unavailable means not fully emotionally present. It's struggling or being unable to access emotions healthily and, as a result, being emotionally distant due to 'walls', which basically act as barriers to true emotional intimacy. Fully experiencing all feelings, whether good, bad, or indifferent, is avoided because they create vulnerability, so feelings are experienced often for a limited time and in bursts, as opposed to consistently feeling on an ongoing basis. Emotional unavailability equates to intimacy issues, which is being afraid of the consequences of getting so emotionally close to someone that to lose them would hurt.

The vulnerabilities are protected by keeping at a distance and/or being involved with similar people so that the risk is minimised. Via this safeguarding, being stretched emotionally or being available is avoided, and even when hurt or 'failure' at a relationship is experienced, it's not '*hurt* hurt' or '*failure* failure' because, on a deeper level, there is recognition that this wasn't going to work anyway and the emotional distance ensures the unavailable person was never truly in it. Being emotionally unavailable has a knock-on effect, so he ends up being physically unavailable as well by doing stuff like disappearing, flaking out, not following through on promised action, or even avoiding sex.

Mr Unavailable's inadvertently complicit partner is you, the **Fallback Girl**, the woman he habitually defaults to or 'falls back' on to have his needs met, while selling you short in the process. Accommodating his idiosyncrasies and fickle whims, you're ripe for a relationship with him, because you are unavailable yourself (although you may not know it) and are slipping your own commitment issues in through the back door behind his. You get blinded by chemistry, sex, common interests and the promise of what he *could* be, if only he changed or you turned into The Perfect Woman. Too understanding and making far too many excuses for him, you have some habits and beliefs that are standing in the way of you having a mutually fulfilling healthy relationship... with an available man. Pursuing or having relationships with Mr Unavailable is symbolic of your need to learn to love yourself more and to set some boundaries and have better standards.

While unavailable is always unavailable, there are two types of unavailability that help to pinpoint the length and breadth of the problem because it's either linked to a specific, recent experience or is indicative of a well-honed pattern.

Temporary unavailability affects even the most emotionally healthy, because when something traumatic happens, such as a breakup, a physically and/or psychologically devastating experience, or we lose a loved one to death, we close up as a natural defence mechanism, because we're afraid of being vulnerable and trusting. If we're typically emotionally available and we support ourselves through whatever has happened, invariably we will *go back* to being available. We live to love and trust again. To be considered 'temporary' the period of emotional unavailability should not last more than two years and typically should involve only 1-2 relationships, or a number of flings. The marker of someone who's been temporarily unavailable but has become available again: they will declare themselves ready to be in a relationship, mean it, and become involved with an available party, plus they don't tend to internalise other people's actions.

Habitual unavailability means this is either the emotional style learned since childhood or, following a painful experience, how we felt about ourselves and relationships changed and being temporarily unavailable has become a *habit*. It's second nature and has a devastating domino effect on interpersonal relationships.

Unavailable, whether it's temporary or habitual, means unavailable for a healthy, mutually fulfilling relationship. Unless you were already involved with them in an emotionally available capacity within a healthy relationship, you as the 'new' person or the one looking to have your needs met or share a relationship, are wasting your time trying to get them to feel more than they're capable of or *want* to at this time. The more you push, whether it's directly or indirectly in more subtle ways, the further they'll retreat. Someone who's temporarily unavailable is far more likely to be upfront about it or bow out when it becomes apparent that they're in over their heads and *stick* to it, whereas if they're habitually unavailable, they've danced this many times before and may not even see anything wrong with their behaviour. Unavailable in simple terms means:

Not ready for a relationship. "I can't give you what you want."

Not over an ex or their past.

Still grieving.

Half-heartedly/not interested but willing to pass time.

"It's me, not you."

Empathy issues and avoiding feelings.

Struggles to be truly honest due to lack of emotionally honesty.

12 SUREFIRE SIGNS THAT YOU'RE A FALLBACK GIRL

The more tumultuous and **dramatic** the relationship, the more likely you are to be in it.

The relationship must offer **little or no hope of commitment**.

The more **baggage** he has, the better. This means that if he comes with a wife, children, an ex-girlfriend, current girlfriend, or multiple partners, the more attractive he is to you.

The more **ambiguous** things are, the better. You don't like asking awkward questions that might give you an answer that you don't want to hear and cause you to have to take action.

There are lots of **'loose' ends** in your love life. Your exes have a habit of popping in and out, and you down tools each time and take them back, only for them to be unavailable again.

You've had **difficult relationships in childhood** or with family and friends.

You have **difficulty getting over past relationships**. In fact, you struggle to deal with rejection.

It might not be what you intended, but you often find yourself **keeping it casual** with one-night stands, flings, booty calls, and Friends With Benefits. Unfortunately, you don't like what comes with the territory: being treated and regarded *casually*.

You have **low self-esteem** and you fear rejection, abandonment, being alone, and being single, and may believe that there are things about you that are unlovable. You often believe that things would be different if you weren't so 'needy'.

You may think that relationships 'suck'. Dating and the attendant emotional woes that come with it have made you **jaded and apathetic**. You're cynical and disparaging of those who are in relationships or trying to be. You've stopped trusting how you feel and you don't trust what men say, feel, or do either.

You and **boundaries** seem to be mutually exclusive. You either don't have any or pay lip service to them, and, as a result, you put up with shady stuff and you don't know your limits, so you stay in relationships long past their sell-by dates.

You get **obsessed with change** – you keep adapting yourself or trying to get him to change. In fact, you like pursuing love against the odds and attempting to get them to make you the exception to their rule of being unavailable or just their plain 'ole selves.

THE UNAVAILABLE MIX

There's a distinct possibility that before you picked up this book, you believed that you're emotionally *available* and that it's him that has the problems with unavailability. However if you have hung around and put up with all sorts of carry-on, you need to address your own availability because, if you were truly available, a relationship with an unavailable man that detracts from you *wouldn't* be attractive and you'd have 'folded' ages ago. You wouldn't participate in the emotional dishonesty and avoidance, because it would be in conflict with you being emotionally available and emotionally honest.

Unavailable relationships arise when you have two people with emotional unavailability issues. It could be two temporary, two habitual, or one of each, but, either way, it adds up to an unavailable relationship. There's always one, more powerful party who dictates the relationship on their terms – *the driver* – and the other party who goes along with it – *the passenger*. The combination of Mr Unavailable and the Fallback Girl is what happens when you hide your often unknown unavailability issues behind his somewhat more obvious ones. You are allowing him to take you on a messy journey through an unavailable relationship.

The premise of a Mr Unavailable and the Fallback Girl relationship is actually quite simple. While we may not realise it, we all choose or align ourselves with people who reflect our beliefs. When they're unhealthy, whether it's because they're negative and/or unrealistic, unavailable relationships are created.

Beliefs are premises that we hold to be true and what we believe is often unconsciously reflected in our actions.

If we didn't do things in line with what we believe, we'd have to adapt our beliefs – for an unavailable person, this is avoided at all costs, for fear of being vulnerable, moving out of their comfort zone and, more importantly, having to *take action*. Each party ends up creating their own self-fulfilling prophecy, which is why, if you've had more than one of these relationships, it feels like you're on a very annoying merry-go-round.

If you've got a 'type' that's yet to yield you a happy, successful relationship or have found yourself in a string of familiar situations that have you feeling bad about yourself, you're engaging in **Relationship Insanity**: carrying the same beliefs, baggage and behaviours; choosing the same or similar guys; and then expecting different results.

Those choices that you're making are working in tandem with your conscious and unconscious beliefs to create a self-fulfilling prophecy that then reinforces those beliefs. What you will learn in *Mr Unavailable and the Fallback Girl* is that what you believe about love, relationships or yourself is not necessarily true in the wider sense, but it *is* true in the context of your beliefs and engaging with Mr Unavailable.

A different set of beliefs, as reflected in your actions, along with changed habits, would create a whole other truth.

Being unavailable affects your ability to connect effectively and healthily with yourself and others. Combined with your background beliefs, it manifests itself in a variety of habits that perpetuate the unavailability by creating situations that allow you to remain unavailable. As a result, when you have these issues it means you automatically have *commitment* issues.

RESISTING COMMITMENT = UNAVAILABLE

Healthy relationships have co-pilots: two people committed to sharing a mutually fulfilling relationship journey. Unhealthy, unavailable relationships generally have a driver and a passenger. Even in very co-dependent, messy, unavailable relationships with what looks like two passengers dragging one another down, you'll still find that one person is, in fact, driving. As the passenger in this partnering, you may have hopped in for the ride and *assumed* you were headed in the same direction, then suddenly realised that his agenda was very different from yours. Or you *knew* what his agenda was (or very quickly found out), and had your own hidden agenda where you sought to change his mind 'en route'.

This is why so many Fallback Girls try to 'win' their guy by attempting to love, adapt, morph, shift, fix, heal and help their way to the relationship they want.

Even when you don't recognise that there are unavailability issues in your relationship, the white elephant in the room is commitment issues because they're intrinsically linked.

Commitment resistance is actively, or in subtle, passive-aggressive ways, resisting being absolute in binding yourself to another person. It's a fear of dealing with the vulnerability that comes with being responsible and accountable for one's self and others, and it triggers resistance through literally avoiding commitment, or sabotaging and stalling the processes that bring it about. Also commonly referred to as commitment-phobia, there are disproportionate fears and beliefs that prevent being able to *fully* commit. Emotional unavailability and commitment are intrinsically linked because if you can't even commit to feeling out feelings, there certainly won't be a commitment to a relationship or definite outcomes. Whether it means putting both feet into the relationship, or opting out and *staying* out, the perpetual indecision and fear means living in limbo in an uncomfortable 'comfort' zone.

The easiest way to avoid commitment is to take refuge in a relationship where commitment is difficult because one's partner shows or verbally communicates that they themselves don't want to put both of their feet in and commit. When faced with the decision of opting out, commitment-resisters flip-flap in indecision, or keep going back to the relationship after it's ended. Failing that, the dominant party in the relationship can always blow hot and cold and pull a variety of manoeuvres to ensure that the show never really gets off the ground. Yep, that's what a very typical relationship between Mr Unavailable and the Fallback Girl can look like.

Now I can imagine that at this point, you might be thinking "Er, what the hell are you talking about?" You might be thinking that *you* don't have commitment issues and that, in fact, you *love* commitment. You probably think you've been working hard at your relationship and that it's a measure of your commitment that you've persisted with Mr Unavailable or even several Mr Unavailables. You actually might think that what stands between you and a committed relationship with him, *is* him. The truth is this:

You want to commit to those who don't want to commit and who actively resist commitment.

This isn't the same as commitment. Much like the Mr Unavailable who told his ex-wife on her deathbed that he loved her and wanted to marry her, knowing that she was going to die the following day (true story by the way), deciding to commit when you know that commitment is unlikely, and they have shown or even said that they're not the committing sort, *isn't* commitment. The same goes for working at your relationship. I don't deny that you've put in effort, but of course it's going to feel like hard work – you're working at a limited relationship with a limited man.

If you keep putting your bucket down an empty well then yes it *is* going to feel like very hard work, but it's highly unproductive and not *real* work.

Often we don't recognise that we resist or have a phobia of commitment because, unlike other phobias, such as a fear of spiders, water, lack of space, people, or buttons, there are no clear, obvious signs of distress. When confronted with a man or the possibility of a relationship you aren't necessarily going to have an overt reaction and freak out, break out in a sweat, panic attack, or run for the hills. You're also having relationships whereas you'd obviously avoid, for example, spider situations.

Instead, commitment resisters tend to engage in subtle and not-so-subtle, conscious and unconscious actions that sabotage opportunities, relationships, and situations that may place them in the zone of having to realise their fear of committing. Often, these actions are in direct conflict with aspirations and desires that are verbally expressed, or desired, but, as with everything, actions do speak louder than words.

Classic examples of commitment resistance are pushing for a 'title' or for the relationship you want from someone, then when they say they'll give it to you, panicking. Or agreeing to do something or be somewhere, then privately looking for ways to get out of it. It's always finding reasons for dates to never go beyond a certain stage, being unable to make decisions, never mind stick to them, even about everyday things, feeling panicky when things are going well or there's no drama, then creating drama, and repeatedly going back to a toxic relationship because you're afraid of finality.

When you're the Fallback Girl, you don't see yourself as being commitment resistant because you are inclined to look for more obvious signs of resistance, plus you think 'saying' you want a relationship or trying to make one work *is* commitment. You're also OK with partial, *limited* commitment, which is why you're OK with him – it's only going to go so far.

Many commitment resisters are the last of the great pretenders, talking a very good game, making all the right noises and apparently leading lives that appear to directly contradict commitment resistance. They are kings and queens of the quiet, hidden agenda. It's not the domain of resolutely single people though; commitment resisters are dating, in relationships, engaged, married, and in-between, and seemingly seeking someone. Commitment resistance doesn't affect one type of person or situation. It can affect anyone and varies to lesser or greater extents. Most commitment resistance can be overcome... but only if the person truly wants to, and is prepared to, address the issues that create it.

I'm not one for advocating the single, attached, or married life, but I very much advocate that whatever choice you make, you make it from a positive place. Instead, I'm constantly finding that people are choosing their relationship status based on fear, insecurity and beliefs they have about that status in the context of their lives. Being single because you fear opening up to someone or relinquishing your 'freedom' is just as bad as being attached because you're afraid to be alone, or married to any old Joe because you believe marriage, *any* marriage, is better than being perceived as some sort of failure.

A relationship status is just that, a 'status', yet people do define and measure their quality of life against it.

This means that fear of commitment can permeate very negatively into every area of your life. This is why there are so many unavailable relationships because not having to commit is so much easier. What we are prepared to put up with and give in our relationships, even when there is no commitment or barely even a relationship, has increased greatly, too. You will find that the great majority of unavailable people don't take enough time between relationships to address their feelings and grieve the loss. Instead, they seek to find someone new to distract them from these feelings. You should know – this is how many a Fallback Girl finds herself in some ambiguous setup with someone who later says, *"I'm not ready for a relationship"* or *"You knew I'd only just broken up with my ex when you met me."*

Until I realised that I had a penchant for men who blow hot and cold and like to be ambiguous about the status of our 'relationship', I considered myself to be the quintessential single girl about town. I thought that I was a bit unlucky in love and that I must have a sign on my forehead that somehow drew in these men. I couldn't understand why it kept going so horribly wrong, but the reality was that I knew the truth deep down; I just couldn't recognise or accept it yet.

I'm not alone – lots of women are just like me. Being afraid of commitment and dealing with unavailability are becoming standard when you're swimming in the dating pool. We attribute these issues and the rocky road we travel as part of being a modern woman in a tougher, more competitive modern world. We actually think this behaviour is normal. This, in turn, tells us that the world is full of unavailable men and that we've put in too much time and effort to leave and we should just keep plugging away at this relationship. It's easy to read stuff in the media and watch the various TV shows that portray the single life or the ups and downs of relationships and end up believing that there is no problem. But there is.

If you don't get wise about unavailable relationships, you will spend your life around men who send a message to you that you're not 'good enough'. This isn't because you're not good enough, but because you're trying to make an unavailable relationship into a committed relationship, which is like trying to make a pig's ear into a silk purse. You recognise that he's not available, but, on another level, you recognise some emotional similarities, or he may even be similar to previous partners or a parent. You, in turn, reflect his beliefs about love, relationships, and himself, and he *knows* that, because you've stuck around for longer than a hot minute, have let him dictate the terms of the relationship, overstep your boundaries, and not have his actions match his words, you're equally emotionally unavailable and are an ideal partner for what he has in mind. Yep, two self-fulfilling prophecies going on here.

In this relationship where he dictates the terms and manages down your expectations through behaviour like blowing hot and cold; you, the Fallback Girl, are the woman he defaults to or falls back on for an ego stroke, sex, a shoulder to lean on and anything else he can enjoy. As you take a backseat in the relationship and try to get on board with his agenda, while at the same time having your own hidden agenda of getting the relationship *you* want, *he* ends up getting all of this with very little commitment and effort. Mr Unavailable often doesn't tell you upfront that this is all that's on offer, so you'll be lured in during the hot phase. Then he'll roll back and become the man of diminishing returns. Like in all unavailable relationships, by him still being around, no matter in how limited, painful, or obnoxious a capacity, you're getting a hint that if you continue to accommodate him, he'll go on to bend and accommodate you. Unfortunately, as you'll discover throughout this book, that doesn't happen.

WHY UNAVAILABLE RELATIONSHIPS DON'T WORK

You may be wondering why a relationship with someone that you fancy or love so much and appear to have certain things in common with *isn't* going to work. In a nutshell, unavailable relationships don't work because:

1. They tick the boxes for unhealthy beliefs that you have about relationships, love, and yourself.

2. They're dictated on one person's terms, which is not a mutually fulfilling relationship – even if you try to comply with the terms.

3. They can't operate with healthy boundaries, which opens you up to disrespect. This includes putting up with stuff like addictions and abuse.

4. If you have good self-esteem, you'll bail when it becomes apparent that they're unavailable. The fact that you don't shows that you have self-esteem issues and you need self-esteem to have a healthy relationship.

5. Neither of you can be truly emotionally honest and without honesty you both lack authenticity and are illusion led.

6. A lack of real intimacy or sabotaging it every time you move forward means that you can never get genuinely close to one another. Healthy relationships progress whereas unavailable relationships go in fits and starts, regress, or come to a halt.

7. Healthy relationships require commitment and, without it, it's like trying to row a boat with one oar. Pointless. A lack of commitment yields lack of responsibility and accountability, which means the relationship cannot be treated like it's truly *valued*.

8. You can never really trust that the relationship is going anywhere because it's inconsistent and imbalanced, and, even after it progresses, it often regresses.

9. Any relationship that requires one or both parties to make dramatic changes before it can work is never going to work, especially if you're not honest or in agreement about what that work is.

10. It's one thing to be in an unavailable relationship when that is exactly what you want, but the moment you want, need, or expect more, the relationship flounders. You will always want more; the less powerful party always does.

11. Any relationship with a solo agenda (the driver – him) or conflicting solo agendas or a hidden agenda (the passenger –you) is *doomed*. Healthy relationships where you want commitment, etc., need a joint, co-piloted, out in the open agenda, something that just doesn't happen in unavailable relationships.

12. These relationships work on a diet of crumbs. When you throw in the fact that he'll be deluded enough to think that these crumbs are actually loaves, you end up selling yourself short and settling for less, while normalising what can often be some pretty shady behaviour in the process.

UNAVAILABLE RELATIONSHIPS IN A NUTSHELL

Emotionally unavailable men thrive because they have complicit, commitment resistant, emotionally unavailable women to accommodate their behaviour. Mr Unavailables are chosen by Fallback Girls because they reflect their beliefs about love, relationships, and themselves.

Women who genuinely want commitment, who are personally happy, and have a healthy level of self-esteem, don't desire or chase Mr Unavailables. If they find themselves involved with them, they also don't blame themselves for their actions and recognise the toxicity.

We chase Mr Unavailables because their behaviour *works* for us. They pander to and nurture patterns within us that, despite being dysfunctional, make us feel *comfortable* in their familiarity.

Mr Unavailable can only be with a woman as long as she's carrying some negativity with her. A personally secure woman with boundaries would make him nervous, plus he couldn't drive things on his terms.

This simple equation demonstrates unavailable relationships:

MR UNAVAILABLE = EMOTIONALLY UNAVAILABLE = COMMITMENT RESISTANT

WOMEN THAT LOVE MR UNAVAILABLE = EMOTIONALLY UNAVAILABLE = COMMITMENT RESISTANT

Hence....

MR UNAVAILABLE + YOU = ONE COMMITMENT-RESISTANT DISASTER

The male issue with emotional unavailability can be rooted in childhood as the product of unhealthy interactions, such as parents who penalise for displaying sensitivity and emotion. By engaging in narcissistically inclined behaviour and surrounding themselves with women who they effectively use, dismiss, and 'fall back' on habitually, their self-esteem doesn't take the same ongoing battering. These men don't think, *"Oh, I'm with an emotionally unavailable woman and that makes me feel bad about myself,"* but they do think, *"Hmmm... if she's with me, she* must be emotionally unavailable, too... OK, well at least we can have a good time together..."

Many Mr Unavailables actually believe they're a good catch!

A Fallback Girl on the other hand thinks, *"I'm with an emotionally unavailable man. What is it about me that won't let him try harder to access his emotions? I know that men hurt me, I know that men let me down, but I can't bear the thought of being alone again. Surely if I show him how much I care, he will see this and be available to me? What is wrong with me?"*

Now, even if the women who some of these Mr Unavailables engage with are not emotionally unavailable when they initially become involved, if the relationship continues, they too end up being emotionally unavailable, in an almost natural reaction to coping with the difficulty of being in the ambiguous relationship which results. And so begins a vicious cycle.

You'll obviously need to have an honest conversation with yourself about whether your dalliance with your Mr Unavailable was a blip in an otherwise healthy relationship history, or whether this is all too familiar territory for you because he's one in a line of Mr Unavailables you've been involved with and may even represent a lot of what you've learned about relationships in your childhood. In fact, he may be a warped version of your father or exactly like him. Either way, in recognising your own unavailability, whether temporary or habitual, you can either nip this in the bud before it becomes a habit, or shake the stranglehold of the pattern.

TYPICAL UNAVAILABLE RELATIONSHIPS

Since I started writing Baggage Reclaim, I've observed, read, and listened to thousands of stories from women who have been involved with Mr Unavailables that all have stark similarities. Below is what unavailable relationships typically look like:

The Casual Relationship Informal arrangements, including Friends With Benefits, as well as those who don't want anything 'heavy'.

The Boomerang Relationship Can't break, won't break – he keeps leaving and returning, and you keep taking him back.

The Rebound Relationship Caught between two relationships, this is recently broken up, separated, divorced or widowed, and still not over the ex, or the hurts from the fallout.

The Affair A messy combo of one person rebelling and the other competing, one or sometimes both of you are cheating on someone else and *you* play second fiddle.

The Dalliance Typically characterised by being short-term, this is a casual fling or whirlwind romance that fizzles out.

The Rehabbing and Remodelling Relationship This is excessive baggage, particularly in the form of problems, including addiction which you try to fix, heal and help, and also relationships where, even if they don't have any major problems, there's a lot of control and demands for change.

The Long-Term Struggle Some unavailable relationships can go the distance in terms of time, but have all sorts of problems within them even when there is history, a title, a legal piece of paper, or kids.

The Fantasy Relationship The combination of illusions and denial, which also includes virtual relationships. This is pure intimacy avoidance.

The Abusive Relationship Full of manipulation, there's a presence of emotional, physical, and/or verbal abuse with use of excessive force and control.

The Secret Relationship On the down-low for whatever reason, it often includes issues with race, religion, and family.

The Excuse Relationship Are they busy, scared, too tired, shy, dealing with a lot right now, or just in a need of an extra day/week/month/year/lifetime to give you what you need? If you or they make excuses, it's to lessen their responsibility.

HOW AVAILABLE ARE YOU?

Which of these statements do you agree with?

1. I'm over all of my exes – this means I'm in a neutral position and am not emotionally invested in either a positive or negative way. I don't have anyone dipping in and out of my life.

2. I've typically been available and have had at least one mutually fulfilling, healthy, committed relationship.

3. While I did find myself involved with a Mr Unavailable, it was a one-time thing and, ordinarily, I wouldn't be interested in someone who behaved in this manner.

4. I'm not afraid to be vulnerable in my relationships and, while I have fears like the average person, I'm not being run by my fears.

5. When I experience a breakup, or someone that I'm interested in doesn't work out, I work my way through my feelings and don't try to avoid them.

6. While I've had a one-night stand or an occasional fling or even a casual sex arrangement here or there, they're few and far between.

7. If someone rejects me/turns me down/my relationship doesn't work out, I don't internalise it and change how I feel about me.

8. I'm OK with being honest or receiving honesty, even in the face of hearing information that I might not like, and I will act upon it.

9. If someone doesn't make an effort or isn't in a position to commit to me, this is a turn-off and I walk away. I don't become more interested or try to push them into a commitment.

10. I accept the responsibility for sorting out any emotional issues that I have and I don't try to get partners to fix me.

11. While I don't mind being kind or helpful, or even compassionate, I know that it's wholly inappropriate to attempt to fix someone else's problems.

12. I don't have a 'type' and tend to look for people who, while I'm attracted to them, share similar values with me. I don't have any criteria about how they should look, their job, how much money, etc.

13. If I met someone and they were still attached, I'd walk away.

14. While there are things that I wouldn't mind improving, on the whole I accept myself and like and love me.

15. While, of course, I don't want to be hurt, I'm not so afraid of being hurt that it affects how I see people and relationships and my trust issues.

16. When I feel uncomfortable I listen to myself and, when I get signals from my gut, I trust the information that I'm getting.

17. I'm aware of inappropriate behaviour and I have boundaries and limits to what I'll put up with.

18. I don't engage in denial, rationalising or minimising,

19. Whether or not I had a healthy relationship with my parents, I have addressed anything from my childhood that is impacting my adult life and/or am actively working on it.

20. There's nothing I'm trying to avoid. Really!

If you disagree with any of these statements, not only does it raise questions over how available you are, but these are all things that, when they remain unaddressed, are invitations for Mr Unavailables to come into your life and wreak havoc. The more you disagree with, the more unavailable you are, although most of these things on their own have the potential to create big problems for you.

HE BLOWS HOT & COLD

If you imagine someone running the hot tap on you for the first time, it feels very hot, so, of course, when the temperature begins to fall to moderate, lukewarm or even icy cold, you're going to feel a very perceptible difference that will jolt you or, at the very least, cause you to feel uneasy. If you've ever come in from the cold, then got into a hot bath, it feels extremely hot, but it's not actually as hot as you perceive it to be – *this* is Mr Unavailable. As he keeps fluctuating the temperature of his efforts and interests, which of course wreaks havoc with the overall temperature of the relationship, you get the impression that he's still blowing hot, albeit not quite as hot as he was in the beginning. Of course, if you keep putting in the same, or even an increased, effort, he actually ends up getting more for less, plus it may take a while before the reality catches up with you.

In John Gray's iconic relationship guide, *Men Are From Mars, Women Are From Venus,* he explains how men have an intimacy cycle comparable with a rubber band.

"Men instinctively feel this urge to pull away. It is not a decision or choice. It just happens. It is neither his fault nor her fault. It is a natural cycle."

Apparently, because we as women pull away when something is wrong, his withdrawal is perceived to mean the same, when, in fact, he's supposedly fulfilling his need for *"independence or autonomy"*. Even more interestingly, when he's stretched the rubber band as far as it can go (he's distanced himself), the urge for love and intimacy will return and Bingo!, he springs back into relationship action, picking up the relationship at *"whatever degree of intimacy it was when he stretched away. He doesn't feel any need for a period of getting reacquainted again."* While John *does* make clear that these withdrawals shouldn't be happening early on in the relationship, this type of behaviour is also very symptomatic of unavailable relationships where your expectations and intimacy are managed down, and it's what most Fallback Girls come to know as **blowing hot and cold** with a dash of **pressing the Reset Button**.

When he blows hot, he gains your confidence and creates expectations he's actually unlikely to deliver on. When he blows cold, he manages down your expectations so that you don't need, want or expect more than he's prepared to give. The net result, should you remain with him, is that your expectations are lessened, his crumbs of attention and contribution get turned into a loaf, you normalise behaviour you'd previously have considered abnormal so that he gets his needs met while yours aren't, and he gets to have the relationship on his terms.

Blowing hot and cold makes it difficult to leave, because he's the source of your misery while also appearing to be the source of your happiness, as he appears to be giving you glimpses of what you think he could be. You keep believing that when you reach the tipping point of loving, giving and trying, that he'll eventually match you.

The Reset Button is where he gives himself liberal license to reset the relationship to whatever point that he feels most comfortable with, which is effectively like erasing the past. With his assumptive, passive aggressive and sometimes outrageous attitude, he operates in a little bubble where he does as he likes and then bamboozles his way around your protests and requests to talk, as he expects you just to pick up where he 'left off'.

He doesn't like 'dwelling', which is code for basically thinking about, discussing, or doing anything that might cause him to connect with his actions and realise that he's behaved in a less than favourable manner to the people he's involved with. If you challenge him, he may penalise you through sulking, withdrawal, and creating conflict, so that you realise it's not worth the aggravation and 'give in'.

28

Acts of resetting include disappearing for periods of time and expecting to return unchallenged, leaving you for someone else and then calling you up or trying to see you behind their back, trying to reach you after you cut contact, claiming he doesn't understand why you're mad at him, making you think you're going mad by denying he said or did things, and often flitting from person to person (or group or relationship).

Many women have asked me why he keeps returning despite being unable or willing to commit or knowing that he doesn't mean you or the relationship any good, and the truth is that, aside from having using inclinations, it's just because he can. He's not meeting any great obstructions and it's like he almost 'resigns' himself to taking what's on offer. What you need to remember is that many guys, unavailable or not, tend to engage in **Chancing Their Arm**.

This is taking a risk, often a somewhat outrageous one, to see if he'll get the desired result. If it pays off, he's quids in. This risk isn't necessarily a reflection on you, or even on the relationship – he often takes these risks just because it's his *disposition*. Many readers have got in touch with me feeling hurt or believing that they're not as healed as they thought they were because an ex has made contact – it's not about you. He's just taking a risk that he'd take regardless.

He lets himself off the hook by believing that you're pursuing things even though he's shown who he is, and that he's only giving you what you want (or his watered-down version of it), when, in actual fact, he's taking advantage of your self-esteem and enjoying the fringe benefits. If his risk pays off, he'll also mark you down for it, so you're often being set up to fail.

He *is* still 'pursuing' you; it's just that it's rarely to the extent that he did at the beginning of the relationship unless he truly believes that he's in serious danger of losing his ego stroke. The difference with Mr Unavailable after the beginning of the relationship is he switches from giving you, let's say, 80% attention and effort, to drip feeding you various levels of attention and effort, to which you respond disproportionately, because he's managed down your expectations.

SPOT THE SIGNS

I'll put it this way: if his 'retreating' involves disappearing, not calling, being disrespectful, shutting you out, and saying/doing any shady stuff to make you feel bad, this isn't independence and autonomy – it's disrespect and commitment issues.

1) Do things feel inconsistent and imbalanced, up and down? This can feel like passion and excitement initially, but eventually it will translate to tension, ambiguity, drama, and a relationship that's not progressing. If he's messing you around when you're together and chasing you up and making big promises when you tell him to shag off, you've got a 'hot and cold'er.

2) Does this feel familiar? If how you feel and his actions are similar to a previous unavailable relationship, you should be hearing alarm bells ringing. Big time.

3) What other boundary busting is going on? Blowing hot and cold doesn't happen in isolation.

4) Are you noticing a negative impact on the relationship? If so, is it because of how you have reacted, or is it because he's behaved in a way that detracts from the relationship? Is he actually retreating, or is he just being independent and autonomous and you're struggling with that?

5) How much of an impact does fear have on your relationship? Differentiate between anxiety based on internal fears tied to your self-esteem and anxiety originating from very real external factors that you're observing.

Basically, there's a big difference between being afraid that they're retreating because it's your natural disposition to perceive them doing their own thing as retreating, and them actually retreating.

Ask yourself: What do I think him doing XYZ [whatever form his retreating takes] means about me? Write it down and question the validity of the beliefs and balance them against real, external evidence of his actions, not just whatever is running through your mind. Does what you believe hold true?

6) Are you co-dependent? If you tend to place all your love on one person, expect them to be around you all the time if they love you, tend to morph into your partners and take on their characteristics, and rely on them for your value and validation while struggling to cope on your own, anything you perceive as not fitting your vision of things will convince you he's retreating, triggering fears of abandonment. It's one thing to have concerns in an unhealthy relationship with a Mr Unavailable but I hear from a lot of Fallback Girls trying to have healthier relationships with Mr *Availables* who end up creating drama or killing it off, due to fears about them doing something as basic as seeing their friends. The best litmus test of whether you're co-dependent or personally secure is to evaluate how much of a life you have independently of theirs – is your life, your worth, your sense of self, based around them?

REMEMBER!

Only unavailable men blow hot and cold. Yes, really!

Disappearing is hugely disrespectful and a rejection of the relationship. If he disappears, don't allow him back into your life.

If someone is being physically unavailable, it makes it pretty damn difficult to have any sense of security about the relationship.

Never allow a hot and cold rinse to go by without questioning it or creating consequences.

I can understand second chances, but that is your *limit*. He's either in or he's out.

HE KEEPS THINGS ON HIS TERMS

What bewilders so many women is how no matter what they do and no matter what he appears to say or do at the time, they keep ending up on his terms. This happens because the combination of blowing hot and cold and the Reset Button facilitates **The Status Quo**, the comfort zone that Mr Unavailable always strives to be in – the level that he's prepared to be expected, needed, and wanted from.

If you imagine your relationship with him on a scale of one to ten, he likes it at *five* – his comfort zone – and everything he does is about maintaining it. Whenever you push for more to take it out of the comfort zone, he will retreat (blow cold or lukewarm) and behave in ways that drag you back to the safe territory of The Status Quo. On the flip side, whenever you tell him to take a running jump, or appear to be losing interest in his fickle self, he will go into a flurry of actions or start chirping all of the right words (blowing hotter) to drag it back to the middle ground. If things move above five, he'll gradually eke it back down with some subtle, passive-aggressive moves and one day you wake up and realise you're back to square one.

If he disappears for a period of time or treats you badly, he will do his damnedest to pick up where he left off and may make some hollow empty gestures and big promises to distract you and quickly ease it above five, with a view to gradually easing it back once he has his feet well and truly under the table. The Status Quo is also in action even when you are broken up, because he may have a comfort zone that involves you being his friend (even if he's not actually your friend), or he may expect to get back together with little or no discussion by liberally pressing the Reset Button.

If you've ever spent a really intense, happy time together, had him share something with you, or been on a holiday as a couple, you're likely to have experienced the very aggressive forms of blowing hot and cold. Mr Unavailables also get nervous around anything that they perceive as a big occasion that might cause you to think that they're in a committed relationship with you, or basically that you're 'special'. Their response is to act badly so that you don't go getting any 'big ideas'.

I've heard from bewildered women who had a Mr Unavailable show up at a funeral or take them to a family/work function and act like The Bestest Ever Boyfriend, only for them to drop off the face of the earth within days.

What happened? They panicked about what these women might think they were capable of.

Even though he'll do all of these things that will no doubt hurt, disappoint, and create a tremendous amount of anxiety, if he's not 'done' with you, he'll expect to pick up where he feels he left off, with minimal conflict, which of course is pressing the Reset Button. This is why it will often feel like you never really resolve any issues, or get a genuine heartfelt apology for anything that happens during these difficult times, because he just wants to erase and move on.

If he's unwilling to look at, or truly understand, what's happened to bring about problems in the relationship, there's nothing to stop him repeating the behaviour again... which is exactly what happens.

All of this flip-flapping is a reflection of his indecisiveness and inability to commit. It's almost like you need to ask him which one of his relationship personalities is coming out today! If you're blowing hot, then it's very likely that he will be blowing at a cooler temperature than you, or it'll be coming soon. He enjoys the newness of what you have and certain comforts of being with you, but aspects of your own behaviour, or reactions to him, set off the trigger buttons that make his tap of attention run cold.

Mr Unavailable has major control issues and he gets to determine the pace, temperature, and direction of the relationship by blowing hot and cold, and, where appropriate, pressing the Reset Button. This is why if you do the running or blow really hot, he'll sprint in the opposite direction, because it's too much for him to handle and removes his fundamental tool of relationship management.

At first, you'll be freaked out by the inconsistency and the messing with your head, but, over time, you end up being trained to acclimatise to it and this is when he goes into cruise control. A major fringe benefit of blowing hot and cold is that, by managing down your expectations, you end up giving them the same or more, for less contribution from them. A major fringe benefit of you letting them press the Reset Button is that, in their eyes, if you've allowed it, then it didn't really happen or it wasn't as bad as it was.

SPOT THE SIGNS

If you can't assert yourself or be equal in the relationship, which means being free to pick up the phone, make plans, be spontaneous and ask questions, he's solo minded.

1) Are you experiencing passive aggression? If he initially appears to agree with you, then subtly, or even aggressively, backtracks afterwards, he's operating on his terms.

2) Can you make things happen? If you're afraid to initiate contact or a conversation about something, are afraid of asking questions or suggesting plans and he basically gets to drive all the arrangements and plans, you're either with someone who does things on their terms, or you've been a passenger.

3) Does he think that his way is 'our' way? If he's not letting you be an equal party in the relationship and is dictating the terms, it's not a joint agenda, it's *his*. He doesn't know best. This isn't a dictatorship.

4) Does he seem to have an entirely different memory of things, especially one where he's Mr Wonderful? Never accept resetting or forced Relationship Amnesia. If you both have different recollections of things – i.e. you remember and he doesn't, this is grossly inappropriate. It's time to ask *why* he remembers differently – trust me when I say there's nothing wrong with your memory, especially if he has a great memory about other things.

5) Can you have boundaries? One thing that absolutely cannot survive in a driver environment is boundaries, because with them doing things on their terms, you have to compromise yourself to stay 'on board', which is a no-go.

REMEMBER!

A mutually fulfilling relationship needs to be co-piloted. There's no room for a driver doing things on their own terms, or a passenger dodging responsibility and commitment.

If there's a pattern, you can be assured you're being yanked around someone's terms.

If he's dampening the relationship when you're together and making big promises when you're not, he's all about his comfort zone.

When he 'can't' make a decision it's because he doesn't want to get out of his comfort zone.

When he keeps changing the terms and conditions of your relationship, it's only changing for you not him – he's still in his comfort zone.

HIS ACTIONS DON'T MATCH
HIS WORDS

You've been spending time with a walking, talking, contradiction. In his mind, because he thinks that *some* of his actions convey the true nature of the relationship and his lack of capability, he assumes that you pick up on these 'subtle' messages, even though he's doing *other* things that not only contradict his so-called intentions, but end up misleading you, too. He's very careless, often saying or even doing stuff to match the moment and then when you're 'out of sight, out of mind', backtracking to something else entirely. It makes him very unreliable and, unfortunately, rather insincere.

You hear, *"I'm really into you. I'll call you,"* but you're wondering where your call is a few days later and replaying the date in your mind wondering what you did wrong. However, it's that he focuses on, giving you the feel-good factor. He wants you to think well of him in the context of the date, even though it just hasn't occurred to him that by misleading you, you're not going to think well of him *after*.

WHY THEY DON'T MATCH

He avoids confrontation. He fears the consequences of being 1) truthful and 2) direct. Of course being indirect misses the point.

He fears hurting your feelings with honesty. He doesn't cast a thought to the fact that misleading you will cause you far more pain in the medium and long term.

He enjoys the short-term fringe benefits of being with you without casting an eye to the bigger picture. He's thinking about things from his perspective, not yours.

He doesn't like to endanger the flowing tap of sex or whatever benefit he's relying on. He wants to be in control of when it stops. If he were truthful, you might cut off his supply.

He doesn't want to be perceived as an 'asshole'. This governs his overinflated ego, because even when he does behave in ways that are hurtful, or downright bad, he's more concerned with how he looks to his peers or to you.

He doesn't know what he wants, but he figures it out on your time. He may never know, but gives himself license to straddle the fence, which basically puts you in No Man's Land and effectively wastes your time.

He does know what he wants, but messes with you anyway until something better comes along. Sadly, many of these men know you're not The One, or are fully aware that they're not capable of giving you what you want, but they see fit to pass time with you.

And then... some of them are **Future Fakers**.

UNDERSTANDING FUTURE FAKING

One of the biggest sources of frustration with Mr Unavailable is that, often, the very expectations he's managing down are those that he's created off his own back without prompting from you.

A **Future Faker**, via his actions and words, gives you the impression of a future, so that they can get what they want in the present. They make veiled, or even direct, references to things like marriage, babies, moving in together, going on holiday, being together the following year and other such things that imply or state that you're a part of their life, then they either disappear or replace the person you thought they were with someone altogether different. Future Faking also minimises confrontation and obstacles that prevent them from getting what they want. There are two types:

Future Fakers who intentionally say and do the 'right' things so they get what they want. Maybe they benefit financially, get their ego stroked, a shoulder to lean on, less hassle about them delivering on promises,   a shag, or whatever. They're particularly passive aggressive because they appear to be going along with you, when all the while they're creeping around behind your back doing something else.

Future Fakers who meant it as much as they could mean it at the time. They *want* to believe that they'll do these things, but due to their overall nature of having actions that don't match words, they're reactive and very 'out of sight, out of mind'. The moment the realisation dawns that they have to commit to what they've said and follow through, they panic and extricate themselves out of things, either in a dramatic manner, or by subtly and passive aggressively shifting their way out of things. Maybe they orchestrate a fight by behaving like a jackass, so that you react and then they can find an excuse to dodge whatever bullet is flying at them.

Either way, each type of Future Faker generates the same net result – a future that doesn't materialise. The intentional ones are confidence tricksters and dangerous users, and the latter unintentional, careless Future Fakers lack responsibility, due care, and thought, and so don't really consider the impact of their grand promises. To do it once, or even twice, can be called careless, but some Fallback Girls dig into their Mr Unavailable's past and discover that he has a long history of 'careless' Future Faking and has of course been liberally pressing the Reset Button, so he can conveniently forget and give himself a fresh start and a selectively remembered relationship history to start over with.

> **As women, never mind Fallback Girls, we've been conditioned to believe that men who don't want a relationship with you or who don't have good intentions, *don't* talk about the future.**

Mr Unavailable has no real comprehension of true love or care. It's like being an alcoholic who's in denial. He doesn't acknowledge his issues, which means that everything is out of whack and feeding into the self-deception, which inadvertently leads to deceiving others. He's the consummate actor and, on some level, he knows that he's playing a role.

You have to understand: it might feel like your situation with him is unique, but the truth is that he's been down this road many times before. He believes that all he has to do is *say* the right things and you won't notice that he hasn't actually followed through. And, let's be truthful, often you don't. You want to believe that he'll be different with you.

Imagine that you spend ages 'nagging' him to take out the bins. You argue about it but he still doesn't do it. Then, for some reason, maybe because you got really medieval on him, he takes it out for three consecutive days, then returns to his normal mode. Initially, you might not say anything, but when it becomes patently clear that he hasn't changed, you confront him and he reminds you about the three occasions that he did take the bins out. This is Mr Unavailable. If he lets you down one hundred times, but he didn't on five occasions, he'll remember the five, and forget the one hundred. If you mention the one hundred to him, he'll call you negative or needy...

It's time for us to realise as women that, yes, some guys do talk about the future, but they still intend to avoid it when it comes round to delivering on it. The 'trick' with Future Faking, and, in fact, with any instance where you encounter someone whose actions don't match their words, is that you end up believing the future, or whatever they intended to do, *was* going to happen, it's just that you must have done something to change their mind. Next thing you know you're burning up brainpower wondering what the hell you did, analysing your actions and conversations and blaming yourself for what's happened.

SPOT THE SIGNS

If you're with someone who says one thing but does another, put yourself on danger alert.

1. Mentally walk through dates and conversations and note anything that he's said, promises, and plans that stand out. Of these things, how many are true or have actually happened?

2. Are you making excuses for him? Write down his excuses, strip them out and what are you left with? Note any excuses that consistently come up.

3. On a scale of 1-10 (10 being the most and 1 being the least different), based on your original perception of him and what you thought this relationship was going to be, how different is the reality? Anything above a 3-4 is significant enough to ring alarm bells.

4. When you follow up about something that he claimed he intended to be or do, what are you met with? Apology, followed by remorse, followed by endeavouring to follow through and actually doing it? Apologising and then carrying on his merry little way and then failing to do stuff again? Obstruction, denial, hostility or even disappearance?

5. Are you hoping that you can change him or are you waiting for him to become a better man in a better relationship? Both of these aspirations point to the fact that his *current* actions are not acceptable.

REMEMBER!

No action means no relationship.

Without action you simply cannot trust in him, his intentions, or the direction of your relationship.

While there are times we can't do everything we intend to, if he doesn't do anything, or very little of what he claims he intends to, it's because he wasn't intending to anyway.

Anyone who is truly a person of action achieves a lot more results through trying to do what they intend and a lot less disappointment, than someone who's full of hot air.

All the fancy things, gestures and words don't mean a thing if you still end up confused, miserable, upset and struggling with ambiguity or settling for crumbs. Make sure that he's walking the walk, not just talking the talk.

HE LIKES FAST FORWARDING

Dating is a discovery phase that provides an opportunity for you to discover whether you both have something that could potentially turn into a relationship. Through the process of getting to know one another through actions, words, and the net result of your interactions, you work out whether there's enough for you to move forward, or whether you need to roll back. This is often forgotten and, particularly in relationships with unavailable parties, it's very easy to get swept up in an intensity that lets you believe that they're actually available because they appear to be firing on all cylinders.

Unfortunately, you miss out on the vital process of doing the due diligence for your relationship, and next thing you wake up involved in something that wasn't what you intended. In these situations, you'll be moving or feeling at a pace that, in retrospect, you'll recognise as being rather alarming.

Fast Forwarding is, in itself, a form of Future Faking and it refers to when someone sweeps you up in a tide of intensity while pursuing and/or being in the relationship, so that you end up missing crucial information about them. While they will Future Fake, they'll also behave intensely by putting so many demands on you (emotional, sexual, wanting to be with you all the time), that you believe that the level of intensity you're experiencing is what is on offer and also reflective of the intensity of their feelings for you. You'll then use a number of the things that they Fast Forward you with as basis to trust them. Fast Forwarders:

- Push for emotional commitment, and often sexual intimacy, very quickly.

- Make you feel like the centre of their universe.

- Distract you from looking too closely at them.

41

- Refer to the types of plans that people who have been in relationships far longer would discuss – marriage, babies, etc.(Future Faking).

- May introduce you to friends and family (including their kids) very quickly.

- Say stuff like, "But it feels like we've known each other for X months!" when you object to something and mention how you hardly know one another.

- Can be petulant and sulky when they don't get their own way, so you quickly learn to minimise conflict.

- Even though they appear to respect an asserted boundary, often quickly attempt to recross it.

- Are very persistent when you're not interested in them.

- Will often quickly state that you're The One.

- Will be eager to 'title the relationship' and demand commitment, even when you hardly know each other.

- Often have strings of high intensity, short dalliances that fizzle out quickly.

- Overestimate their level of interest.

- Veer between deflecting questions about themselves, oversharing, or telling lies and using selective omissions.

People who tend to Fast Forward as part of their general relationship habits can go through their cycle in a few hours (ever met an intense person online who sent you several emails, pestered you and then disappeared?), a day, a night (one-night stands, for example), a few dates, weeks, months, and, in some cases, some can play the long game and draw it out for a year. But it will stop, and, when it does, it's often painful.

Even though you may have had concerns about him, you'll use the intensity to cloud them out.

But let's be real: it's flattering when someone seems to fancy the arse off us so much that they can't seem to want to stop ripping off our clothes or saying we're the best thing since sliced bread.

The key 'weapon' with Fast Forwarding is intense *action,* which throws you off guard, because it's not like you're hanging your hopes just on words. However, this action is unlikely to be consistent and, eventually, it will form part of the hot and cold cycle. As a Fallback Girl, being swept up by someone in a grand romance is very attractive anyway. But with your habits of not always recognising inappropriate behaviour and your eagerness to be validated and loved, you don't recognise that being Fast Forwarded in itself is an unhealthy marker for the relationship.

Even without anything shady, by Fast Forwarding the relationship, you'll both create great expectations that may stifle the relationship before it has a chance to prosper. If you took things a bit slower, you could actually get to know one another. The intensity is impossible to sustain and, when it stops, it feels like you've crashed and burned. The relationships that healthily survive Fast Forwarding are those in which the two people have slowed down but are, in essence, still the same two people who first met; there isn't a dramatic shift in character and behaviour.

If he's around in a year or two and your high-intensity dalliance has yielded into something steadier, then good for you. However, the problem with people who Fast Forward is that they can't cope with steadiness. They also make the mistake of being so OTT that they create expectations they cannot deliver on.

Mr Unavailable overestimates his level of interest because, often, the uncertainty of not knowing how you feel and the need to 'win you over' and 'suck you in', is what triggers his desire for you.

When you get swept up in the intensity, you'll bask in the adoration. Of course, when he disappears or replaces 'the model' you got with a pared-down version, you'll wonder what was wrong with you to cause the loss of adoration. When the relationship stops being new, he panics about what you may be expecting, and, as he's sure of your interest, the desire loses its 'erection'. If you don't hear from him again, he'll have moved on and pressed the Reset Button with someone else... and lather, rinse, repeat. If he's still around and things are going from bad to worse, you'll be getting the hot and cold treatment, while thinking, *"It was so great in the beginning! What happened to that guy?"* and then sinking all your efforts into attempting to retrieve the beginning of the relationship.

SPOT THE SIGNS

Does it feel like your heart, mind, emotions and life have been dominated by him, even though you hardly know him?

1) Have things significantly 'dropped' off from an intense beginning? While things calm a little, they shouldn't calm so much that you have to question what the hell has gone wrong.

2) Has he broken it off/disappeared? You can be pretty damn sure if he went from super intense to up in smoke, that you've been Fast Forwarded.

3) Have you found yourself agreeing to things that you've come to regret and are not reflective of your values or even how you feel about him?

4) Do you feel like you have to go along with the speed of things out of fear of losing him or being regarded as a 'spoilsport'?

5) Of all the things he said he'd be and do, how much has *actually* happened? Walk your way through the relationship again and focus on times when it was particularly intense, where he made promises or even demands – how different are he and your relationship from what you thought they'd be?

REMEMBER!

Anyone who actually intends to be around and be themselves *doesn't* need to speed you through the beginning of the relationship.

If you give in to the speed and get swept along, you not

only miss out on actually getting to know them, but vital signs of whether this relationship is good for you.

When he comes back making big promises, watch out, because this is a mixture of Fast Forwarding and Future Faking. Take your time.

A significant change in action is at minimum a code amber. This means stop, look, listen, assess and do not proceed until you understand what is happening in your relationship.

It's not necessary to go so fast. You shouldn't need to go at high speed to make someone feel more secure, as you'll ultimately end up far more insecure.

HE LOVES CASUAL RELATIONSHIPS

As Fallback Girls, we'll often convince ourselves that keeping it casual is the way to go, because we're still hurting from a previous relationship or we're risk averse. When you throw in the fact that some of us have high sex drives and/or *overvalue* sex, he recognises that playing to the enjoyment of it, or tugging the insecurity strings, is highly advantageous, making sex (or the prospect or withdrawal of it), a very powerful weapon. Unfortunately, it's important to acknowledge that:

You may be thinking that you're in a relationship of sorts with him, but he may see you as little more than a Fuck Buddy, Friends With Benefits, Hook-Up, or a Booty Call.

He might not attach these particular terms to you, but this is often what you amount to, and he may be putting in about as much effort as it would take to order a takeaway a few times a week (or however often he gets in touch).

MORE FOR LESS

The difference between a one-night stand and a booty call? Not much. It's just a one-night stand on repeat.

It's pulling the same 'con' more than once and actually managing to get away with it. For that to happen, you're pressing the Reset Button *yourself*. Booty calls happen because they chance their arm, possibly do a little more Future Faking, and you *accept*.

If you believe that you're both friends, either because pre-sex you had a friendship or he's played the 'friend card', you may feel you're 'above' a booty call and are doing Friends With Benefits. Really, using the word 'friend' legitimises what would under other circumstances be unacceptable behaviour, especially if you weren't friends in the first place and only started referring to them as such to justify sticking around.

While friendships can survive a one-night stand, a fling, or even sporadic encounters with mutual care, trust, and respect but no emotional attachment beyond friendship, if one crosses the line, it's very difficult to recover the friendship, especially if the other party seeks to continue the dalliance anyway.

It's logical to believe that because of your friendship and sleeping together that a relationship could and should happen.

It's been drummed into us that the best relationships are ones where the couple are friends as well, and we've seen enough romantic comedies and read enough 'chick lit' to cement this notion. However – and it's a big however – you're forgetting two crucial pieces of information: you're a Fallback Girl and he's a Mr Unavailable so you are both stepping into murky waters. While he may be a great guy, I've read enough tales to know that, as Fallback Girls, we're often attracted to the same qualities in male friends that we are in relationships.

Particularly if you were both genuinely friends, he may *assume* that you know what he's like. You, unfortunately, assume that you're exempt from his treatment due to the 'friendship'. Yep, *messy*.

While these arrangements can appear to be mutual, like anything that has Mr Unavailable in it, it's not actually as mutual as you'd like to think and one party (him) is dictating the terms. Even though we'll bullshit ourselves, the truth is that in *any* casual relationship, there is always one party (you) who wants more, or has more expectations. He knows this, but, if you're knowingly participating, whether you put a name to it or not, he lets himself off the hook by telling himself that you know it's casual or that it's obvious that it is, so he gets to sleep easier at night.

SEX & THE DISAPPEARING ACT – FAST FORWARDING EXTRA FAST

Many a woman has slept with a man thinking that it was the start of something beautiful, when, in fact, it was the end of something that had never really started for him. He knows from the outset that he has no intentions of calling again, or that he's not interested in having a relationship, but he allows her to believe that it's a possibility. His ego loves the idea that she's falling in love, desiring and trusting him; he's not interested in being with a woman who 'just' wants him for sex.

This is Fast Forwarding in days or even *hours*, which may be when you experience a one-night stand or an 'amazing' date that never makes it to a second.

If he comes back for more, despite disappearing or blowing lukewarm or cold, it gives strength to the misconception that he finds it difficult to resist the sex, which then places it at the centre of the relationship, creating a false emotional tie. You connect the fact that you enjoy the sex so much and that he keeps returning with the idea that he must be 'The One'. What he's doing however, is extracting maximum value by turning it into a no-strings, unemotional arrangement. When he thinks about having a 'good time' and getting a warm reception, he thinks of you.

DOUBLE STANDARDS & ENTRAPMENT

Casual sex is more prolific now than it's ever been, yet women, *not* men, continue to be penalised for being sexually liberal. On top of this, even if you're not looking to indulge in casual sex per se, many of you still engage in some level of sexual activity in the early stages of dating. It might be because you think that you're having such a great time so, *"What the hell?"* or you don't want to be perceived as a spoilsport because you're turning them down. While sleeping together on the first night, or soon after, works out for some, more often than not, it will leave you empty-handed, especially when that sexual partner is Mr Unavailable and he doesn't play fair.

His egotistical conflict doesn't stop him from having sex and essentially setting a trap. You have to wonder: why would he sleep with you, or even be on your case for a shag, knowing full well he'll mark you down for it if you agree? Because he can. For him, if one woman 'slips up' and gives it to him 'too easily', there are plenty more where she came from. You're being set up to fail.

This is entrapment and feeds back into his beliefs. It *suits* his agenda to sleep with you and discard you, or mark your card as a 'Passing Time Candidate' who's good enough to screw and use, but not good enough to be The One. That's not because you *deserve* this treatment or that you're anything you've been deemed to be by him, but, whether it's because he slept with you early on or you're keeping it casual with him, he draws negative conclusions about you that confirm his beliefs, even though he's just as much a party to creating the illusion of a false connection.

He's often chancing his arm to see how women react to his advances. If the risk pays off, he has sex with you and writes you off. If it doesn't pay off, he'll overestimate his interest until he finds another way to mark you down. The reality is that you're damned if you do and damned if you don't.

SPOT THE SIGNS

If sex is the dominant aspect of your relationship, this shows up imbalances in other areas. If you're having sex in an undefined or 'casual' relationship, it's a sexual arrangement.

1) List any and all concerns and incidences that have upset you. Don't deny anything and put down as much as possible. If any of the things that you write down are crossing boundaries and symptoms of you being treated without love, care, trust, and respect, sex is the *least* of your concerns.

2) Is your relationship undefined or defined as casual? If it's ambiguous or casual, or you're too afraid to ask, it's because you're not in a relationship.

3) Are you only in contact around the times that you're getting together? What is the contact like between your dalliances? If he's disappearing *and* you're still having sex, it's casual. If he takes you out and expects sex afterwards and then nothing until you meet up again – casual.

4) Your interactions and conversations are very sexual in nature. Graphic texts, virtual sex, phone sex, actual sex but not much else going on – yep, it's about the sex, which means it's casual.

5) Have you slept with him on more than one occasion thinking that you were getting back together? If so, you're being fooled by the same con.

REMEMBER!

Just because someone can sex you well, that doesn't mean they are The One – it means they're good at sex and pleasing you.

Lose any ideas out of your head that someone who you have a sexual connection with is someone that you can have a relationship with. Fast.

Sex with him may feel familiar and good but, if you've broken up, it means you're not in a relationship anymore.

You may think things would be so much better if the sex improved or the relationship materialised, but both absences tell you that there are some fundamental pieces missing from the foundation of your relationship.

It's bad enough putting up with shady relationship behaviour, but to put up with feeling bad about yourself because of how you're treated about sex with them – major no-no. He's just not that special.

HE DEALS IN CRUMB RATIONS OF COMMITMENT

Whether it's committing to being with you, or to breaking up and moving on, he fears either option in equal measure. Mr Unavailable is afraid of commitment. Period. The Status Quo, his comfort zone, keeps things at 'five', probably at your expense. He wants it all on his terms. As a result, not only does this leave you between a rock and a hard place, but his commitment resistance means that he says and does things to cater to each side of the fence, which, of course, sends out conflicting messages.

Remember the core issue here – he's unavailable – and this means that he won't even commit to a feeling, so you expecting him to commit to a *relationship* is quite a leap. When he feels what to others might seem like the start of something wonderful, he backs away from it and blows lukewarm or cold to get back into a neutral zone. If he starts experiencing any negative feelings, he'll avoid those and start blowing hot to feel better. This means, of course, it's never really about you; it's always about him.

HEAVY EXAGGERATION OVEN USER

Doing some simple basic stuff that *available* people take for granted takes a lot of effort for him – just the mental effort of showing up feels huge. When you question his commitment capabilities, if he's deluded enough to actually believe that he can and will commit, he might remind you that he bought you something, took you out to dinner, stayed the night, has moved in, or has claimed that you're exclusive because he thinks that this is what commitment takes. If he acknowledges that he's not ready to commit but he's unwilling to step up his game (yeah, that would be all of them) or leave (yeah, that would be most of them), he'll try to sell you his crumbs as a loaf, as if you're supposed to be grateful for them.

He keeps throwing you crumbs that 'magically' become a loaf in transit.

He doesn't view his capabilities in reality and may see himself operating at as much as 100%. The very deluded may think it goes beyond that. His 100% is not an available person's 100% because he has *limited capacity*. It may feel great to him, but if what results is contradicting words and actions, within relationships that lack progression, commitment, etc., his capacity is limited. The more you put up with it, the more you see a limited capacity as full capacity and the crumbs get magically turned into a loaf.

Just because it's all he's capable of doesn't mean it's enough for you, and just because he gives what he's capable of doesn't make him great. This is exaggeration of the worst kind and it will set you up for a fall. Ever seen someone settle? It's because they decide that something is better than nothing, but that something may be very insubstantial. It's like you're saying, *"Wow! Look at how much of a limited contribution is coming from a limited man!"*, which is like celebrating the obvious and championing mediocrity.

Looking at him in context – based on the sum of his previous actions, contradictions, and what he's doing currently – realise that what he has to give is what he has to give. In some instances, it may dwindle further, particularly if he finds that when he gives less, you try more. If he's giving very little, he has very little to give. If he used to give a lot, but he's gradually or suddenly withdrawn and replaced that with less, what he initially gave was for show and what he's consistently showing and giving now is what he has to offer.

The key is to stop overvaluing the crumbs, too, and making them into a loaf, because if you saw them as crumbs, you'd have left.

HE'S JUST NOT COMMITTING

The reason why Mr Unavailable doesn't see a committed relationship with you is because he doesn't see a committed relationship with *anyone*, or at least not the type of commitment that you're looking for – healthy, positive commitment. Obviously, if you have unhealthy ideas about commitment, you'll meet your match with him, but that's a different matter!

If he does envision commitment, it's often a short-lived fantasy. When he has to deliver on it, he undermines the commitment he supposedly made – yep, Future Faking, Fast Forwarding, blowing hot and cold, et al. If you're involved with him and don't run for the hills from his flip-flapping ways, he'll read this as a signal that you can't be that interested in commitment either.

If, while involved with him, aside from his own patent inability to commit, you also lack personal security (which means having a reasonable level of self-esteem, being authentic, and having your own life, desires, and interests), you may do stuff like creating drama, having little or no boundaries, being a human transformer and basing your life around him. These actions reaffirm whatever shady ideas he has about commitment and inadvertently legitimise his resistance.

You having your insecurities doesn't make you responsible for his resistance, because he's resisting anyway, but you are, by continuing to contribute to the dynamic, enabling his behaviour.

The truth is, if you had more personal security, you wouldn't participate in whatever he has to offer and you'd be OK with walking away because you'd be secure enough to recognise how it would detract from you. Many a Fallback Girl has burned up valuable brain energy wondering what she said or did to stop him from committing, especially when he has stated or implied that it was in the offing – his inability to commit isn't about you; it's about him and his beliefs and behaviours. It's not about you.

UPFRONT OR UNDERCOVER?

Rewinding your relationship with him and playing it back, you'll recognise key indications that he wasn't commitment able. He was either blatantly obvious about it or he thought he was doing a good job of covering his tracks, but commitment resisters always show themselves because their actions don't match up with their words.

The Upfront Commitment Resister shows you, through words and actions, that he's incapable of giving you a committed relationship. He tells you he's no good, that he's screwed up, and that he's not ready. In the meantime, he's not calling when he says he will, slipping in and out of your bed, making you feel needy for asking for the basics, and generally behaving like someone who no woman in their right mind would chase commitment from. By still being around, you think that there's something about you that will potentially inspire him to change. As far as he's concerned though, he's told and shown you all you need to know and if you still want him around in spite of this, he'll jump on board for the free ride.

The Undercover Commitment Resister tells you that he's really into you, tells crap stories about why he's currently messed up, promises to be different and to be patient with him, and, essentially, makes all of the right noises. Unfortunately it all leads to the same, miserable, outcome, because there's only so long that he can pretend that he's a great catch, or you eventually realise that he's incapable of committing and that he's not as into you as he's led you to believe. Your brain tells you that if he's saying the right things and is still lurking around, he might eventually deliver. When you end it, he'll come at you full force and beg for another chance after making lots of big promises that he'll break again.

SPOT THE SIGNS

If you're feeling hungry in your relationship, it's because it lacks substance.

1) If you've broken up more than twice, you've got commitment issues.

2) Is he saying that he's got other things going on or bigger priorities? You know all the excuses he gives? Those are the 'other things' and 'bigger priorities' and you're being relegated.

3) Has he said you're in a relationship? Have you both said you're in the *same* relationship? If you haven't both said it, it's not a relationship and it's too ambiguous. If you aren't both in agreement about what your relationship is, it's not a committed relationship.

4) Is it only you who's committed? One-sided commitment is like a three-legged horse or rowing a boat with one oar – a pointless waste of time. It takes two for relationship commitment.

5) Has he expressed concerns about committing? Don't play them down or act like you know better – you don't. He's telling you why he's unavailable for the relationship you want. Unless the core reasons for the fear go away, your relationship is going nowhere.

REMEMBER!

What is the rule? Not just the general rule – what's the rule with this person, with this situation? If it's familiar, you know the rule.

Don't be hard of hearing or see meaning where there is no meaning. When he says, *"I don't want a relationship,"* it means abort mission. As women, we spend too much of our lives trying to figure out other people's 'why' instead of addressing our own.

When someone says that they want to commit but it doesn't materialise, something's very wrong. *'Want'* is about a desire for something, so if it doesn't materialise, they don't want it that much.

A crumb is a crumb is a crumb. Unless you're an ant, that crumb doesn't look like a loaf. Either get your eyes tested or take off your magnifying rose-tinted glasses and get wise about what healthy relationships look like. Oh, and take him off that pedestal you've put him on while you're at it.

There's a guy out there who will commit to you (when you're ready to commit) but that's not going to happen if you stick with Mr Unavailable.

HE KEEPS A FOOTHOLD IN YOUR LIFE

Let's cut straight to the chase – he can't keep control of you and maintain The Status Quo outside of the relationship if he doesn't have a foot in your life and is unsure of your interest. He's all about his comfort zone, so, aside from having a comfort zone for when you're involved, he equally has one for when you're no longer together. In his mind, you're either going to be together on his terms or apart on his terms. As a result, he's quite frankly a pain in the bum.

From pushing the 'Friend Card', to poking around in your life, to chasing you for contact, attention, and even sex, he's devised a number of means to attempt to maintain control even when the relationship is over. He can't commit – whether it's to being with you or leaving you the hell alone – so he's ensuring that you're an option should he change his mind or have a use for you, while feeding his ego with the security of what he perceives as your affections for him. He's rarely upfront about this so, of course, this wreaks havoc in the lives of any and all Fallback Girls that give him the time of day.

The moment that you appear to be moving on is when he'll home in on you, blow hot, and set you back ten steps. You'll readily accept his offer of his friendship because you don't want to let go either and you keep reminding yourself that he's so nice, what great qualities he has, how 'connected' you are, and how he's so like your soulmate except for the small problem of him being emotionally unavailable and unable to commit. Let's just cut to the chase:

He's *not* your friend and he exploits an innate human desire to be perceived as being friend-*worthy*.

When he suggests that you should be friends or comes back and dangles the 'Friend Card' when he's trying to squeeze his way into your life on lesser terms, it's because – if you won't give him the time of day, let alone your friendship, aside from the fact that it will be very tricky for him to keep a foot in your life – you not being his friend communicates that he might not be as 'wonderful' or 'innocent' as he believes.

There's a universal belief that if someone is still prepared to be your friend after you've broken up, it means you're a 'good person'. Securing friendship and respect, even if it's undeserved, becomes of paramount importance. What he's failed to realise is that these are things that are earned and if he's that bloody concerned with being perceived as hurting or wronging someone, it's about time he sought for his actions to reflect this.

You know when he asks to be friends after the breakup and you don't hear from him for a while? It's because, in you saying YES, he's secured enough of an ego stroke that he only sees the need to get in touch with you to check that it still stands.

You know when he pesters you about hanging out, catching up, or whatever to show that you're 'friends' and then you agree and he suddenly goes 'dark' or the arrangement falls through? He secured enough of an ego stroke through your agreement that he sees no further use for you. For now.

You know when he badgers you to understand things from his perspective, or for your forgiveness, only for him to go off and mistreat you again? It's because he's gained what he wants – forgiveness – so the slate's been wiped clean. Even though he may do more stuff to piss you off, in his mind you're 'friends'.

The truth is: only people who are undeserving of your friendship have to badger, railroad, and guilt you into being their friend. If they were someone who acted with love, care, trust, and respect, they'd have a relative comfort in knowing they acted well enough that there is a possibility of friendship, but they equally would respect your need for space and not assume that they have a right to your friendship.

POKING AROUND

It's easier to keep in touch with minimal effort, and with so many of us sharing aspects of our lives online, that often link us to mutual friends and acquaintances, it has never been so easy for someone to poke around in our lives.

When he's in 'investigative mode', he's looking for clues, either from you or third-party sources, that 1) you haven't moved on, 2) you're still the person he thought you were, and 3) that you're still an option. Unfortunately, Fallback Girls are inclined to see poking around as something flattering – we think it's a reflection of his feelings and inability to resist us. Be under no illusions – he's poking around to maintain The Status Quo. Nothing more, nothing less.

If you haven't heard from him, little do you realise, he may have done the poking around he needed without having to let you know about it. He may have asked mutual friends about you, who told him that you're OK but suffering (he thinks you're still into him), or checked your Facebook profile and seen that you're not happy or people sympathising with you (he thinks you're still into him), or seen you walking around the office or town looking like someone has died (he thinks you're still into him), seen a 'tweet' about how much your heart hurts (he thinks you're still into him), or heard how you tried to date but decided to stop (he thinks you're still into him).

Equally, he may have got confirmation that you're still an option from _you_.

He may have got a call, text, or email from you checking in to 'see how he's doing' (he thinks you're still into him), or another message wondering why you haven't heard from him (he thinks you're still into him), or you told him he's an asshole for treating you XYZ, but still responded to his next contact (he thinks you're still into him), or you quickly reply to messages or agree to meet up (he thinks you're still into him).

When you get the frenzied poking around, where he's calling, showing up at your work or home, etc., it's highly likely it's because you're not responding to any of these, or have responded in a drastically negative manner, and he hasn't found third-party means to confirm your interest. While for a lot of Mr

Unavailables even a very negative response is still attention in their eyes, for some, a very negative response will trigger that out-of-control sensation, and – yep, you guessed it – they start pursuing you, thinking they want to get back together, Future Faking, etc. If you eventually move from very negative to positive again, which confirms your interest and validates their ego, they'll bail or turn into Mr Not So Interested.

LOOKING FOR A HANDOUT

Much like there are so many more casual relationships, there are so many more casual *breakups*. Often because of how he conducts himself, how things are left may be ambiguous.

You know you're involved with a Mr Unavailable *and* a pisstaker when he seeks to get what he had from you in the relationship outside of it.

Respect isn't his strong suit and he absolutely doesn't want to give you the basic courtesy of having enough space and time to grieve the loss of the breakup and heal, because if you do that, he can't keep a foothold in your life! By continuing to seek what he's already defaulted to and 'fallen back' on you for when you were together you start believing that you're needed and wanted and don't realise that if you give him any of these things, he's now done a bait and switch where you've ended up 'giving' on *lesser* terms.

As a Fallback Girl who's looking for validation and hasn't made the distinction between quality attention and crappy, self-serving attention, you'll see him reaching out for a 'handout' as a sign of his feelings for you because you'd rather be in his life on some terms, rather than no terms. Particularly now that you're broken up, you hope that extending yourself to him will demonstrate your greatness and help you win him back.

If pushed on why he's treating you this way and effectively using you, he'll blame you.

He'll claim that you know what he's like, that you didn't have to give him what he asked, pushed for, or even coerced you into (and in some instances pulled yet another 'fake-off') to secure 'the goods', and absolve himself of any responsibility for any hurt you feel. This is yet another important reminder that, even in the face of making uncomfortable decisions and suffering some short-term pain, never, ever, *ever* allow someone to use you, especially when the relationship is over. When you break, you *break*.

SPOT THE SIGNS

People need to be 'in' or 'out' of your life, not keeping a foot, toe or toenail in to be disruptive.

1) Can you actually call him your friend? Think about all the other friends you have: Is he like them? Yeah, I thought not. Unless you have friends who mess with your head and use you for what they can get and exploit your desire to win them over.

2) Can you call him up whenever you like? Yep, just like you would an actual friend.

3) Has he asked you to sleep with him? Are you finding yourself having sex, stroking his ego, listening to all his problems, writing out cheques, etc? You're being used.

4) When you respond to contact from him, do you find that he pulls back? You're being toyed with.

5) Have you ever dropped a date or ended a relationship for him only to flake out on you again? He's like a dog in a manger – only wants you when he knows he can't have you and loses interest as soon as he can.

REMEMBER!

Friends don't try to fuck you or fuck around with you.

If you settled for crumbs *in* the relationship, I can assure you that you'll have a crummy friendship. Don't try to keep him in your life on some terms rather than no terms, because you'll end up being disrespected while selling yourself short.

All relationships, good, bad, or indifferent, need a period of 'silence' before touching base or trying to be friends. If the relationship was under three months, make sure at least a month has gone and you're over him.

People who behaved in a friend-worthy manner in the relationship are confident enough in themselves that they don't need to force a friendship down your throat.

Remember that for some people, agreeing to being friends with them means you've forgiven, or even forgotten, past wrongdoings. If you haven't, I wouldn't go down the friend route.

HE USES 'TIMING' TO MANAGE YOU

Time is a wonderful thing for Mr Unavailable because, by his reckoning, he seems to have oodles of it; or, at the very least, he hasn't a care in the world about eating up *your* time or, as a friend of mine says, "using up your good years". He's always moments away from a crisis, a disaster, a heavy workload, a cat up a tree, or a match that he just *has* to watch tonight.

Time is something that he clings to like his life depends on it.

Time helps him avoid confronting the reality of the here and now, because he can always stake himself on a future that he'll no doubt avoid when it comes rolling around.

Time is that thing that he counts on when he recognises that he may have overstated or misled you because he thinks that he'll just deal with it 'later'.

Time is the indefinable thing that he uses to stonewall you and avoid responsibility for anything to do with you or the relationship.

'Timing' helps to avoid having very difficult conversations about the relationship or having to move it on.

As a result of entering his space-time continuum where he's *super* busy, suffering a time shortage, not thinking past the short term, avoiding the future or faking one, claiming he needs 'more time' or that he's not ready 'yet', you end up waiting around for the 'right' time, assuming that this is all that stands between you and your happiness with him, when in fact, it's never the right time.

BUSY BEE WITH A TIME SHORTAGE

I took to 'jokingly' calling one Mr Unavailable 'Busy Bee', as I was always sandwiched in between stuff, often with him 'conveniently' wanting to hang out when he needed to spend the weekend in London and use my parking, and he essentially made himself look and sound like The Busiest Person Ever.

If world leaders can find the time to attend to their families, have a social life, be friends to others, etc., why the frick can't Mr Unavailable?

His repeated talking about time actually manages down your expectations and has you grateful for the crumbs, yet again turning them into loaves of time. It's not that he can't free up time; he doesn't *want* to. He has the same 24 hours, 7 days a week that the rest of us do.

There's no such thing as not having time for a relationship –people *choose* not to. He sends a very consistent message that his time is more valuable than yours.

Often, what he blames his time shortage on are the very things he's constructively used to avoid intimacy and commitment. Often the workaholic Mr Unavailable isn't as needed or under pressure at work as he makes out, but being a workaholic allows him to avoid dealing with the discomfort of someone else's needs. The issue isn't the management of his time or the factors that he claims are the time suck; it's that he values safeguarding himself more.

SHORT-TERM THINKER

If Mr Unavailable gave some genuine thought processing over to considering the medium and long-term, he'd be a very different person. That, and your 'relationship' would be over a lot sooner. He's all about the now. He has no qualms about getting heavily involved with you for the short-term fringe benefits.

He gets to have his emotional needs catered to whilst shafting yours, gets the sexual benefits while sustaining the false connection, enjoys the social benefit of having a woman at his beck and call to spend time with when it suits, and essentially he's moving along one day or one isolated get-together at a time.

The avoidance of commitment when thinking about time means that when his thoughts stray, even for a few moments, to the 'future' (read: in a few hours, tomorrow, the following week and beyond), it brings about uncomfortable feelings that he quickly squashes. If he *does* dwell beyond the short term, it's actually when he's most likely to disappear, create conflict to orchestrate tension or an exit, or go to some lengths to remind you of the lack of a future. You, in the meantime, spend so much time staying in the moment that you forget to look at the bigger picture – this is why Mr Unavailables get far more relationship play than they should.

FUTURE AVOIDING & FUTURE FAKING

Where there are 'future' issues, you've got problems. He's either Future Avoiding by stonewalling attempts to discuss the future, make plans, or commit; or he's Future Faking. The net result is the same – the future that you'd like or that's been promised to you doesn't materialise.

Avoiding commitment to time means that, for a future-avoidant Mr Unavailable, making plans, sometimes even the simplest of ones, is agonising. This is where you'll get non-answers, tension, or outright avoidance, through stonewalling, disappearing, and conflict. I knew a Mr Unavailable who couldn't commit to something as basic as a night out. When he heard we were going on holiday, he created a fuss and said he 'might' come, spent a week in indecision. In the meantime, we went ahead and booked our trip.

With Future Faking, he's actually avoiding the reality of time because he's putting more effort into creating the illusion of a future than he is into making an actual future with you. This, of course, is a ticking time bomb because it's only a matter of time until that future catches up with him.

PLAYING FOR TIME

If you listen to his bullshit excuses, you'll think it's all just a matter of time because you're focusing on the wrong aspects of the excuse.

I'm not ready for a relationship You think that he just needs to be convinced of the merits of one, forgetting that if he's not ready for a relationship but he's still sleeping with you, etc., that you're casual.

I need more time You think that literally with some time and patience he'll come around to your way of thinking but you forget to ask what he needs more time for. To make up his mind about you? To be casual? To try to work things out with his ex?

I need a week The sense of urgency lets you believe that once this super-important obstacle is attended to, he'll be yours in a week. You forget to ask what the hell he needs a week for? He's stalling you until the next excuse.

If only things were different, I'd be with you You get the impression it's circumstance and bad timing, instead of recognising that things aren't different and the issue is him.

The truth is, he isn't ready and, depending on how he chooses to conduct his life, he may never be. What he's actually doing is buying time. He assumes that you have all the time in the world to sideline your feelings and goals.

Some of them do hope they'll get with the program at some point and acclimatise to a committed relationship. They'll look at you and know that, on and off paper, you're pretty damn special and they fear someone else enjoying that specialness, yet they don't value it enough to give you the relationship you deserve. So they hold on to you, even though in doing that they're still left wondering why they can't step up and *feel* and *do*. So they buy some more time. They figure it must be something about you that's not pushing the right buttons; but, like the Fallback Girl, they're the common denominator to each of their relationships.

SPOT THE SIGNS

Time waits for no one, including Mr Unavailable, which means you certainly shouldn't. You're not more powerful than time itself.

1) Let's crunch some numbers. How long have you been together? How much of your relationship has been consistently good? So, for example, if you've been together for a year, and only 3 months were consistently good, it means that 75% of your relationship consistently hasn't been.

2) Fits and starts, regressing, and flatlining – progression issues. If it's increasingly difficult to spend time together, or you've found that the time you have is shrinking instead of increasing, you've got timing issues as well.

3) Have you got scheduling issues? Your relationship requires a joint co-piloted agenda. If his 'schedule' of how available he can be for the relationship, or even what he wants out of it, is significantly different from yours and he is not breaking his neck to adjust his life and find a solution you both can live with, you need to drop him from your schedule.

4) Is he 'switchy'? If he's chopping and changing his moods, chasing and then backing off, saying stuff and then denying it, he's incredibly switchy and living in the short-term.

5) Are you experiencing delays, postponements and cancellations? Occasional is fine but regular occurrences of it or big plans not happening = commitment and availability issues. Do plans have to be on his terms? Does he back out of your plans? Are you afraid of broaching subjects and asking questions?

REMEMBER!

He's just not that special. Really – he hasn't been awarded special status or less time in the week than the rest of us.

Too busy for you, equals too busy for a relationship, equals unavailable, equals time to move on to someone who doesn't have to scratch around to rustle up the basics.

Anyone who is reactive and stuck in the short term is a pain in the arse to be with. You cannot progress a relationship that's stuck in a short-term time warp.

When people think beyond the short term, they consider the consequences.

HE'S AN EGOTIST SEEKING PERFECTION

Mr Unavailable blindly assumes that he acts as he does because he's never met the 'right' woman. His ego forgets to remind him that in his unavailable state, he's not the right man – for anyone. By playing silly games (even if he doesn't think he is), he gets to let himself off the hook and continue looking to the future where he thinks that his perfect woman exists.

He's failed to recognise that his resistance in relationships isn't caused by the women he's involved with, but by himself.

Perpetually dissatisfied and seeking unattainable perfection, he always has an eye cast over the shoulder of his current Fallback Girl, ensuring that he avoids looking too closely at his own actions.

His quest for perfection is inherently based on the premise that he fundamentally recognises his emotional shortcomings, even though he may deny it, but he believes that when he finds what he's 'looking for' in a relationship, or it finds him, that he'll suddenly, spontaneously combust into an emotionally available, commitment-willing man with great relationship habits, and all of his problems will magically vacate his life.

Deep down he doesn't truly believe that this perfect relationship exists or that he can be a better man in a relationship. He then resigns himself to being Mr Unavailable in an unavailable relationship, often making out that he can be and do better, but not being emotionally open and willing enough to do anything to bring about change. He then reminds himself that it's not his fault; he just hasn't met the right woman yet.

MAKING IT WRONG

At the start of the relationship, when you often get the Mr Unavailable that blows hot, he's likely feeling, being, and doing a lot of the stuff he thinks should be part of his 'perfect relationship'. He has negative and unrealistic beliefs and at the same time has conflicting beliefs and desires that fuel this vision.

Unfortunately he panics on experiencing this 'perfect relationship' and undermines it because he'll feel vulnerable. He either doesn't believe in his capabilities to have a relationship and meet your needs, or he's said and done things that are not wholly representative of him, making them somewhat difficult to sustain over an extended period of time. Or the effort of the hot phase combined with what you subsequently may want, need, and expect may set off his flight/sabotage reflex. When you throw in the fact that he may recognise your own unavailability, the whole experience ensures he ends up finding reasons to confirm his beliefs.

If he doesn't blow particularly hot at the outset and makes it clear, via actions and words, that he's a limited man, that he's not interested/half interested/only out for himself, etc., he may still have a remote hope that the 'right' woman will provoke change. Unfortunately any efforts are being severely undermined because, by you engaging with him in spite of his lukewarm or even cold behaviour, he recognises that you don't have the healthiest relationship habits.

MARKING YOU DOWN

He's hiding his commitment issues behind what he perceives as your own shortcomings – shortcomings I should stress that either aren't actual shortcomings, or, if they are, they're ones that he's happy to exploit for the purpose of getting the relationship he wants. On some level he knows that he's behaving unfairly or downright awful at times, and if you're accepting it, and even in effect rewarding him for it, he'll regard this as a major flaw in you. He'll often mark your cards from the moment that you give him the time of day. He has a contradictory belief that the perfect woman for him would never put up with the very behaviour that he engages in.

Often when you share information about your relationship history or childhood, he draws the conclusion that you're just as screwed up as him. When you combine this with him perceiving you to have little or no boundaries, depending on what and how much he can get away with, he may think you're the same as him or similar. While there is some comfort in this, overall that type of 'synergy' is not part of his perfect vision. He subsequently uses the information garnered to rationalise that you can't actually want to be in a fully-fledged relationship – after all, he doesn't, even if he does neglect to mention this...

MR UNAVAILABLE'S MENTAL SCORECARD

She lets me sleep with her	-10
She let a guy mistreat her	-20
She jumps when I call	-30
She's needy	-40
She wants me even though she knows I'm no good	-50
TOTAL	-150

If you appear to be very physically attractive, outgoing, ambitious, and lots of other perceived positives, but you're still single and, on top of that, you're interested in him, he will make the assumption that there is something wrong with you. He may have no clue what it is, but the surety he has that this 'flaw' exists means that he can subconsciously justify his inaction with you while no doubt doing things in the relationship that will expose the so-called 'flaw' that he is looking for. Don't make the mistake of thinking that you can change to suit his perfect ideal – you can't, because the goalposts keep moving. The biggest joke though, is that the 'flaw' that he can't quite put his finger on, is him...

SPOT THE SIGNS

An imperfect man seeking what basically amounts to perfection is an oxymoron.

1) Has he got a 'schedule'? If he breaks up or starts long-winded discussions about how he expected things to be a certain way by now, you're with the guy with a perfect vision of things that he keeps killing off with his demands and unavailability... while blaming you.

2) Has he got a list? He's either admitted to a list of requirements or during the time you've been together, he's littered your relationship with references to 'how he likes things'.

3) Do you feel like you can't do right for doing wrong? Yeah, you're with the guy with whom you can't win.

4) Do you ever privately laugh to yourself about how deluded and demanding he sounds? It's because he's being deluded and demanding! These are not attractive qualities!

5) Are you trying to be and do everything you can in the hope of pleasing him? You're with the man who will find every reason on earth not to be 'pleased' because he's not *available*.

REMEMBER!

Let me say it again – he's just not that special.

There's a reason he's not in the 'perfect relationship', or he's never settled down. It's not because he's such an 'amazing' man or there are no perfect women – he's a pain in the bum!

If the relationship isn't as 'great' as he would like, he is a part of that reason.

It's not your job to make him a better man or even an available man – it's his.

Twisting yourself into a pretzel trying to please him is just too much back breaking work for *anyone*. Untwist yourself and find a man who accepts you as you are and accept *yourself* while you're at it.

HE BREAKS OUT THE SOB STORY
& EXCUSES

As women, society has taught us to either frown upon expressions of emotion from men, or to think we've struck gold when they do shed tears or tell us a *'weally, weally personal story',* as we interpret it as a sign of how special we are to them. The middle ground is that sometimes men *do* cry, just like sometimes *we* cry, and sometimes they share intimate details of their past, but, by the very nature of your interest in Mr Unavailables, you're bound to believe that a show of 'emotion', in the form of tears or 'sharing' their past, is something amazing.

You can be incredibly sympathetic and compassionate about a lot of stuff and, while these are good qualities in appropriate situations, with Mr Unavailables they become your Achilles heel and blind you. For him it feels like all of his Christmases have come in one go because not only are you on sympathy and compassion overload, but you'll even do some of the hard work for him and make up excuses for him.

AN EXCUSES-LED MAN

I've had a lot on with work/really busy.

My battery ran out. Again. Yes, really.

We were on a break. Oh, we were together then? My bad.

I'm keeping you a secret because I want you all to myself.

My family just isn't ready for our relationship yet.

If I leave her, she wouldn't be able to handle it and might even do something to herself.

I'm trying to find the right moment to tell my kids.

I wouldn't have done it if you'd let me do [whatever boundary-crossing thing you denied him].

I didn't say anything because I knew you'd react this way.

It doesn't mean anything.

I didn't feel that you needed to know.

I knew you'd get the wrong idea.

Mr Unavailable has realised the value of making excuses, no matter how thin or even outright dumb they may be, and what's helped him to inflate the value of these excuses is being able to get away with them time and again.

An **excuse** is a reason that is given to justify an offence or fault, but Mr Unavailable, in particular, uses excuses to lessen the responsibility and the blame.

The truth is that it's only in unhealthy relationships that you have to put up with someone making excuses. In healthy relationships, while one may give a reason for something happening, they don't seek to lessen their responsibility.

Excuse-led men like Mr Unavailable end up carrying on as if they're so much more important. Relationships require each party to treat each other as valuable and as a result, there is no room for excuses because, by lessening responsibility, it lessens the commitment and honesty in the relationship. Having that responsibility and honesty ensures that more connection is made between actions and the impact on you.

THIS ONE TIME AT BAND CAMP

Mr Unavailable and his tales of woe remind me of that scene in the film *The Social Network*, where the girlfriend of Mark Zuckerberg's character emphatically states that she's ending it with him because he's an asshole and not because he's clever and misunderstood.

Inspired by the line from American Pie that's synonymous with the girl who wouldn't shut up about her band camp experiences, **This One Time at Band Camp** represents Mr Unavailable's 'sad stories' that millions of us have had to listen to.

All Mr Unavailables have something they repeat every time things get tough. Most have at least one tale of woe about a woman from their past who screwed them up and left them the way they are. They all have excuses and tales to lay the foundations for extricating them out of the relationship or responsibility at a later date. These stories reap hassle-free sex, reduce pressure, and give the impression of a wounded man who needs more time, tea and sympathy.

The first few times he told the story, it was heart-wrenching and cute, but, over time, you realise that it's just a story and he's so disconnected from himself that he's giving you the watered-down version where he has no responsibility and he gets to pretend that he was this totally available 'victim'.

"And this one time... at band camp... this woman let me down a really long time ago. She made me feel so useless and she wouldn't even sleep with me anymore or give me a blowjob. Then I found out that she'd been cheating on me and I've just never been the same since... And then... this one time at band camp... I was devastated when this woman knocked back my proposal... and... and..."

You hear this and think: *"Oh, the poor guy. No wonder he can't fully express his feelings to me. He's hurting and he needs the support of a good woman to help him through this. He'll open up eventually. I know that I can make him feel like a man in the bedroom and I've got a whole closet full of lingerie and massage oil that will make him feel like king of the castle. I don't mind giving him blowjobs and I'm going to make sure that he never even has to ask for one. Cheated on? God, I know that if I had been cheated on, I'd be very distrusting so I'm going to show how reliable I am and how I can be trusted..."* and so it rolls on.

The real story was more like this: He *was* let down a really long time ago after she got sick and tired of him perpetually disappointing her. She discovered that not only had he been sleeping around, but that he was trying to hit on someone from their office. Outraged because they'd been sleeping together regularly, in an act of revenge she cheated, too, with a guy who'd been chasing her for a while. She *did* give him blowjobs; she just didn't feel like giving them 24/7. He *did* propose to an ex, but it was after she'd cut contact with him and he used it as a last ditch attempt to win her over. He wasn't actually intending to get married, although he'd swear blind that he was.

If women presented themselves to men and said that they were screwed up, some guy had messed with them, or any of the other stuff that comes rolling out of his mouth, we'd be labelled 'needy' or 'psycho'.

What's scary is that these tales are often exaggerated, watered down, or outright fabrications! You only find out the truth as he 'fluffs his lines' or pulls the **Drip-feed Manoeuvre**, which is where he drips extra bits of his story at a later date, when he thinks you can handle it. Either that or you meet his ex and find out the horrifying truth.

TEARS OF A CROCODILE

Crocodile tears are false and there's little or no sincerity in them. It may start out innocently, but the person gets savvy enough to recognise that they get what they want when they shed them.

They may not see it that way but people who 'cry' them do so because it generates their desired result. Ooh, that's a bit harsh, you might think. Well, here's the thing: there is a genuine expression of emotion in crying– it's spontaneous, it can't be helped, and there's a realness in there.

Ever had him cry his eyes out and beg you not to leave him, claiming that he can't bear to be without you, and then when you stay he goes cold on you?

Ever had him weeping down the phone saying he can't believe you won't speak to him and then when you do, he's back to his usual self?

Does he only seem to cry when you want to deal with issues?

Does he cry and tell you about how hurt he is that you left him and then next thing you hear is that he's been shagging someone else behind your back? [This actually happened to me.]

Does he cry and say how lonely and devastated he is that you've cut contact but when you go around there he's shacked up with another girl or you hear he's been trying to hit on your friend/co-worker?

These are just some examples, but, the point is, they're *hollow* tears used to shift the agenda and manipulate you. Oh, he might believe they're real, but it's a bit like the way he believes he's going to give you the future when he's Future Faking yet again. It's called being *reactive* and that's what these guys are.

He's unavailable, hence if he cries, you misguidedly believe that he's emotionally available. You might believe he's remorseful and on his way to being a half-decent guy in a committed relationship and believe you're seeing a different side – that he's being vulnerable and letting you in. Ladies, it takes a lot more than crying a few tears to be emotionally available – you've all cried plenty of times and you're still not available yourselves.

Have you ever been in a situation where you're crying and you don't know why? Or you're crying but you're not actually crying about whatever is unfolding but about something else? This is something that you not only need to understand about crocodile tears, but also about when he chases you up after you tell him to beat it and appears to be contrite:

When things feel out of control because it's not being dictated on his terms, this feels unfamiliar and extremely uncomfortable to him.

Crocodile tears make an appearance when his ego's been dented, he's reminded of a similar situation that upset him, or he's pulling a passive-aggressive manoeuvre that plays to the you who's desperate for some validation of his feelings, knowing that you'll be affected by this 'production'. The moment that you react in the way that he expects (example – he texts, you respond), he switches off because it's back on familiar ground again and the urgency and his reaction to it passes.

SPOT THE SIGNS

He may be wounded, he might be sad, he might have had a bad experience, but if he's using these as reasons for why he can't meet your needs or excuses for why he's treated you poorly, he's telling you he's unavailable.

1) Have you ever thought, "Oh, here we go again!"? It's because he's rolling out the same old tales and excuses.

2) Have you found yourself rationalising his excuses? It's because the original excuse was crap.

3) Does he take responsibility? I don't mean saying "Sorry" and hurrying you to move on, then repeating it, but actually being genuinely apologetic, expressing remorse, taking responsibility, not trying to blame you or whatever else he can latch onto, and endeavouring not to repeat the action.

4) Do you feel more bothered by his story or tears than he does? Be careful of being manipulated.

5) Is he drip-feeding you new bits of a story? This means he wasn't being honest and upfront when he told you and is engaging in mind fuckery.

REMEMBER

There's only so many times he can tell the same story and then it's time to change the record.

A genuine story or expression of emotion doesn't have a predetermined idea of what you should say or do as a result of it.

If he's honest, responsible and respectful, he won't expect, or even demand, that you accept an excuse, story or tears as a way of lessening responsibility.

If he's the only one who can make excuses, tell stories and cry, there's a lack of empathy going on here. Danger alert!

Strip out all the excuses and what are you left with?

HE ONLY THINKS OF HIMSELF

When I've been in 'relationships' with lazy or reluctant 'partners', it's been comparable to trying to cycle a tandem bike on my own with the teammate on it, with the addition of a flat tyre. Very tiring and a pain in the arse.

Mr Unavailable is that reluctant teammate and he's very much a solo thinker and player with empathy reserve issues. He basically projects his vision of things and, after establishing the relationship on his terms (while of course crossing your boundaries), he assumes that, if you're still there, you're on board because he's Me, Me, Me, It's All About Me. He can't see past his own nose and thinks that what he does in his interests is in your interests and he doesn't have any incentive to change.

Say this to yourself as often as necessary: **He takes as much as I give him. He gets away with as much as I let him. *What* has he done for me lately?**

Mr Unavailable does and thinks about things on his terms and from his perspective. As he's a solo thinker who believes that he can take care of himself and that everyone is out for themselves, he assumes you'll take care of yourself also. While there are certainly some really shady ones out there, a lot of Mr Unavailables are, for all intents and purposes, relatively OK guys with shit relationship skills, issues with commitment, and, of course, the solo mentality. These are the guys who catch you out with their selfish relationship habits because you expect more of them.

He makes decisions about the relationship without giving you a heads-up.

If he starts out thinking you were great and that he could see a relationship, and then the chase wears off and he changes his mind, he often says nothing. The first you know about it is when you have an awkward conversation and he starts squawking about how he's not ready for a relationship yet and yadda yadda yadda. It either hasn't occurred to him that this is something critical that you need to know, or he has thought of it and assumed you'll see it from his actions, or he has thought of it and decided he'll enjoy the ride for now and pass time with you. After all, he wouldn't want to endanger the shag, etc. He may also assume that because his feelings have changed, then surely yours must have, too.

GIVING WHAT HE WANTS TO GIVE

Mr Unavailable thinks about what he is able to give and decides what you need on that basis. Now, bearing in mind that he's not exactly honest and connected with himself, he often believes that his limited contribution is far more than it actually is.

Fallback Girls often wonder, 'How the hell can he think that anyone would be happy with those crumbs?' but to him they're not crumbs; they're his effort and, even if it's based on a 10% capacity, to him it feels like a lot especially with women overvaluing them, too.

Thinking about others is what committed people do and when he contemplates meeting your needs (not the ones that he's conjured up for you, but the ones that you've stated or even kept badgering him about), it creates uncomfortable feelings that he, of course, is looking to avoid.

Some Mr Unavailables have very little empathy, so you can explain till the cows come home, but if their disposition is to think of themselves and not really give a rat's about others, it's like you're speaking gobbledygook while trying to force them to have a skill that they don't possess.

Some Mr Unavailables are selfish in their relationships, but can appear giving and generous to others, which no doubt is frustrating for you. You'll wonder how he can have loving relationships with friends or family or help out the little old lady down the street, but it's important to remember that thinking about others outside of a romantic, committed relationship context is different. He may not make the same associations about giving and doing to others as he does in a romantic relationship.

He may feel that the opportunity to be vulnerable is limited in these other interactions, plus, on top of this, a romantic relationship has different expectations and demands and is ideally beyond short-term moments and experiences. This is why he seeks to keep managing down your expectations, so that you only want, need, and expect what *he's* prepared to give. If you go beyond this, you'll experience negative consequences.

NO INCENTIVE TO CHANGE

He keeps going back to the 'all you can eat' Fallback Girl relationship buffet until a sign goes up on the establishment declaring it closed down. He takes whatever is on offer and pushes for and asks for extras to see how much he can squeeze out of you. If you have little or no boundaries, he'll squeeze you dry until you either go bankrupt or have the good sense to stop offering the 'service'.

To be honest, when most of us are given the opportunity to have our cake and eat it, we do, although if we are emotionally healthy and hanging around like-minded people, the opportunity to be taken advantage of or take advantage is minimal. As he only thinks about himself and is patently selfish, he'll happily relegate you to dubious roles such as *The Other Woman* and *Yo-Yo Girl* and enjoy all of the fringe benefits of a relationship even when you have expressed discomfort and he knows that you want and expect more.

While he fannies around pretending that he's going through an agony trying to figure out his life so that he can be with you, or claiming that he's trying to be a better man in a better relationship, he's actually keeping you on ice and in the position of Fallback Girl.

He has absolutely no incentive to be any different from what he is because you have already shown that you are prepared to be and stay with him when he has nothing or very little to offer. For him to suddenly have a conscience about what he has been doing is expecting a benevolence that I wouldn't go holding your breath for.

From your perspective, you're thinking that love and a relationship are an incentive to change, but that's not how he views things. Knowing that others will be with him if you won't means he doesn't really feel there are any major consequences for not changing his ways.

SPOT THE SIGNS

Someone who's all about the 'ME' doesn't have room to consider you and as a result can never truly recognise your needs or the impact of their actions (or lack of them) on you.

1) Does he tell you what you need? You'll find that you can talk till you're blue in the face, but he doesn't actually listen to and do what you ask, even when he's asked what you what. No. He just does something entirely different and claims he's trying to do what he thinks you want.

2) Do most of his relationships tend to have similar lengths? Some Mr Unavailables literally cannot go beyond a certain point, as it makes them feel like they're considering someone else too much. Ever been with Mr 90 Days, Mr Just Under Six Months, or Mr 2-3 years?

3) Does he actually think that what he wants should be what you want if you want him to be happy? This is pure laziness. It would be better for him to go out with his reflection or a cardboard cut-out.

4) Do friends, family, etc, express surprise about him being involved? A lot of solo guys are *known* for being solo.

5) Does he claim he's "never had this problem before"? Yes he has, he just doesn't want to admit it. You'll rarely find that they have a 'clean' relationship history and he's likely guilty of the same behaviour in other relationships.

REMEMBER!

No relationship can have a chance of growing so much as an inch when you're involved with someone who cannot see past their nose.

Being with selfish people is hard work. Let me say it again – he's just not that special.

Selfish only works when you only have yourself to consider. Commitment in mutually fulfilling relationships requires you to be selfless at times.

Don't fall into the trap of believing that if you accommodate selfish people that they'll match your efforts. Selfish people don't register your efforts and, in fact, have a sense of entitlement.

If you can't share in a relationship, you certainly won't be able to care or empathise – major problems.

THE WHYS OF MR UNAVAILABLE

Every year I clock up thousands of searches via the likes of Google for answers relating to emotional unavailability and figuring out Mr Unavailable, and a post that I wrote about *How to Spot Emotionally Unavailable Men* has been read over a million times.

When people discover my site Baggage Reclaim, they're looking for a solution to a problem. Ideally they want that solution to be me saying, *"Do A plus B and you'll get C and convert him into an available man."* Many readers believe their situation is unique and that the strange relationship that they've found themselves in is a direct result of something that they've said or done. They often think they've misunderstood something, that they're going crazy, that they need to change themselves so that they can 'win' his love and commitment, or they wonder what they can do to change him.

What they, of course, discover, like you have, is that the situation *isn't* unique and it's not something you've said or done that's 'made' him this way – he was this way before you met him, while you were with him, and will be long after you're gone, until he sees fit to address his reasons for being unavailable. You haven't misunderstood, although you may have applied meaning where there is none. You're not going crazy, you don't need to change yourself for him (although you do need to address *your* love habits), and you *cannot* change him. It's upsetting, but also empowering because you can stop making his problems *your* problems.

You, like many a Fallback Girl who has come before you, and will no doubt follow, have probably spent far too much time and brain energy trying to 'figure him out', which is like rationalising the irrational. On top of this, you may have emotionally bankrupted yourself in the process of playing Columbo and trying to be loyal. Here's the thing:

Wondering why another person's emotional style is to be emotionally unavailable is like asking, "How long is a piece of string?"

Some of you will think that you know the reasons, and you might, but, equally, you may be barking up the wrong tree. In fact, more often than not, you're way off mark because, in trying to understand the who, what, where and why of someone else's emotional behaviour, you're looking for a solution and an answer that you can involve yourself in. You're also applying that energy and those attempts to understand to the wrong person. You will never have 100% of the answers to someone else's behaviour. Hell, you won't always have 100% of the answers for your own.

This chapter is focused on providing the core and most common reasons why Mr Unavailable is... Mr Unavailable, and, along with the previous chapters that break down how he operates, the aim is to provide you with more than enough information to validate the concerns you have, understand the flaw you have in your grand masterplan of trying to get a commitment-resistant man to commit, and more importantly, empower you to address the thing you can control: you.

I want you to see that his behaviour isn't about you so that you can stop making yourself responsible for making him into a better man.

You can pretty much group the reasons into fears, beliefs, emotional schooling, some confusion and badly learned relationship habits, and past experiences that have left a negative imprint and created poor associations with being vulnerable and intimate. All of these factors feed into one another and result in emotionally, spiritually, and sometimes physically, unavailable men.

FEARS AND BELIEFS

Mr Unavailable is very driven by fear although he may not be fully aware of exactly how deep these fears run and how they're affecting not only his ability to emotionally engage in relationships, but his actions, or lack thereof, that result. He's afraid of commitment and the responsibility that comes with it; being truthful and seeing himself in an authentic light; and of failing, missing out or essentially experiencing anything that he views as an uncomfortable or unpleasant emotion. That's a lot of fear.

Fear is an emotional response to a perceived danger – for him that danger is the consequences of commitment and intimacy.

The danger isn't *you* per se; it's all the things that you and your expectations, needs and wants bring to his life. He's afraid of being absolute in promising himself and the responsibilities and situations that that brings. He's afraid that if he allows someone in and is emotionally *available,* that, by risking himself, he'll experience negative consequences.

His way of safeguarding himself from the perceived 'dangers' is to take refuge in relationships that cater to his beliefs and that don't cause him too much risk. Those relationships are with... you.

Just like you, he's catering to his own self-fulfilling prophecy and that's why you trying to change him or waiting for him to change is futile, because he just finds another way to legitimise his thinking.

The truth is that everyone has some level of fear of commitment and being vulnerable, but he allows it to transcend everything. Unfortunately he has a fear of failure and making mistakes, hence why he maintains a best of both worlds position. He's thinking, "If *I'm* not in it and minimising the impact on me, how the hell can I be impacting her so much?

He doesn't genuinely believe that anything is his fault - most things are 'seemingly' totally out of his control and a byproduct of the interaction and the other person not safeguarding *themselves*. He may assume that because he's safeguarding himself that you are and, that if you're not, it's some sort of 'fault' in you. He won't be held accountable, as it equates to being vulnerable, so if you call him out on his behaviour he'll only turn it around on you or deny it.

Being noncommittal means that when he thinks about 'sticking' with you, he panics that there may be a better option. When you tell him to "Jog on" he panics that you *are* his best option, so he uses fear to continue keeping his options open.

This all goes back to basics, because women are socially conditioned to believe that they need a man in their life pretty much as soon as they become adults, whereas men are programmed to sow their wild oats and spread their options. Unfortunately, while he's terrified of missing out, his friends all drop off the radar and settle down, and after a while he becomes the odd one out, clinging to his bachelorhood and claiming that he hasn't met the 'right' woman yet and that they're all 'psychos' or 'too needy'. At some point, he'll probably have a midlife crisis and panic himself into his version of commitment to some poor woman who thinks she's hit the jackpot.

EMOTIONAL SCHOOLING

Many men discovered as children that when they didn't suppress perceived weaknesses such as expressing emotion, displaying vulnerability and sensitivity, and communicating their feelings, it was often penalised. It's no wonder that as adults, they struggle to relate to women who are asking them to share themselves and their inner emotions. It's incredibly confusing, because they are thrust upon the adult world and expected to have access to a whole range of emotions that they're totally unfamiliar with.

If he's out of touch with himself and his emotions, how can you expect him to know how he feels and, even more importantly, communicate it?

It's not that he's sitting on a wealth of information about how he feels – it's not there and, even if it were, he wouldn't know how to access it. Some men just don't *feel* these feelings. What they attribute to feeling something for someone is comparable to an awkward concern for a pet. In fact, they often feel more for a pet!

The key issues that arise are:

Making negative associations with normal emotions.

Perceiving any show of emotion that they don't like as dramatic.

Feeling that if they're needed, wanted, expected from more than they want to be that you're 'needy'.

Finding it difficult to empathise.

Selfishness.

Believing someone else's feelings took precedence over theirs, so going to extremes to avoid being in that situation again.

Being afraid of abandonment.

Being afraid of feeling so much for you that it would hurt to lose you.

Having little faith in people so carrying trust issues into every relationship.

Being unable to identify how they feel about anything – he may almost be vanilla and lacklustre about everything.

All sorts of experiences can contribute to why he behaves as he does and it's important to recognise that these are part of the same reasons why *you* may be attracted to him and experience chemistry. He may have very legitimate, even very sad, reasons for why he is the way that he is. But... it's not conducive to a healthy relationship.

He'll talk about how he has a 'mess' to fix.

He'll say he's afraid of getting close to people.

He may tell you that he sabotages his relationships.

He'll tell you he drinks (or whatever) a lot to numb the pain.

He'll say stuff like 'I can't do *this*' and 'This is too much for me'.

In conflict he may accuse you of behaving like a parent.

He'll become childish and freeze you out during conflict.

He'll send long emails/letters detailing all of his fears.

He'll say that he needs to go off and sort himself out.

He'll cry post-breakup and tell you that he misses you, but *still* doesn't' address the issue.

These are problems that existed before you met him and they are his to resolve, or at least find a way to handle them and live with them in a healthier manner. They are *reasons* for why he may behave as he does but they are not *excuses*.

I'm often asked what makes a Mr Unavailable genuinely change: serious consequences. As humans, we have a disposition to only really step outside of our comfort zone when we experience negative impact and the consequences of not changing start to appear to be greater. You also have to remember that two ideas about changing are cancelling each other out:

Mr Unavailable thinks that it takes the 'right' woman to change him and you think that you *can* change him which means that neither party is applying the appropriate effort to the right person.

It's also important to recognise that, in adulthood, men continue to be emotionally schooled by external factors such as society and the media. Women are the big purchasers of self-help books and, much like the male attitude to therapy, much of what is written in books about having healthier and better relationships isn't picked up by men. Instead they read stuff about pickup techniques, which are about gaming the system (us) and taking shortcuts without having to put in the proper emotional work and healthy relationship habits. All of these 'techniques' are geared to people who don't want to change the habit of a lifetime of being unavailable so it all just perpetuates a well-honed cycle.

Regardless of what your experiences have taught you, the difference between these 'trainees' and normal men is that the latter try because they want to live more than a disconnected experience. That and the less screwed-up men don't try to leapfrog over the basics of a relationship by duping women.

NARCISSISM

Many emotionally unavailable people have narcissistic tendencies, so they exhibit *traits* that are typical of an all-out narcissist but they don't fulfil enough of them to actually be one.

A **narcissist** is someone who displays excessive self-love, is devoid of empathy and has delusions of grandeur, which means that they'll pursue their own agenda to the severe detriment of others. They can be a real bully and, when they're nice to you, it can feel pretty amazing but when they 'turn', it's horrendous. They're incredibly defensive when in conflict and may become very abusive if you call them out on their behaviour, especially when it pierces this illusion of grandiosity. Everything is about them. They experience problems and never see themselves as a part of it – everyone else is at fault. They can also be hypersensitive about any perceived criticism and have fierce boundaries while completely bulldozing yours down and having a lack of any sensitivity to you.

It's important to realise that all narcissists are emotionally unavailable but not all emotionally unavailable people are narcissists.

According to the Narcissistic Personality Disorder (NPD) group **Narcissistic Personality Disorder** is "an all-pervasive pattern of grandiosity (in fantasy or behaviour), need for admiration or adulation, and lack of empathy, usually beginning by early adulthood and present in various contexts".

To be a narcissist, there are nine criteria, of which five need to be met:

1. Feels grandiose and self-important.

2. Is obsessed with fantasies of unlimited success.

3. Firmly convinced that he or she is unique and, being special, can only be understood by, should only be treated by, or associate with, other special, unique or high-status people (or institutions).

4. Requires excessive admiration, adulation, attention and affirmation.

5. Feels entitled. Expects unreasonable or special and favourable priority treatment.

6. Demands automatic and full compliance with his or her expectations. Is "interpersonally exploitative", i.e., uses others to achieve his or her own ends.

7. Devoid of empathy. Is unable or unwilling to identify with or acknowledge the feelings and needs of others.

8. Constantly envious of others or believes that they feel the same about him or her.

9. Arrogant, haughty behaviours or attitudes coupled with rage when frustrated, contradicted or confronted.

Source: NPD (http://www.runboard.com/bnarcissisticabuserecovery)

In general, the points that I've highlighted in bold reflect the most common complaints from women about their 'relationships' with Mr Unavailables. I'm not a doctor; I'm just an expert on inappropriate behaviour and if you *have* been involved with a narcissist, you'll have experienced at *least* five of the above criteria.

Mr Unavailable looks in the mirror and thinks, *"Hmmm, I've still got 'it'. I work hard, I pay my bills, I don't beat up women, I'm not a prick, and I go to the gym five times a week. There are a lot of men far worse than me. I'm doing the best I can. I've got a lot going on. It's not my fault. If X would just lighten up a bit and appreciate what she's got, I might just think about getting serious with her..."*

When he tries to get an ego stroke, that's like a **Narcissist Supply** – narcissists cannot get enough attention and spend their entire life seeking small, medium and large-sized doses of it from anyone and everyone. If they don't automatically get them, they'll contrive a situation to extract attention or even demand it.

While many Mr Unavailables *are* a pain in the bum with their need for an ego stroke, the difference between your run-of-the-mill one and a narcissist is that the latter is *always* looking for that 'fix'.

One of his activities that will have you believing he's a narcissist is Mr Unavailable's tendency to have a stock of women on tap, more commonly known as a **Narcissistic Harem**.

This is typically a number of women clucking around him giving him an ego stroke. Why extend yourself to a one-on-one relationship when you can have a host of women pandering to your whims and making you feel like The Big Man? In the Narcissistic Harem, they can be ex-lovers, friends, colleagues, family, etc. No matter how 'platonic' they all claim it to be, there's at least a few of them with designs on him... or if they can't have him they try to ensure no one else will. They're like a fortress of his own making and they are the perfect foil. When he thinks about why he has not managed to hold down a relationship, he'll claim he hasn't met the 'right' woman and feel he can legitimise that view with the validation of his expert team of cluckers.

I make a point of firmly differentiating between Mr Unavailables and narcissists because they're two different things and I see a lot of women eager to apply the term to exes and partners so that they can 'diagnose' them. That's not to say that some Mr Unavailables don't cross into outrageous, even abusive territory; but as much time as we can spend researching someone else's problems and diagnosing them, this is an unproductive and somewhat misinformed path to continue down. There is a simple reason why you shouldn't be too quick to 'diagnose' *all* Mr Unavailables as narcissists:

Fallback Girls become involved with Mr Unavailables because you're both emotionally unavailable. If all Mr Unavailables are narcissists, then all Fallback Girls are too and that's simply not true.

I understand your frustration. I've had enough experience of self-involved men to last me a lifetime but if you *have* been spending your time investigating the behaviour of narcissists, you've missed the most vital piece of information:

92

A true narcissist is dangerous and a no-go, code red, abort mission, do-not-pass-go situation.

You cannot change them, you cannot win —- the best thing, in fact the *only* thing you can do, is get away from them as quickly as possible and have absolutely *nothing* more to do with them. They'll use you ruthlessly after luring you back in with unbelievable charm and then they'll turn.

Making it a medical reason can imply it's out of his control, which implies your actions are out of *your* control. There's also the uncertainty if he's undiagnosed, but if he's behaving so badly you believe he's a narcissist, it's a sign that you need to eject from a very unhealthy relationship.

I'd certainly seek some form of counselling and, as first port of call, check out forums and sites online such as the Narcissistic Personality Disorder group (http://bit.ly/narcb). Whatever you do, don't run home and tell him that he's a narcissist. You have no idea how he will react and it could even be dangerous.

THE BREAKUP

Regardless of whether or not he's been emotionally schooled since childhood to be unavailable, breakups can go a long way to shaping his perception of relationships and himself in that context. If he's been heartbroken, experienced what he perceives as a 'proper' failure or a 'fail *fail*', has lost someone to another or to death, it may have caused him to shut down, or to shut down even *further*.

Many Mr Unavailables are not over one particular person, no matter how long ago it was.

When he experiences a breakup, he doesn't do the healthy route. If he's not trying to keep a foothold in an ex's life, he's instead making sure that he doesn't feel too much of the breakup, by ensuring that he buffers his emotions by taking up with a new Fallback Girl to airbag him. He's never really processed any of his breakups, especially not any that he believes he felt 'deeply' in.

He may feel that he can't allow himself to be fully available to somebody because of a negative relationship experience from which he's now safeguarding himself emotionally. Often there's a woman in his past who's essentially an invisible barrier that appears to prevent the two of you from moving forward.

It may well be true that he once made himself emotionally available to someone in a relationship; or it's possible that, actually, he wasn't emotionally available in that relationship either, but she wouldn't put up with his bullshit and it stung. If it's the former, if he was extremely hurt by another and even had his trust breached because she, for example, cheated, he may have decided that he cannot take the risk of loving and trusting someone again. These are incredibly difficult situations to get over, but it can be done, although it's hurt that they need to resolve before getting into another relationship because, until they do, it's a safe relationship where they're not intending to be 'in' anyway. The other person will also be an emotional airbag and always a hop, skip, and a jump away from being distrusted.

If it's the latter, while I'm not saying that his feelings weren't hurt, if he was as unrealistic about his contribution and actions back then as he is now, suffice to say that it's highly likely that he's in denial about the *real* reasons the relationship didn't work out. Remember that ego often reigns supreme when it comes to breakups and if he wasn't in control of how the relationship ended, he'll feel ill-done by.

If he doesn't feel in control of the terms of how a previous relationship ended, he will believe he feels more deeply than he actually does.

Mr Unavailables almost always struggle to understand a breakup and will feel more interested if they weren't the one to initiate. It's an unfamiliar territory because they're normally the 'driver'. It's either that they can't understand how you got behind 'the wheel'; or they can't understand why, even though they may have been the one to end it, you don't want them hanging around in your life; or why you went off and met someone even better, thus removing their options. Suddenly you feel like 'the one that got away'.

It's all ego and when they experience rejection they feel wrong-footed despite not making a genuine effort and contribution into the relationship.

This is why you'll have an ego-driven battle with him, because, in not rejecting his behaviour and sticking by him through thick and thin (in spite of the fact that he didn't deserve it), he wrote you off. Now he latches on to the perceived rejection because he can't accept that the same woman he wrote off told him to take a run and jump, even though if she hadn't told him to take a run and jump, it wouldn't have worked out anyway. Yeah, exhausting, I know!

CONFUSION FROM MIXED MESSAGES

There has never been a more difficult time to navigate the shark-infested waters of relationships. It may be the twenty-first century but, in many respects, we've taken two steps forward and then hovered back and forth in confusion. We've had the feminist movement, we're supposed to have equality, and the battle lines have been fiercely drawn between the sexes, but nobody seems to have equipped the parents of children growing up into this new world of modern dating, or the adults crashing around in it, with the appropriate skills to cope with this transitioned world. So what we actually have is a world of laws, norms, and expectations about how both sexes *should* behave but both sexes are still programmed like it's 1909.

The modern Mr Unavailable knows no different because he's play-acting at being an 'evolved' man and the modern dating world is confusing as hell.

In the Nineties, there was a lot of talk about 'New Men', the modern day answer to the species with a penis. The 'New Man' was caring, sharing, in touch with his emotions, willing to let us do our thang and not be threatened. He understood that the male-female relationship dynamics had changed and that he couldn't cling to his instincts. When was the last time you heard people bandying around the term 'New Man'? You haven't, because by the time the new millennium rolled around it became clear that the rules may have changed, but *they* hadn't. There are plenty of men who will unashamedly declare that they are 'old school' and that's how they like it... and there are a lot of fronters out there.

Mr Unavailables and some of their shadier siblings – 'assclowns' – are effectively 'playing the game'.

Some do it consciously and many do it as a force of habit. It's all about pushing down the urges and the instincts, but often they fail at it. The real man always comes home to roost and issues rear their ugly head. Pretending that they share the same values as you and that they're nurturing, sensitive, and supportive can only last for so long, especially if their natural inclination is to be a solo player.

They're very adept at changing the 'terms and conditions' of the relationship, which is essentially shifting the goalposts to suit their own agenda. This means that what they deem to be important for them to make the leap to commitment today could easily change tomorrow. He could be OK with you being an independent career woman and tomorrow he could declare that you being an independent career woman makes him lack confidence in whether the relationship would work.

In order to be ready for the rigours of the modern relationship and not run into emotional issues, he'd need to be equipped (ideally by his parents), but, unfortunately, unless he's coming out of his teens now, it's unlikely that this 'New Man' ethos has actually been taught to him.

Whether a man is 2 or 52 at this moment, there are in-built factors at play about how he emotionally interacts with others.

If we accept that for the majority of men, there is no big evolution of the male species going on as a result of the empowerment of women, we will start to see many of the men we date in a different, more real, light. Truth be told, the modern woman doesn't appear to want a 'New Man' that much and, in fact, doesn't appear to know what she wants, period, which is why Mr Unavailables go hand-in-hand with the problems of the dating world.

Unfortunately, we live in a time when men don't know whether they should open doors, pay for dates, let you pay, be nice, be bad, be strong, stay at home, be a provider, let you be the provider, or whether they're even needed. Men of every type watch these contradictions take place every single day and for many it leaves them confused, ambivalent, dedicated to their form of behaviour, and sure of the notion that women don't know what they want. Whichever type of man they choose to be, there are women out there who will want them, regardless.

If you've ever met a pretty decent guy and gone running for the hills in favour of a Mr Unavailable who gives you the runaround, you'll have experienced these contradictions for yourself.

To add even more to the confusion, it's important to acknowledge the impact of the increase in casual relationships. It's never been so easy to not only have sex, but to get a lot of the fringe benefits of a relationship without having to actually commit. This in itself sends out huge mixed messages because the value of a bonafide relationship gets devalued in the process. Let's be real - sometimes we as women participate in casual relationships to be 'down with it' and more importantly because we'd rather be 'in' on these terms than out completely. When we change our minds or start looking for more, they get confused because they don't want the same things and wonder how on earth they've been caught out again.

With this in mind, what's the incentive for certain types of men to change when they know that there are many women who are emotionally confused, with low self-esteem, commitment issues, and a disconnection from themselves and their desires, who will welcome them with open arms, even if they have a wife and kid in the background or they treat them like something they stepped in?

The dating arena has no consistency and code of behaviour, unlike, for instance, when our parents dated and there were more understood norms and expectations. Now anything goes and the price that we all pay is that it leaves us wide open.

TAKE THE FOCUS OFF HIM

Be careful of projecting your view of things mixed in with his insecurities. It's also important to recognise that his reasons may not be the *true* reasons for his behaviour if he has got used to telling himself a story that allows him to keep behaving as he does. This is why it is helpful to know the type of reasons that someone might give or that might be behind what they do – it's recognising that the presence of the reason is one major code red alert in itself, especially when they say that it's down to *you*.

It's absolutely pivotal in your quest to overcome this destructive relationship pattern that you stop concerning yourself so much with what he wants and thinks, and focus on what *you* want and think, identifying whether you want something that originates from a positive or negative place. Don't look for loopholes to justify a continued investment in him because when it walks like a duck, quacks like a duck, and looks like a duck, it *is* a duck. Mr Unavailable does not truly want a relationship.

He wants a moment and a passing feeling, but he doesn't want an extended version of anything.

From the moment that they started pulling back from you and failed to deliver on that initial promise displayed or became an entirely different person, or started treating you in ways that completely overstepped your boundaries, it was a glaring signal that you needed to get the hell out. Mr Unavailable is not about permanency and building a relationship, so you both want different things. Blaming yourself and trying to love him to death so that he sees how wonderful you are is a total waste of your time and a serious depletion of your self-esteem resources. Take the focus off him and bring it back to you.

HE BLOWS HOT & COLD... YOU BECOME THE PURSUER

I've yet to come across a Fallback Girl who didn't feel her 'spidey senses' going in the early days of the relationship, yet most do very little with this feedback. While many Mr Unavailables *are* deceptive, Fallback Girls are guilty of blindly pursuing their own agenda, despite indications that they should be backing off.

You slot in with him blowing hot and cold, because, aside from catering to your drama meter, *you become 'the pursuer'*. Those giddy, heady times when you first met and he made you feel like the centre of his universe are *gone*, and instead, when you pursue him, despite the shift in temperature and respect, you become the pursuer. No matter what takes place after this, you're the Fallback Girl who's pursuing her idea of the relationship and him, that's beyond the capacity of what he has to offer, and he's just the passive, lazy Mr Unavailable that's along for the ride because you *keep pursuing* and *you keep offering yourself.*

It's a classic **Bait & Switch**: you've been wooed and lured in and you've eventually taken the bait and now that you're hooked, you've been tossed back into a reality where he's not so interested anymore, the attention has faded, or what you thought was on offer isn't. By pursuing him, he now gets the same or even *more* contribution from you, with *less* contribution from him.

You've become so heavily invested in the idea of him and the relationship that the reality of who he is hasn't caught up with the fantasy created by your betting on potential. Despite his actions, you're still trying to make the quintessential pig's ear into a silk purse. You're not only ignoring clear indicators of who he is and what you're going to get, but you're ignoring what he says or shows he wants because *you think that you know better.* You think that your love is all that he needs and you've decided that you're going to love him so he's got to love you.

This is difficult to digest because in most Fallback Girls' minds, you believe that your Mr Unavailables are doing the bulk of the pursuing but, in actual fact, it's *you.*

The only reason why a woman pursues a man who is a total flip-flapper who doesn't know his arse from his elbow is because she has low self-esteem and is afraid to let go of the *idea* of him and the relationship and accept the reality.

You pursue because him pulling away **triggers your flight or fight reflex** and you're too scared to walk away, so you fight for it instead, even if there's not much to fight for.

You pursue because **you believe that something you've said or done has triggered his pulling away**, and to make things 'right', but instead show him that you don't care enough about yourself.

You pursue because **you're focused on the initial great behaviour** rather than the reality of the *majority* of his behaviour. You believe the beginning is an indicator of the end.

You pursue because **men like this seem far more attractive when they appear to be *less* interested in you.**

You pursue because **it sets off your internal fears**, which combined with the very real external fears (his behaviour), sets off the drama meter.

You pursue because **it's your relationship pattern**.

You pursue because you're **heavily emotionally invested**, even though there's very little substance, because you want to *justify* your investment.

But, most of all, you pursue him because you want to demonstrate that you're the 'right' girl for him, so that he can validate you and you can avoid rejection. You can just about cope with the 'small' rejections caused by each withdrawal, but if you don't win back some attention from him that would be *total* rejection.

You pursue him, you pursue your own agenda, you pursue the relationship, and you pursue the dream that's arisen from betting on potential. After a while, you're so blindly focused on what you believe your feelings are and, of course, the anxiety and insecurity generated by your fears, that the reality of the situation and who he is no longer matter. You're in blind pursuit.

BREAKING THE CYCLE

We all have our off days and can be impacted by stress, tiredness, and a variety of factors that may not actually be related to our partners, but it shouldn't be a 'chore' to be in a relationship and you shouldn't be at the mercy of some guy's emotional menstrual cycle that 'comes on' when he feels overwhelmed and he has to bail so he can desire you again.

Pay closer attention to *actions*. You can only get sucked into the hot and cold cycle if you're words and imagination-focused, otherwise you'd recognise the disconnect between his words and what results, plus the fact that, overall, things aren't *progressing*.

Under no circumstances should you accept someone disappearing out of your life periodically, whether it's physically, where you have no idea where they are; or you do, but they refuse to participate in the relationship; or whether it's in terms of contact.

Don't allow anyone to press the Reset Button, which is where they just pick up where they believe they left off, usually from a convenient point that erases any wrongdoing on their part. You'll know there are serious issues if when you question their retreating or disappearing, they stonewall you, create conflict, or just disappear. Respectful partners recognise that an explanation is the *least* they can do.

No chasing them around, especially in the quest for validation. Make that one call and wait for them to return it and get on with your life in the meantime. If they don't respond, don't keep calling, texting, showing up at their door, and emailing.

Validate your own feelings – you have every right to be pissed off when he bails on the relationship each time things progress. Your feelings are *valid* and if you owned them, you'd be less inclined to accept shady behaviour.

Fear derails relationships and also creates bad ones but we also need to recognise that sometimes our internal fears can have us either believing that someone is retreating when they are *not*, or can cause us to believe that they're going to retreat so that we behave in ways that bring about the outcome and create a self-fulfilling prophecy - us playing out our fears pushes them away. If you do either of these things, this will create a dubious intimacy cycle that's actually of your own making.

REMEMBER!

Don't chase, *meet* them. Chasing is one-way and exhausting, tag means the chase doesn't stop, and *meeting* them is *mutual*.

There's a fine line between chasing and desperation. As it's open to interpretation, it's best to drop chasing once you've established you're in a mutual relationship, or if the feeling isn't mutual, stop chasing.

You know when a parent has to go out roaming the streets to get their child to come home? Well that's you when you're chasing him.

If you're drama inclined, sit on it for at *least* twenty-four hours before you take action. Don't be reactive otherwise you'll fuel *and* enjoy the cycle.

HE KEEPS THINGS ON HIS TERMS...
YOU MAINTAIN THE DRAMA METER

You've learned to believe and trust that an attractive relationship will create sparks, excitement, and drama. When you meet a guy who wants nothing more than to treat you well and pursue a relationship, you'll struggle to be interested, as he appears to lack these things, when, in fact, he lacks the negativity that you're typically attracted to. Instead, your relationships need to have fleeting highs and plenty of lows from him blowing hot and cold and often having more baggage than an airport terminal.

By being a *drama seeker*, even though you may swear different, you're happy to pick up the baton and pursue him to get the relationship you feel that you're entitled to from him. When things don't fall into place, it ends up bringing out your fears and insecurities, so you keep playing to them, which, of course, creates more drama, so it's a vicious circle.

Now bearing in mind what he's doing, you'll be acting like you want as close to a '10 relationship' as possible, so your energy's focused on getting him to change or revert back to the Mr Wonderful from the beginning, so you can get what you want.

The middle ground 5, actually comforts you because it appears that things are chugging along, albeit nowhere, but you also *like* things going below or above 5 as this to-ing and fro-ing back and forth is your drama, excitement, and passion.

It's a perfect validation opportunity – either your negative beliefs are confirmed or you get a temporary 'fix' by getting the attention and action you were looking for.

His blowing hot and cold signals that you should get invested and prove yourself, plus it caters to your negative beliefs, which feeds your cycle of drama, which triggers the very uncertainty and anxiety that you profess to hate but that you actively create and seek because you think this is what 'love' feels like.

Fallback Girls think drama equals a 'normal' relationship.

As you're unavailable, your fears become disproportionate and combined with his hot and cold, you get sucked into the drama. This is how it can work:

During the hot phase at the start, it feels close to a '10 relationship' and you lower your defences, often overriding any concerns. If you were distrusting, drama may have resulted as he worked to win you over. Or you may have 'given in' to the attention.

He panics that you may expect, need and want too much when the relationship is a 7/8/9/10 (or you perceive it to be due to his Future Faking), so he backs off to manage down your expectations. This creates a **"What the Eff? Moment"** because it's either a serious jolt from previous behaviour or he feeds it to you slowly but surely, until it creeps up on you that he's backed off.

As things slide to 5 (you may think it's less), you wonder what you did to cause the change in him, etc., and react by either pursuing him or calling him on his behaviour – not because you intend to bow out like you should, but because it puts you in the zone of fighting for the relationship. Or you may spend time alone creating your own dramatisation out of things in your mind and to anyone who will listen until he thinks it's safe to creep back in (the Reset Button).

You'll be anxious and in drama-seeking mode. Below 5, he feels out of control and so he'll blow warmer so that you're manageable, possibly edging things up to a 6, 7, or 8 – you rarely get back the 9/10 guys from the start.

However you don't trust it even when it's good so you'll sometimes act up to confirm your beliefs, which may take it below 5. Your Status Quo is below 5 – this confirms your beliefs and effectively gives you the relationship you *expect*.

At this point he'll blow warm enough to increase to 5, or a bit above to cushion, and then gradually ease back. As you're trying to 'win' him, he'll come to discover that due to your eagerness to be validated, he actually gets away with putting in less effort for the same or even more effort from you.

As the 'relationship' progresses (or doesn't but you feel emotionally invested), your expectations increase so you'll question his behaviour, and look for or demand solid indicators of his feelings that he can't give. You'll basically push for more commitment, which results in discussions, anxiety, and stonewalling, or overpromising and underdelivering from him. You're creating and seeking drama because you know that this is doomed.

Eventually he'll learn what to expect from you and eventually, on some level, you learn that nothing comes of the drama but it's what you know and you like the initial positive feeling that's created by it - you can be as much of a short-term thinker as he is. You don't actually feel comfortable at *any* stage of the relationship scale because of your unavailability.

Each stage of happiness or unhappiness brings out other fears and different levels of distrust.

Below 5: catering to negative beliefs.

Coasting at 5: anxiety about progressing and realising potential.

Above 5: waiting for the catch.

You like drama. In fact, you love and crave it. There was a time when you knew that drama was about the pursuit of excitement and may have even believed that it was a phase, but when you've attempted to go out with available guys, you were uncomfortable and now you believe that real passion, love, connectivity, and companionship are found with unavailable men who make you jump through hoops.

Drama is now the only thing that many women recognise as a consistent feeling in their relationships, which in turn translates to 'love', so even when you're involved with men that aren't offering drama, you'll create it. You may not know this but:

Men know that women who like drama aren't cut out for a healthy relationship. Some men also know that it's far easier to attract and keep women when they treat us badly.

Fighting to get a '10 relationship' from a stuck-at-5 man is your competitive spirit. Winning will confirm your worth and validate you by giving you love against the odds. Unfortunately, he's still a 5 man so you're catering to your self-fulfilling prophecy and creating drama. You might want happiness but you're keeping it at bay.

BREAKING THE CYCLE

Drama 'works' for you and you could say you love *Relationship Crack* – getting high on the bad stuff and driving yourself crazy... and then returning for more – because, even though you know it's no good, you felt more comfortable, loved, showered with attention, and in control of things when you were on your high. But remember, that like any crack, it takes its toll pretty damn quickly and you will end up being an emotional wreck – not just for this relationship, but for any relationship you walk into because you'll continue to create the pattern, over and over again, to get the feeling.

Identify your Drama-seeking Trigger – the feeling or thing that sets you off. Whatever it's rooted in, it's because something about the situation is familiar, or your overriding fear plays out and you act on it. All triggers come down to fear. For example:

Boredom Fear that everything is going stale and that you need to inject some excitement or else the relationship is doomed.

Loneliness Fear of being alone.

Abandonment Fear of being abandoned, scared that you're losing him. You're wondering what you did to chase him away or scared that you *are* chasing him away.

Feeling neglected Fear of being unheard, unloved, not cared for, and not needed. Fear that your efforts don't count.

You're with men who reflect and amplify every last damn thing that scares the crap out of you! That's what Mr Unavailable represents – the sum of all of your fears and your uncomfortable comfort zone. Even if you did find a Mr Available, you'd question it due to your fears, hence, you could end up turning *up* the drama meter just to see what happens to the relationship and prove that your fears are founded. *You get to be right.*

Internal Fear vs. External Fear. What you need to assimilate is whether your triggers are rooted in your own fears or whether it's his characteristics and behaviours that trigger the fear? This is a huge way of calming down your life because you get to listen to internal feedback and external factors to work out where you're coming from.

What this means in simplest terms: are you going into all of your relationships, irrespective of the quality of the man that you are engaging with, carrying negative beliefs and fears that override the reality of the relationship? Or do you still have all of these beliefs, plus he's actually behaving in the negative ways that trigger those fears?

At the end of the day, is it real external fear, or is it internal fear tied up in you? If what you fear is happening, it's a huge indicator to opt out. The likelihood is, you're probably experiencing a bit of both. In either case, the fear takes precedence and you're not addressing what's triggering your fear and giving yourself a reality check.

Get out of the short-term 'hit'. You act on the feeling and the fear. You have no patience. Much like when you can't stay away from him or you're wondering when the hell he'll call, you just can't bear the short-term feeling and feel like you must react to it. Hence, you wind up in bed together, feel good for a day, maybe a few, and then BOOM!, the high from the relationship crack wears off. Or you call him twenty times, he doesn't pick up, or he does and he's the same twat he was before you called, and BOOM!, high wears off. When your trigger kicks in, you have to take control. Be aware. Know that this is a temporary madness and that it's powered by fear and own it.

By being aware of what kick-starts the madness, you can begin pulling yourself back to a rational reality. When you feel the urge to Drama Seek and get your Relationship Crack high, the feeling of tension that results from the fear and the euphoria you would feel if you were to react to the tension are short term. The low and the negativity will actually last longer, so you need to start telling yourself that the only thing that's going to last is the *shit feeling*. Let's say you are at level 4, you react, get your relationship crack and you get to level 8; when the high passes, you'll be back at 3, 2 or even 1. You then have to work much harder to pull yourself back to 4 and beyond. Teach yourself to ride it out and know that you feel like crap right now, but the feeling will pass.

REMEMBER!

One of you *will* tire of the drama. I suggest you make the break first. You may think that it's your 'thing' that creates passion in the relationship, but I've seen it too many times where one of you overvalues the presence of the drama and the other one gets sick of it and moves on.

You can't be your best you when you're living a life with *Dynasty* levels of drama. It's unsustainable and, as many a drug addict has found out, you have to increase your fix in order to get the high you're used to.

Do you want a relationship or a soap opera? Unless you want a seven-days-a-week drama to play out, recognise that no relationship can survive on a diet of attention-seeking.

Not all attention is created equal. If you were in an available relationship, you'd be receiving and experiencing healthy attention.

Drama isn't love. Pain isn't love. Drama is drama. Pain is pain.

HIS ACTIONS DON'T MATCH HIS WORDS... YOUR ACTIONS CONTRADICT YOUR WORDS

As a Fallback Girl, you can see the immediate contradictions arising. All you have to do is think about wanting to be loved, cherished, happy, to be in a committed relationship, to be their number one priority, and not be abandoned, and then think back to the various men you've dated to see that your past doesn't reflect what you profess to want or need. This happens because of engaging in **relationship insanity**: carrying the same beliefs, baggage, and behaviours; choosing the same guy/different package; and still expecting different results.

You keep trying to get a healthy relationship out of a Mr Unavailable, which is a bit like trying to get water out of an empty well.

If you want to know how you truly feel about you and what the negative things are that you believe about yourself, look at the man you profess to like or love. The easiest way to show how contradictory you are is this:

You actively pursue and experience relationships you say that you don't want.

You're heavily emotionally invested in relationships you say that you don't want.

You want him, but you don't want him in the package that he comes in. You just need him to change a little...

Much of your contradiction arises from inaction. Like attracts like, so he masks his fear of commitment by just refusing to commit to an outcome and seeing what he can get en route, and you mask your fear of commitment by taking up with men who are the least likely candidates for giving you commitment and then spending a lot of time thinking and talking, but rarely actually doing anything. The one thing you are both doing right is finding people who are most likely to give you the relationship that you want.

You're committing to *not* committing.

The trouble is that you'll commit to anything that comes in the package of Mr Unavailable. If he comes in the package of, say, a Half-Decent Guy who's available, you can barely commit to an evening out with him, never mind a relationship! In fact you commit at these crucial points:

As soon as you meet. You see so much potential, you're straight into the future. You may not even see that much potential, but you're gagging for companionship and affection. **You're the Fallback Girl who doesn't like to be alone** and thinks every guy she 'connects' with might be The One.

When you realise that he has issues because you feel comfortable around wounded souls, guys who scream hard work and drama, because you feel that you can be the one to make him better. **You're the Fallback Girl who's a sucker for a sob story and baggage.**

When you realise that he's not going to leave his wife or his girlfriend, or make that separation official by becoming divorced, because you think that if you show your commitment, that you'll be rewarded. **You're the Fallback Girl who commits when it becomes clear that he's definitely *not* going to commit.**

When you realise that your interest isn't reciprocated. You're the Fallback Girl who commits to the *idea* of him and the relationship and to feeling rejected and living in a fantasy.

To the cycle of drama. You're not that sure about him until he starts catering to your fear of abandonment and making you jump through hoops, and, after a while, you're not really going out with him, you're going out with the high created by

Relationship Crack. **You're the Fallback Girl who commits even though you weren't really that interested** until he started messing you around and got your attention.

YOU THINK YOU'RE AFRAID BUT TRYING

When you're involved with Mr Unavailable, you recognise that even though you may be very different and you don't like a lot of the stuff that he does, that there's a familiarity to being with him, not least because he caters to your beliefs about love, relationships, and yourself. To you it feels like you're fighting for your relationship, that you're trying to overcome your fears, and that surely you shouldn't be too harsh on him. You believe that you're afraid and trying so he must be afraid and trying, too. Or you wonder why he can't try if you are. Now, I appreciate that to an extent you *are* trying, but it's time to hear a home truth:

There's a massive difference between trying in an available relationship with an available party and being emotionally available yourself, and trying to iron out your own fears in a limited relationship that reflects your negative or unrealistic beliefs about relationships, love, and yourself.

Throwing a lot of effort into a futile activity is going to feel like you're working very hard, but it's totally counterproductive. Unless this is your first encounter with a Mr Unavailable and you got out relatively quickly, you *know*, even if you won't admit it, that this relationship is not going to work. You *know*. That's not trying; that's going through the motions and creating limited pain for yourself – it hurts, but not as much as you fear it would if you truly put yourself out there.

BREAKING THE CYCLE

Relationships are 100:100, not 50:50, contrary to popular assumption. Anything less than being authentic and putting in your whole self and full effort is subjective and keeping score. When you're being honest, available, and living authentically with your values, you can smell a rat that's not stepping up in the relationship.

Don't expect of others what you're not doing yourself. You may think you're working hard in this relationship, but you're not. You're working hard at trying to dig concrete with a plastic shovel. You don't need to be taking your cues from Mr Unavailable – you need to take your cues from *you*. If you're basing your actions (or inaction) around what he will or won't do, you become just as lazy as him in the relationship. **What can you do in this situation?** If he doesn't take action, make a decision, etc., what will you do? If the answer is similar to wait/do nothing/have another conversation, you're inactive.

Make a list of what you're waiting for, because you know that inaction is often waiting on others or some random cosmic shit to come along and make things easy for you. Be specific and if there are quite a few things, I'd put them into small (accomplishable immediately or in the short term), medium, and large. Now go through the list and mark what can be tackled by you and then mark the ones for which you're waiting on external factors. If the majority – over 90% – are down to others, your life is not within your control and influence. Assign some of these to yourself (because you know you can do *some*thing) and make sure that the bulk can be addressed within the short to medium term.

Are you holding the answer but hoping it's something else? Most inactive people are shutting out vital information because they don't like it. They hope that if they sit tight, something else will present itself, ideally without too much intervention from them. Much inaction comes from relying on others to provide answers to questions that we already know the answers to, or waiting for them to do things that we know they're not going to do or that we could easily take charge of ourselves. Classic example: waiting for him to call it a day when you can.

REMEMBER!

Love is an action as well as a feeling. If you're loving in an inactive, unproductive environment, your efforts are limited.

**Don't expect anything from him that you cannot be and do yourself –
commitment.** You will create unrealistic expectations and set yourself up to fail.

**If your life and your relationship are looking hugely dissimilar to what
you claim you want, something's going wrong with the action.** You're the
only person you can control so it's your actions you need to tackle, not his.

Step up to the relationship table as an equal party. When you arrive as Miss
Available, healthy beliefs, fears in check, not attracted to shady behaviour, etc., you
will be an active party in your relationship investing yourself in healthy, productive
activities and opting out when he won't.

Life is happening now. Dwelling in inaction with a view to banking on Mr
Unavailable and being happy at some arbitrary point in the future is nothing short
of silly – you need to be doing things to be happy right now.

HE LIKES FAST FORWARDING...YOU DINE OFF ILLUSION

If someone doesn't see themselves as they really are, there's very little that you can do, because even rubbing their face in it won't connect some of the disconnected. But you are on the receiving end of their actions. You are the one who feels the pain, the humiliation, the abandonment, the deceit, the confusion, the ambiguity, the contradiction, the anger, the sadness, and so much more, and yet you deny it.

When you live in **denial**, you basically find the truth unacceptable so you work very hard to shut it out, because to acknowledge it would pierce the very carefully constructed illusions that you have about them and the relationship. Sometimes denial can be 'healthy' in that, for example, when you grieve the loss of someone, it allows you to gradually process what you can handle and move through the grief stages until you reach acceptance. However, denial as a habit is dangerous, and it creates false relationships chock full of illusions. You use denial to avoid making uncomfortable realisations and decisions, taking action, and seeing the truth in some of your own actions.

Part of this problem of not seeing the reality of your relationships is that you get caught up in chasing a feeling, and trying to extract things from him that are missing in yourself. You want him to have faith in you and see your potential, so you have faith and see potential in him in the hope that he'll reciprocate – the potential you see isn't realistic and the faith is misplaced.

You're often reluctant to let go of the illusion, which can actually be an act of passive aggression on your part. You don't like the fact that things are not what they used to be or haven't met your expectations of what you think he could be, so, rather than accept the 'new' reality and reassess your position, you stand firm and insist that he get on board with your thinking because you either want him to go back to what you thought he was or to realise your vision of what you believe is 'right', even though he's resisting.

There are five key things that create illusions in relationships:

Projection. Crushing on Mr Unavailables and then projecting your feelings on them and deciding they should reciprocate.

Thinking that your feelings are big enough for the two of you. You lose all sense of proportion and become so consumed in how you feel that you want them to be swept up in all the love you have to give, believing that one day they'll catch up to how you feel and return it. Trust me, they won't.

Avoiding relationships by living in a dream world for fear of being rejected in the real world. In choosing men who are aloof and unlikely to be interested in you, or who are physically remote (for example, online relationships), you avoid the type of hurt you fear the most. Instead, you build sandcastles in the sky and then feel rejected by your own daydreams, because the reality is that you need some sort of inspiration for these illusions and they're not a part of your life.

Not wanting to let go. Even if it's the most toxic thing to continue feeling as you do or being involved with someone, you continue, not only because it's a bit like 'I've started so I'll finish', but also because even when there's nothing or it's crap, you hold on tight because you still think it's *something*.

Loving and trusting blindly. Even when you receive information via their actions and words that should change your feelings or your trust levels, or even what you envision the relationship to be, you proceed blindly so you end up in a false relationship. While the feeding of illusions *is* partly down to them, you have expectations irrespective of whatever is taking place in front of you.

It's important to remember that it's a bit difficult to make him accountable for something that's a grand illusion in your head, when you could have been making him accountable for real behaviours. Likewise, you can't wonder why he isn't being and feeling what you want him to be when he's not partaking in the relationship.

Mr Unavailable has to deal with his own issues with reality so it's a bit like a clash of the great illusions.

In his world, his behaviour is fine and, even if it's not, he's OK with it, and even if he's not OK with it, he has no real burning desire to change, because he doesn't match his actions with his words. From the moment that you're willing to accept his crumb-filled contribution, he registers that you can't think too highly of yourself if you have so much faith in him. He may even think you're deluded. Often you're one in a long line of people who've placed faith in him.

In your world, you want the fantasy so much that you don't want the reality, which is why he can not only get away with the likes of Fast Forwarding and Future Faking but why, even in the face of experiencing these things and not experiencing a reality that reflects their promises, you still hold tight and demand your fantasy.

Irrespective of his behaviour, you still need to remember that, by refusing to accept the reality and projecting your own version of things on him, you're being disrespectful because you're always seeing anything other than the person who's in front of you and living in a fantasy relationship. It starts to seem like it doesn't matter if he's there because you're making up your own version of events anyway and, if he's of the more opportunistic and somewhat dangerous variety, he'll abuse this. Respecting the reality of someone gives you the opportunity to re-evaluate whether what's on offer is what you still want.

BREAKING THE CYCLE

Dropping the illusions to be action-focused, while daunting, enables you to live authentically and you can start creating a real life on real terms. In order to find personal happiness, never mind happiness within a relationship with another person, being honest and living honestly is paramount and that cannot happen when denial is part of how you cope with life. While I don't doubt that it can be hard to let go of what you believed him to be or what you thought you had, if you don't, you will actually open yourself up to much more pain.

Recognise that certain levels of intensity are a code red. While it's flattering for someone to tell you they love you within days of meeting, it lacks sincerity. Being super intense, suggesting plans that others don't talk about until they at least know each other and have spent a reasonable period of time together, and basically trying to speed things along so you don't look too closely at things, are a major sign that all is not well, especially when there's a significant shift from hot to cold.

If you're serious about finding a loving relationship, slow down. Don't just get swept along – slow down so you can go in with eyes and ears open, with your feet on the ground. You have a duty of care to assess the risk.

Have an honest conversation with yourself – have you been Fast Forwarding? You have to recognise that when you expect certain levels of intensity fairly early on, feel that you have to sleep with them, push them to confirm their feelings, try to get pregnant after a hot minute, start pushing for engagement, etc., you are Fast Forwarding. It's a good time to address your beliefs and attitudes about dating because you're setting yourself up for failure. In fact, I'd ask yourself how serious you are about finding a relationship, because exerting this type of pressure so early on in the relationship not only tests men out to see if they can meet your emotional demands, but a lot of the behaviour in Fast Forwarded relationships is quite unhealthy.

Why do you need to demand so much of the person and the relationship so early on?

How much validation does your ego need?

Isn't this all a bit like an elaborate prank that goes way too far?

If you gain agreement from them via actions or words, what do you think that this tells you about you? Is this true? Does this belief hold up in the medium and long term? Yep, short-term thinking.

If in doubt about his actions and motives, put your foot down and press 'Play' and see how the relationship copes at a steady pace. If it's already over, 'Rewind' the relationship tape and mentally play it back and you'll see all the signs.

REMEMBER!

Words, especially those that prop up relationships, need actions to solidify them and you could cut back a lot of your misery if you became more visually aware.

If you're going to have faith in someone, make it evidence-based. It needs to be based on the consistency of their actions, and, if they change their behaviour, you have to adjust your field of vision and ask yourself if what you think about the person and the relationship still stands.

You can enjoy yourself, but it's time you became aware of inappropriate behaviour, boundaries, and matching actions with words. This means you can ground yourself and ensure you don't wash up in a painful relationship.

It doesn't matter what he says; it's his actions that tell you the real story and let you know exactly what's going on. Words allow you to believe in the fantasy, in the potential, and in the hype. Unfortunately acknowledgment of his actions and what they mean kills that all off.

HE LOVES CASUAL RELATIONSHIPS...
YOU CONFUSE SEX WITH LOVE AND
A CONNECTION

Even if he never utters a damn word of care or doesn't do anything nonsexual to show it, if you're having great sex, you think that it reflects his true feelings. If you're having bad sex, you think it's reflective of your flaws so you think that improving it will show that you're lovable and worthy. If you're having no sex, you think it's reflective of how 'rejectionable' you are so you'll make it your vocation to try get sex so that you can feel accepted and validated. Sex plays too big a part in unavailable relationships. If you allow it to cloud your judgement, you may also believe that you can sex your way out of problems or into someone's affections – you can't.

Sex is the low-hanging fruit that's easier than actually being emotionally intimate.

You mistake a sexual connection for an emotional one, an indication that there's more to the relationship than there actually is. And if you're getting bad sex or no sex, you mistake the emotional connection that you think you have as a reason to keep pushing ahead so that you can try to make the sexual connection. When you find someone attractive, feel a supposed chemistry, your libido goes crazy, or you swing from the chandeliers while having orgasms, just as they cloud your judgement, you may also believe that all of these things equal a love connection - they don't.

GREAT DYSFUNCTIONAL SEX

In talking to many Fallback Girls, it seems that irrespective of whether you're getting good sex, or heaven forbid, bad sex, you're still heavily invested – they just generate two different types of relationships.

I call sex (both good and bad quality) with dubious partners **Great Dysfunctional Sex**, which is any sex where there's a significant shift in the balance of power; or where ambiguity, insecurity, dependency, high drama, strung-out emotions, etc., exist; or there's the existence of another person (i.e. they have a girlfriend or wife). The 'greatness' in dysfunctional sex is really about the size of its relative importance to the relationship, not necessarily the quality of it, and Fallback Girls greatly *overvalue* sex so they ultimately end up *devaluing* themselves. If you have bad sex and still pursue a relationship, it's because you believe 'the problem' is something that you need to work on and that the moment you're lovable enough, the sex problem will be solved, which just increases the level of dysfunction.

Ever wondered why:

The last sex you had before you broke up was off the chains and mind-blowing?

Sex with a person who actually 'belongs' to someone else feels so damn good?

You're losing sleep over a man who mistreats you and can't even sleep with you right?

Sex with Mr Unavailable leaves you clinging to him with orgasmic joy and may even push you to tears?

Make-up sex is soooo good (only applicable if you have make-up sex very frequently)?

All the breaking up and making up, the confusion, uncertainty, ambiguity, not knowing how to interpret his latest behaviour, add to the heightened sexual tension, and, the reality is, that if the sex is great, it's heightened by the absence of reality. If you ever got real about him, you'd find that the sexual connection diminished rapidly.

Ask anyone who's been No Contact, then fallen off the wagon – more often than not the sex is utterly disappointing. This is because, even though your self-esteem hasn't grown quite enough to stop you from falling off the wagon, it's grown enough to know that there's nothing but hot air and an emotionally vacant man lying on top of you, who quickly shifts to his usual mode of disappointing the hell out of you soon after.

YOU'RE CHASING A FEELING

I get it: sex feels good and even when someone isn't up to much in other departments, it's easy to convince yourself that because you feel so good during sex that you just need to extend that feeling for longer periods of time and expand it across your relationship. Unfortunately, the very premise of things being focused on sex is very short-term thinking.

You must stop chasing the 'feeling' created by sex and quit living in the moment or clinging *to* 'moments'. This is a sexual pitfall for you, and he exploits this short sightedness, your libido, and your confusion about emotions and sex.

There will always be sexually opportunistic people, but you don't have to provide the opportunity.

It's easy to kid yourself with your vagina and your overactive imagination that the feelings created by sex, or the supposed attraction and chemistry you feel, can correlate to the rest of the relationship. Great sex, no matter how great, has a sell-by date, and after a while you need some substance behind the penis.

FEELING SEXUALLY REJECTED

Something has gone very wrong when you're prepared to take anything just as long as you get a semblance of a relationship. It stems from fear of being alone, of not finding somebody else, that this is as good as it gets, of letting go, and ultimately having to deal with your own issues. Fear, fear, fear, fear, fear draws in mean, mean, mean, mean, *mean*! It's important to recognise that feeling sexually rejected doesn't just stem from bad or no sex - if you're only good enough to have sex but not a relationship with, that's sexual rejection in another guise.

Fallback Girls feel sexually rejected when they're used for sex, feel they can't please their partner, or aren't having sex.

The desolation you experience if you're feeling sexually rejected alongside what already feels like rejection of you in terms of a relationship, can make you dependent because how you perceive yourself becomes intrinsically tied to how successful or unsuccessful your relationships are. You end up believing that something about you is unlovable and that if you can just be everything that he wants, then POOF!, great relationship *and* great sex will appear.

So, along with trying to extract a decent relationship out of someone who doesn't want to give or be in one, you find yourself trying to turn him into Mr Loverman when all he wants to do is 'get' his... and get out with minimal fuss or drama. If you're not trying to do this, you're trying to turn him into Mr Relationship – that's why I get so many Google searches and advice queries asking, "Can a booty call turn into a relationship?" This is exhausting, redundant work.

Take this man off his pedestal! If you're being used for sex or having bad or no sex, he is an equal contributor to this paltry situation! Why the hell are you assuming the sole responsibility for the success or failure of the relationship?

Of course you're not going to leave: you wonder, "What man will want someone who isn't good enough to have sex with or is only good enough to have sex with?" Your confidence is shot. You figure you might as well stay and keep trying because no one will want you anyway and, of course, you might get validated. If he's your first relationship or sexual experience, or you're involved with him while you're already feeling vulnerable from a previous experience, you'll believe that this relationship defines you.

Sex becomes a weapon that we can be controlled with because, no matter what type of sex you're getting, him 'deigning' you with the opportunity to pleasure him becomes 'affection' and 'attention'. For all intents and purposes, you could be a cardboard cut-out – I've often joked that that's what they should be left with.

THE JUSTIFYING ZONE – THE GREAT COVER-UP

You have some sticky areas that, when addressed, will change your dating and relationship experiences, and more importantly, improve your self-esteem. When you stay in relationships long past their sell-by dates or pursue even the flimsiest of dalliances, it's because you have a reluctance to admit that you've made a mistake, you get carried away, and even in the face of knowing you've made a mistake you cannot handle it. What results is that you become a habitual resident in **The Justifying Zone**.

This is that slippery slope that many women find themselves on, especially after they have sexual contact. We feel that we need to justify our emotional and sexual investment and this justification is effectively attempting to close the door after the horse has bolted. The Justifying Zone will always appear when a man fails to live up to the initial promise he first exhibited or does something inappropriate to raise a major red flag that could potentially scupper the possibility of the relationship. So, for instance, when the ambiguity increases along with all of his other core behaviours, the potential to stay in the zone and cling to it for dear life becomes even bigger.

As women, we tend to look for the smallest of things to make ourselves feel better about sleeping with someone or just plain ole liking/loving them, and this often causes us to spend more time on a relationship than is necessary. We see gold when, in fact, it's brass or even rusty ole copper, and often we use the Justifying Zone as the launch pad for betting on potential and basically hoping that a cockroach will turn into a frog, then, eventually, into a prince.

Why? Well, to be fair, who wants to feel like they've had Yet Another Dubious Dating Experience? You have to remember that you have unhealthy relationship habits and measure the value of yourself based on your interactions with men. You don't want to have another Here We Go Again Moment and you'll bet on the potential, even if he never shows an ounce of decency ever again.

Sex, of course, is the biggest booby trap. You will definitely find yourself in this zone if you sleep with him too soon, or sleep with him and things don't prosper and develop as expected. Many women still equate sex with someone as a signal of a bigger, deeper connection and, if we're left feeling empty, unfulfilled or confused, we'll remind ourselves that there *must* be strong potential if we slept with him in the first place. This is too big an assumption to make.

You don't want to feel devalued by the experience, even though the subsequent lack of return on investment that you experience by being in The Justifying Zone only serves to devalue you further anyway. The Justifying Zone is an excuse, and if you find yourself there, it means that there is something wrong with the relationship. End of. You don't justify and make excuses or accept crumbs in healthy relationships with good men, period.

BREAKING THE CYCLE

The primary issue isn't the sex, even if it *is* an issue. The real issue is that you're involved with Mr Unavailable. You can go left, right, up, down, round the houses about it, but all routes lead back to unavailability. The sex isn't what needs to be worked at – it's his availability – and the only person who can work at that unavailability is him. This means you're wasting your time and, if you put both feet in reality and strip the denial and excuses out of the relationship, you'll see that not only are there many other things wrong with the relationship but that it's *not* the sex that's caused it.

Unless you're OK with being casually regarded, don't participate in 'casual relationships'. If you want something 'light' don't let it go beyond 3 or 4 occasions and for no more than a month. Trust me when I tell you you'll save yourself a lot of trouble. You cannot upgrade – don't waste your time. You're not in a movie!

Don't try to have the type of relationship or feelings that some people take years to achieve, in just a few short days, weeks, or months. Take your time, otherwise you will set yourself up for some mighty falls and end up getting hooked on sex in a hollow relationship.

Frustrated by having sex that you thought was 'special' that turned out to be casual? While there are no guarantees for avoiding some of the shadier Future Faking types, I'd steer clear of being sexually intimate in the early stages of dating, especially if this is what you have already consistently done. While sex isn't all of the problem, I can assure you that it's blinding you. You'd see some of the mind fuckery a lot quicker if you weren't too busy getting screwed in other ways.

Deprioritise sex. This doesn't mean that sex isn't important, but it's not *so* important that it should be used as an excuse to continue going back to an unhealthy situation, especially when you're saying you actually want a relationship. Sex can be passionate, but if it's the only source of passion in the relationship and the only area that 'works', you're on borrowed time.

If you know that you're not in a position to handle the emotional consequences that can arise from sleeping with someone, don't sleep with them until you can. Get to know and respect you and, if you're the type of person that sex means a lot to and goes through a lot emotionally post-sex, honour yourself by going slowly. That means asking yourself: Am I comfortable with what I know about him so far? Do I know where I stand with him? If not, don't assume that you'll be 'standing' in a relationship just because you slept together. Has he done anything so far that, at best, causes me to stop, look, and listen or, at worst, signals that something is very wrong because he's crossing boundaries? Does he, at the very least, act with sincere care, trust, and respect?

REMEMBER!

Sex can't make a relationship and it can only break a relationship that's broken in *other* areas. Take off your rose-tinted glasses and stop denying the other issues.

Don't mix the business of getting to know someone with the pleasure of sex. It gets very confusing if you're not self-aware enough.

I suggest you get the relationship connection first before you go and stake yourself on a sexual connection. Sex can be worked at, so can relationships, but focus on the relationship first.

You are better than this. If you stay in a relationship where you're controlled by sex or feel sexually rejected, all that's going to happen is that you're going to be controlled or rejected further.

The sex is only a part of the issue here, so if you're thinking you can sex your way out of the problems, you might as well get out now and save yourself the energy, lubricant, lingerie, and the headache.

Never, ever, ever, ever, *ever* allow yourself to be demoted from girlfriend, to Friends With Benefits, to booty call. If you're not good enough to be in a relationship with, you're not good enough to screw.

HE DEALS IN CRUMB RATIONS OF COMMITMENT... YOU'VE BECOME A DISGRUNTLED CUSTOMER

When you find yourself wishing for someone to get back to how they were in the beginning, you're like a disgruntled customer who believes she's purchased a product with a particular package that's subsequently expired. When you ask for it to be reinstated, nothing happens and now you're left with the pared-down version. You're pissed off! You wonder why the product has stopped being what you thought it was and fondly remember the good times. You don't want a refund – you just want what you thought you were paying for.

You're the disgruntled customer who wants an exchange. You feel violated by the Trade Descriptions Act, but you're also a victim of your own inflated expectations that are based more in what you perceive the product can do in your capable hands as opposed to what it's actually capable of doing based on its specifications and performance. You're like someone who doesn't read the instructions, sets up the product blindly, then wonders what went wrong.

You want more than he can deliver, and even though he has, in many respects, misled you to believe that there's more on offer, you've had more than enough tangible proof in his contradictory actions and words, to know that what you want and what you're going to end up with are two totally different things.

CAN'T HE JUST CHANGE 'BACK'?

A person isn't just about the beginning of the relationship and, in actual fact, they're not just about the good times, so you need to see them as a whole and the relationship in context. I've had women ask me why he can't go back to being the guy he was at the beginning when they've been with him for eight years and struggling for 7.5 of them! You do the maths on that one! You need more than 'good times' and 'moments' to justify sticking in a relationship that's been consistently struggling for longer than it's been consistently good.

Why can't he 'go back' to being that guy? Because he's not that guy all the time. The guy he is, is the one he consistently shows you over a longer period of time – trouble is, that's not the one you want. Let's call him Love Bobby (remember Fun Bobby, the good time guy from *Friends* who Monica dated?)

At the beginning, probably after a good ole press of the Reset Button, Love Bobby 'genuinely' believed that things could be different this time. He felt excited, horny, affectionate, loving, jealous, possessive, out of control, or whatever, and he correlated that with his level of interest and started talking up a storm, making plans, and being a Future Faker. Unfortunately, he overestimated his level of interest and capacity for a relationship.

If he has to go 'back' to or 'become' something, it's a major sign that you're stuck in the past or betting on potential.

Unless you're planning to somehow trap yourself in Groundhog Day and put the beginning of your relationship on repeat, it's impossible to maintain that feeling of newness that someone with the attention span of a gnat needs. If you're looking for commitment and consistency, you need someone who is actually more than OK with the relationship progressing – he's *not* 'that guy'. He can't go back to being 'that guy' because he isn't and wasn't that guy in the first place – you had him on temporary hire and your loan key's expired.

YOU WANT TO BE THE EXCEPTION

Fallback Girls make a rod for their own back by deciding that they don't want love and commitment from a healthy source. They try to get it from unwilling, unhealthy, limited sources, because the pain endured en route feels like the love is more worthwhile.

You think that it's not a love worth having if you haven't got someone to make you the exception to their rule of behaviour.

This 'exception' thing is, sadly, a recurrent theme throughout all relationships with Mr Unavailables. You hear anomalies and urban myths about women who were given the runaround by their guy and then he miraculously changed into a better man and gave her the relationship she wanted, guys who left their wives and lived happily ever after with the Other Woman without any scorch marks left behind, and guys who realised that the booty call that they'd treated like a sexual skivvy was 'The One'. These are the exceptions, not the rule, and pain and suffering shouldn't be a benchmark of the type of relationship you want to get involved in.

What you're looking for is a fairy-tale ending to a situation where you've had low self-esteem, little or no boundaries, and have at times been treated 'less than'. That 'ending' is a shortcut and the reality is there's rarely a good outcome to these situations and the overwhelming majority of you are taking a huge gamble.

BREAKING THE CYCLE

In being a disgruntled customer who's trying to be the exception to the rule, it's important to know the rule and acknowledge it. If you truly acknowledged what the rule is, you'd recognise what an insurmountable challenge you've set yourself up for. It's another example of not trying – you want someone to revolutionise the wheel rather than be with someone who is the relationship wheel.

Accept that if you're disgruntled, he's not being the man you thought he was or that you expected him to be. Relationships aren't like Ikea, where you can keep bringing back products or collecting missing pieces until you get what you want or at least get your money back. Stop rejecting the information you're receiving loud and clear. Accept it. There's no refund or exchange policy here, so you've got to accept who he is and his actual actions and work out whether this can work for you or whether you need to opt out. Staying and banging the counter to push him to change and practically acting like a protestor *isn't* the way to go.

What's in it for you? Why are you continuing to gamble with yourself? At what point do you say, "Enough!"?

Do you know *your* rule? If your rule is to be suspicious and distrusting in every relationship, guess what? You have to play your part and learn to have faith in yourself, so that you can trust in others and either increase or roll back the trust accordingly. Distrusting people always find more reasons to distrust. Where they don't, they make it up. Why? Because they don't trust themselves. If your rule is to keep going out with unavailable people, and/or people who mistreat you, guess what? You have to opt out and not try to turn a pig's ear into a silk purse, because you have enough experience to know what the rule is.

What is the rule? Not just the general rule – what's the rule with this person, with this situation? If it's familiar, trust me, you know the rule. **Are you trying to be the exception?** If you can answer these two questions by looking at what consistently does and doesn't happen, and apply the knowledge to make appropriate healthy choices, you'll be happier and will find yourself in healthier relationships. If you keep trying to be the exception to his rule of behaviour or even wider life rules, it's like peeing into the wind – a waste of time, messy, and bound to backfire.

Learn to admit when you've made a mistake. The customer isn't always right. Sometimes you make a bad purchase that's not suitable for its intended use, or you don't do enough research before committing to purchase. Not admitting the mistake is costly because you keep throwing more energy and investment into it. If you can admit when you're wrong, you'll learn to trust when you're right.

REMEMBER!

Commitment enhances already healthy relationships, but seeking commitment in an unhealthy relationship will not make your relationship better. It's like using a hammer when you need a drill.

The efforts you make in trying to have the type of power to get partners to change and make you the exception to their rule of behaviour needs to be turned on yourself. It's time to make an exception to your previous rule of behaviour and make some big changes.

Wanting to commit to Mr Unavailables isn't commitment – it's lazy. When you're trying to commit to an available man and being available yourself, *that's* commitment.

I'm not saying change doesn't ever happen, but it's time you worried about why you need someone to fundamentally change themselves so that you can have the relationship you want.

We all have egos, but people can and do change their feelings and intentions. While some of these people have hidden agendas and were never honest about their feelings and intentions, it's best not to take up the role of disgruntled debt collector hunting them down for the relationship you believe you're owed.

HE KEEPS A FOOTHOLD IN YOUR LIFE... YOU KEEP LEAVING THE DOOR AJAR

Every day I receive emails and comments from women who are trying not to have contact with their exes. Most of them veer between having great days, shaky days, and desperate days when they fall off the wagon and either open the door and let them in, or signal their continued investment by leaving the door ajar for them to step through. Here is the reality:

Mr Unavailable operates on an open door policy. He considers your door open until he either gets a better option, you very firmly turf him out of your life, or you find somebody else.

Until you either get really hurt by him or you get over him and change your relationship habits, you'll veer between leaving the door swinging wide open or at the best, ajar. For most Mr Unavailables, if you so much as leave the door open a crack, they perceive it as 'open' and 'service as usual'.

Why do Fallback Girls leave their proverbial doors ajar? Like Mr Unavailables, you don't like endings and finality, you want to believe you're an option and have them on some terms rather than no terms, and, with the combination of your beliefs combined with your constant quest for external validation, you just won't let things be. Your Achilles heel is trying to be what you think a Good Girl is. Unfortunately, something's getting lost in translation.

In your world, you think Good Girls don't have boundaries because you equate having no boundaries with unconditional love. The Good Girl is ever loving, ever forgiving, ever trying, ever nice. No matter how long her guy disappears for or how poorly she is treated, when he does creep out from under his rolling stone, she's there, and when he says things will be different for the 50th time, she believes him. When it gets to the 100th time, even though she is weary, because she's 'good', she'll force herself to smile even though it doesn't meet her eyes and she'll believe him again.

You think you're showing how much you love them; he thinks you're an access all areas doormat.

The Good Girl loves and trusts blindly because she wants to believe the best in every situation and person even when there is evidence that suggests otherwise. The Good Girl has worked out What Good Girls Do, and even though she has been doing it and yielding negative results, she believes that, eventually, The Good Girl 'wins', no matter how dangerous a gamble and on one of these days – between luck, fate, a man falling out of the sky, or one of these guys deciding to make her an exception to his rule of behaviour – her prince will come. You're too caught up with how you 'look' and in trying to be the Good Girl, you forget about how you're acting.

NO ENDING, NO FINALITY

When Mr Unavailable keeps his foot firmly wedged in your life, you make the mistake of either 1) taking him at face value or 2) deciding that, in time, he'll want to be more than friends again and that you should just be patient. You need to realise that when Mr Unavailable diminishes the already poor contribution that he was giving you down to friendship, the last thing you should do is reward him by breaking him off a piece! If you'll screw him as a friend, what is the impetus for him to go back to being your boyfriend? Nothing!

You keep opening the door, and, each time, you believe that bestowing this man with the benefit of your change in door policy will be rewarded with a relationship. Instead, as usual, he fails to deliver. A common scenario with major repercussions is when someone that you regard as a 'childhood sweetheart' or even 'The One That Broke Your Heart' gets in touch with you 10, 20, or even 30, years down the line. He often arrives just as the separation starts or the divorce is going through, and peppers his emails, calls, and dates with anecdotes about those 'amazing' times you had together, even though you may remember things differently.

However, most of us do subscribe to the idea of a fairytale ending, so the idea of a guy you dated ages ago, swooping back into your life now seems perfect, even though neither of you are in reality, because you both treat each other like you're way back when as if however many years haven't gone by. If you're fresh out of a breakup or divorce, or have had a long period of being single, him 'showing up' will seem like wonderful fate. Of course, if this guy is a Mr Unavailable, then things go sour very quickly and the woman on the receiving end is left devastated.

You allow him to keep a foothold in your life and keep leaving the door open at various degrees of ajar because you don't want the finality of an ending, because you don't want to let go of the idea of him and the relationship, even though you may recognise how damaging he is to you. Mr Unavailables will never disappear out of your life if they have to be the one to decide it (they're like cockroaches), so you have to be the one to close the door on them. The responsibility is yours.

SEEKING VALIDATION... AGAIN

Fallback Girls stay friends with even the *worst* of Mr Unavailables because feeling like we're not even good enough to be a friend would only further dent our already bruised self-esteem. It's the last chance saloon to salvage something decent out of the wreckage and, the truth is, you hope that by dignifying him with a friendship that he doesn't deserve, that you'll ultimately give him an opportunity to miss you, regret not making the most of being with you, and 'win' him back. In recognising that there is some level of commonality between you with the unavailability you both share, you think it's wrong to have boundaries with people like him or not be his friend because you feel like you're being hard on *you*.

You make a rod for your own back, because you beat yourself up with your conscience and your busy mind. You also panic that if you don't stay friends, or at least have a way into his life, you won't be able to keep an eye on him and it scares you that he might become a better man in a better relationship... with someone else. You're hooked on being 'right', but you're sending the wrong messages about yourself in the quest to be validated. It's almost like you're saying, 'See, I'm right! He *is* unavailable! He's a shit relationship candidate!' and putting yourself through the pain because at least you get to confirm all of your beliefs, stay in your uncomfortable comfort zone, and avoid fully dealing with the consequences of your choice to be with him.

YOU'RE OK WITH BEING AN OPTION

The critical thing in managing Mr Unavailables is that you need to operate a closed-door policy. That means that they can knock... but they get no answer. When he gets the message via your actions and general receptiveness that you will be there for him no matter what, it communicates another message – that he's free to never commit himself fully and keep his eye over your shoulder for other options.

Even when you end things and know that you were accepting crumbs, you're unwilling to close the door 'just in case'.

What you have to recognise is that you can't have it both ways – you can't complain about him keeping tabs on you and keeping a foothold in your life, if you keep leaving the door ajar, then opening it again. The power of contact lies with you, not him, because as long as he can dip in and out of your life, he will, so if he feels like dipping in and out of your life for the next 50 years and you want to let him...then this is how long it will go on for.

BREAKING THE CYCLE

I have a book dedicated to the No Contact Rule (NC), which is basically cutting contact until you are over an ex, or even permanently, so you can not only break up, but break an unhealthy cycle. NC is a delicate balancing act between taking back control, booting someone out of your life (even if they don't know it) and not going crazy. You apply it when you are in a relationship that just won't die a death, even though it's dead as a dodo, when he likes to dip in and out of your life whenever it suits, and especially when you keep flogging a dead horse and chasing him, in spite of his unavailability and treatment of you.

It's about closure and closing a door even when you don't get to have a 'conversation' or a big breakup moment, and this is what most women struggle with.

You love to have the conversation and you need to have the breakup moment, because you think it's what you need for closure and you like wondering, "What if?" But you need to forget these and focus on you. So what does NC involve?

No calling, emailing, texting, Facebook, Twitter, stalking him on dating sites, faxing, message in a bottle, communication by osmosis, Morse code, or anything.

No contact means no contact. It's that simple. Sit on your hands, tape your dialling fingers together, reward yourself for getting to milestones but do *not* contact him.

Don't allow any of the following things to break NC:

You're hormonal. You're horny. You're drunk. You're lonely. You're nostalgic. You're weak. You have an emergency. You're out of another breakup with someone else and seeking comfort.

If you react to any of these booby traps, you will not only end up regretting it, but you'll have to start the whole process all over again, whilst he sits there thinking, *"Ah, so she does still want me. Mmm, yeah I still don't wanna be with her though..."*

No contacting him via your friends.

Instruct mutual friends not to come to you with any information about him, unless he has 'the clap' or some other such STD that affects your health. You need to move on and forget about him, not be hearing out -of-context information where people make more out of something than actually exists.

No sex. No quick fumbles, slippery snogs, one last shag for old times' sake, or any bodily contact. Ever.

Get rid of his contact details.

I'll let you keep his number for three months and that's only so that you know it's him if he decides to call and you'll know not to answer. Otherwise wipe out all information you have on him because no contact means you're breaking up and closing the door on that chapter in your life.

If you fall off the wagon and break contact, that's OK, as long as you get back on the wagon and you don't make it a regular thing. You need to commit to you and you need to grow some proverbial balls of steel because you have to be bigger than your 'urges' and your 'fears'.

Most Fallback Girls doing NC ask whether it's permanent. Why? Because they think they want to be friends with him at a later date. If you were friends before your relationship and he was a good friend in the relationship that didn't bust up your boundaries, knock yourself out being friends once you're over him. If he was an asshole as a boyfriend (or whatever he was), he'll make an asshole friend though. Stay on the wagon until you're free and clear of your feelings for him and use the time productively to be 100% focused on you and addressing your availability.

REMEMBER!

When you break... you *break*. The relationship has ended for a reason. Do not aim for or continue friendship with a view to extending the relationship dynamic.

When your relationships end treat them as *over*. This ensures that you don't end up keeping your options open or being an option for them and ensures that you fully process the end of the relationship. It also flushes out Mr Unavailable's dubious intentions.

Don't tell him it's over to play games. This is manipulation.

If you keep leaving the door open, you lose all credibility. It's like having 'Mug' stamped on you.

You're not an option. I can't say this enough - you are *not* an option. Don't behave like one, don't ever allow yourself to be regarded as one.

HE USES 'TIMING' TO MANAGE YOU... YOU SEEM TO HAVE ALL THE TIME IN THE WORLD

You use 'time' as a justification for sticking around because you deduce from his various feeble excuses, that if now is not a good time, there will be one at some point. While he's playing for time, you don't realise what you're doing with your time – hanging around in an unhealthy relationship.

Fallback Girls, in effect, hear a Mr Unavailable say that the time is bad and yadda, yadda, and they think, *"Well... he hasn't actually said that there is no possibility which means that there is possibility,"* but this is like playing one-in-a-million odds with one man, which represents being made an exception and the fairytale.

You engage in breaking a fundamental boundary that erodes your self-respect – you wait around for him to make up his mind about you on *your* time. Mr Unavailable is wasting your time, but you're right there with him wasting your time because waiting around on him is a distraction from you.

TREE FOCUSED

You're a reactive person that doesn't give enough thought to the medium and long term, beyond betting on his potential and fantasising about the relationship you feel you could and should have with him, which is highly unproductive because it creates illusions. What would make a huge amount of difference is realistically considering whether what you're doing has anything beyond a short-term gratification.

Fallback Girls are too busy looking at the trees to recognise that they're in an unavailable wood.

A classic example of being reactive is when you recognise that the relationship with him isn't working and you end it. Post breakup, as you attempt to come to terms with the sense of rejection you feel because he wouldn't be the man you wanted and love you, the fear that, *Poof!,* he might turn into a better man in a better relationship causes you to start second-guessing your decision and panicking that you've not been understanding enough.

When you then feel bored, nervous of finding out too much about yourself and having to take action, afraid, or experience negativity in another aspect of your life, you calling him/sleeping with him/getting back together becomes an attractive prospect.

Any emotions you're experiencing are a natural part of grieving the loss of the relationship, but by avoiding them and seeking attention and validation, you halt the feeling of rejection – *this* is why Fallback Girls keep returning to the scene of the crime. Of course, you get a short-term fix and a longer-term hangover. Particularly if you've been down this road before, you actually have some level of awareness about what the potential consequences are, but you deny them or put off dealing with them until a later date because you prefer the short-term gratification.

MISGUIDED LOYALTY

Often the first inkling you might get that he doesn't appreciate your show of solidarity is when you have one of those big, emotional arguments where you get upset about his lack of contribution into the relationship and you remind him of how patient, understanding, and loyal that you've been, or whatever it is that you think is your 'contribution' and he retaliates with, *"Well, I didn't ask you to wait, did I?/I've told you that I don't want a relationship/I didn't ask you to do those things."* This enables him to absolve himself and shift the blame to where you're ready to welcome it. The trouble is that if he *is* responding with some of these things, depending on the circumstances of your involvement, what he is saying may be true if you have continued to pursue your vision of things.

None of this is based on the solid foundation of a relationship; it's based on an idea you have formulated in your mind about who this man can be and what relationship you can get. At this point when you realise that he isn't appreciating your efforts, this is your Get Out Moment, but the great majority of Fallback Girls feel that their personal investment is too high to walk away and instead pretend that they're not waiting, effectively pretending that their expectations have shifted to his, and adopt another wordless plan of action because they don't want to let go of their commitment. You're now looking for him to say or do any minuscule thing that will indicate that you're right to wait, so if he turns around one day and says something like, *"I'm glad that I can count on you,"* this will be your bingo moment and your waiting will seem validated. Or you argue and discuss with him till he says something remotely close to what you want to hear. When you finally get wise to what is going on, you realise it's time for you to start showing some loyalty to you.

RELATIONSHIP AMNESIA

I remember hanging out with the Mr Unavailable that I spent five months of ambiguity with. I'd been thinking about finishing it with him, because I hated not knowing where I stood, then, while we were lying on the couch, snuggling and watching TV, he said, with a contented sigh, *"I've really missed... this,"* and, honestly, I felt like my heart would burst at what I felt was a show of emotion and I went back to the waiting game. It was only when another few months had gone by that it occurred to me that I had no idea what 'this' was. Dipping in and out of my life and having me eagerly awaiting a visit?

This is like having **Relationship Amnesia**, which is where you seem to suffer partial or total memory loss about events, feelings, and experiences relating to the true nature of your relationship. Typically, it's when they say or do something positive and unprompted that promptly drowns out all the negative stuff, or when you mentally latch on to even the smallest of what you view as positives. In particularly unhealthy and dangerous relationships, it may be that something bad happens (a 'trauma') and to cope with continuing to be with him, you block out anything that pierces that denial bubble.

When you keep returning to a poor relationship, you're definitely 'suffering' from memory loss and by continuing to operate off the short term – chasing a feeling and living off moments, hopes, and pipe dreams – a lot of time passes, often without you realising. In the past, whenever you recognised how much time had gone by, the likelihood is that the realisation didn't make you come to your senses; instead it made you feel more invested and like you had even more of a reason to try and get the relationship to 'pay off', which, of course, means that you go back to your 'memory loss'.

Unfortunately, for a woman who's staked her future on Mr Unavailables, she may find that she wakes up one day and she doesn't have time left to, for instance, have a baby. Or she starts believing that she has passed her sell-by date and that she's not as attractive to men any longer because she thinks her prime years have passed her by. At the end of the day, the sad reality is that men *do* have more time. They're not penalised for ageing, society lets them believe they're a great catch no matter what age they are, and they can make babies for as long as their sperm works. Society and some of our peers let women believe that they are operating on borrowed time when they enter their thirties, and by the time the forties come round, they treat you like you should just give up and accept defeat. Time... these men... and society, are just not very kind.

BREAKING THE CYCLE

When someone tells you that it's not the right time, it means a mutually fulfilling healthy relationship is not going to happen. Walk away. If the right time rolls around then you'll be quids in if you're still interested, but if it doesn't, at least you won't have wasted your time hanging around. When someone shows you that it's not the right time because they hang on to you while being unavailable anyway, it's also time to walk away and keep walking.

If you *have* been waiting, you must own that choice. Even if they have made promises or stalled you, you have made the decision to stay and you must be honest about your reasons for doing so, in order to recognise what you need to address within you.

What are you avoiding? What is you waiting for him providing a distraction from?

Have you had to change your deadline more than once? You're staying in a relationship past its sell-by date.

Has he broken promises and had actions not match his words? Yeah, he's Mr Unavailable so of course he has.

Are you waiting for him to change? This is a very bad sign. If you have to wait for him to change so you can get the relationship you want, the relationship is doomed.

If someone tells you not to wait, please don't decide you know better – you don't. You might be thinking that with a little time they'll change their minds and see their error and your greatness – don't gamble your life away. If they've told you to move on, it's time to write down your reasons for hanging around.

What are you afraid of? What are you afraid of experiencing? Of feeling? Of having to be responsible for happiness in your own life? What are you afraid he might be or do? What's your rationale for waiting? If you're 100% honest with yourself – no lies and denial –does that rationale hold up?

Here's the truth: Someone who tells you not to wait for them is saying, "Please don't continue to have faith in me, you're wasting your time. You can wait, but it's your own fault if you do."

Value yourself and your time. When you truly value you and respect your own dreams, aspirations, goals, values, and life, you won't be so quick to fritter away what time you do have on an unavailable relationship. Write down short, medium, and long-term goals – this will help you to refocus on you and also get perspective on time, where you're at, and where you need to be. I've heard from many a woman who has sidelined a career and aspirations such that by the time she realises how much time she's fannied away on Mr Unavailable, she's lost confidence in herself. Don't let that be you. Get a life, because when you have a full and rounded life not focused on him and waiting, your need for him will dissipate.

REMEMBER!

No time for you, no time for the relationship. NEXT!

Don't ever, ever, ever, ever, *ever* wait around for someone to hopefully become interested in you – you have one life to live and your self-respect.

If you've been waiting and they've been feathering their nest elsewhere by cheating or starting a new relationship, bounce their arse out of your life fast.

There *is* no perfect time – you're either in or you're out. Simple. There will always be things that can come along and snatch our time but oddly when we want to make time, it opens up.

If you do decide to wait for someone (this must only be in exceptional circumstances), make it three to six months tops. That's short term and the time is for them to get themselves organised, not to make up their mind about their interest or commitment to you. Beyond that you're into medium and long-term waiting and that's seriously unhealthy.

Time waits for no one. Unless you want your gravestone to say: '*Here lies [name]. She was a great woman that dedicated her life to waiting around for Mr Unavailables,*' I suggest you find better things to do with your time.

The risk of waiting isn't worth the reward. It's easy for them to say that they'd wait if they were you – they're not you and they're not in the same position.

HE'S AN EGOTIST SEEKING PERFECTION... YOU'RE SEEKING A 'FEELING'

Fallback Girls don't really look at the key components that actually make up a decent guy and the foundations of a good relationship because they're too busy chasing an elusive feeling, trying to recapture the man they thought he was and living in the past.

Over the years, I've asked women why they're 1) so attracted to their Mr Unavailable or 2) struggling in a long-term relationship, or 3) not interested in a Mr *Available*, and the word 'right' has come up repeatedly.

It just feels 'right' with him.

Things need to be 'right' before I'm willing to believe that he's truly ready.

It just didn't feel 'right' with him.

If your beliefs are rooted in negativity and unrealistic, how would you know what 'right' is? More importantly, what is this 'right' feeling?

Do you know when it actually feels genuinely right? When you're in it for the right reasons and you recognise what a healthy relationship is. With healthy self-esteem, you learn that there are situations where love cannot take root, prosper, or survive, and you opt out. If you're saying it feels so 'right' when you have little or no boundaries, and you're either not in a relationship with them or are in one that's struggling and catering to your unhealthy beliefs, it's because you don't recognise that you're mislabeling. What feels so right is patently wrong for you. Learn to listen to yourself and observe what is taking place around and to you.

RECAPTURING

Why do you think it's so easy for certain Mr Unavailables to dip in and out of a woman's life over a period of years? She's not focused on the time that's elapsed; she's focused on the 'feeling' she had on each of those occasions with him.

I've spoken with many women who insist that the 'type' that they believe is 'right' for them is necessary and of course, 'right'. When I ask them exactly how many successful, healthy relationships they've had with their type – zilch. When we don't understand the important factors in a healthy relationship, we latch onto more superficial or wholly unimportant qualities and so, for instance, we feel that because he looks like how we always wanted the 'right' man to look and maybe he's great in bed, has a great job in a similar field, is respected, has a dog, his own home, and yadda, yadda, yadda, we deduce that he must possess other values that we want in a partner and then get caught short when we realise that he doesn't. Until we realise this, we keep chasing a feeling that we think a person we aspire to be with will create. If we experience that feeling at the beginning of the relationship, but it disappears after a few months and only makes occasional reappearances, we keep trying to recapture and extend it.

You're effectively shooting yourself in the foot over a feeling. But feeling 'right' starts at home, and so the biggest question you have to ask yourself is do you feel right with you?

LIVING IN THE PAST

It's like you're only remembering the relationship up to a certain date – the day before things changed – and you're basically living in the past. Unfortunately, if when you talk about him and this relationship, you're saying how great things used to be, how you wish he'd go back to being *that* guy, and how you've invested too much to walk away, you are talking about a relationship that's over, even if you haven't said it yet. What you're talking about are your reasons why it's hard to walk away from him, but hard as it may be for you to hear, those reasons are not based on the present. If you were looking at your relationship and him in full, you'd recognise the disconnect between what was and what *is* and understand why your relationship isn't working. Remembering the past is not enough of a reason to stay.

BREAKING THE CYCLE

Acknowledging your present, seeing the relationship in its entirety, and not being stuck on replay lets your feelings and efforts catch up to the now. While past actions can be indicative of future action, when you get stuck in the past, there's a whole period of time since then that tells you who this person is. I've heard from women who have stayed for *years* in relationships based on the first few months – it's not just about recognising that you've been seeking a feeling from long ago, but also the significance of the contrast between who they were then and who they've been since and now.

Say goodbye to chasing the feeling. You cannot even begin to fix a relationship when you're not in full acknowledgement of who and what you're dealing with. You also can't say hello to a better relationship with someone else and a better you, if you don't let go and say goodbye. If you had the relationship, you wouldn't have to be so focused on finding the feeling. You need to get into living as chasing, whether it's him or a feeling, is kinda exhausting. Get into the real world and focus on building feelings through building a relationship with a foundation.

Stop looking for things to be 100% bad before you'll leave. This means that you're waiting for the relationship to be your version of truly awful before you'll bail and that could be incredibly dangerous, not least because you may already be playing down seriously unhealthy behaviour.

Even if your relationship is '50%' bad, that in itself is a sign that you both need to seriously address issues. Your relationship is an unhealthy seesaw. Fact is, if you have to look at your relationship as a percentage of this and that, you've got problems. People in even moderately decent and healthy

147

relationships aren't tracking their happiness on a subjective index of percentage points. They don't have to divide it into good and bad –they're too busy living.

While you're living in the past, you're missing out on your present and your future. That 'past person' is gone. Acceptance is a fundamental part of relationships and this means you either work with what you have (healthily) or let them go. Chasing a feeling or staying and complaining are all highly unproductive.

If you (or they) have not addressed the issues that have you in unhealthy relationships, The Most Perfect Person That Ever Did Live in the Universe won't make a blind bit of difference. The responsibility for personal growth is yours, not another person's, and if you can't do it independently of them and off your own steam, it's lazy, limited change. You can work out your issues even if he won't. The fact that he's happy being who he is like a pig in shit, doesn't mean that your chances of helping yourself are nil – you're not the same person and you are coming at this unavailable malarkey from entirely different perspectives.

REMEMBER!

There's no such thing as a perfect person. However, that doesn't absolve you from the responsibility of distancing or cutting yourself off from people who don't behave in ways that are conducive to forging even the basics of a mutually fulfilling healthy relationship.

Anybody who will mark you down for being you and have you jumping through hoops trying to be 'perfect' is not a relationship worth staying in. Whether they hold the hoop out for you or you make the decision that you need to change for them, it's a sign that you're not yourself in the relationship, so whether you stay or get out, you must be yourself.

It's tiring, disrespectful, and, at times, demoralising to be involved with someone who's made it clear that you're not good enough as you are and that change is needed. It says, "I don't accept you; I reject you." That cuts both ways.

Short of living in his pocket or installing hidden cameras on him, you have no idea what his new relationship is like. Stop worrying about someone else getting a better him in a better relationship and start focusing on you being the best you in a better relationship.

If you're not the 'right' person for them, they're not the 'right' person for you *either*. When you insist that they're the one for you while they've already declined, there's something wrong with that equation – you're saying, "The right person for me is someone who doesn't want me or value me."

HE BREAKS OUT THE SOB STORY & EXCUSES... YOU INFLATE YOUR EMOTIONAL AIRBAG

If I had to sit with a Mr Unavailable and listen to his sob story, you would see me rubbing the tips of my thumb and forefinger together as I played the smallest violin in the world. I only wish more of you would do the same.

You experience a lot of Bingo Moments, which are like lightbulbs switching on internally every time you register and latch on to something that you think gives you a reason to believe that he feels more, or provides an excuse, or what you believe is a valid reason to believe in him and your vision of the relationship. Some of your Bingo Moments are very subtle and not-so-subtle things that signal that he's Mr Unavailable, and these trigger your interest because now you know that he's the type of guy that ticks your Fallback Girl boxes.

I want you to picture yourself as a human emotional airbag – it's like each time you have a Bingo Moment, you run over and wrap yourself around him or throw yourself behind him so he can land on you. Hurting from his ex? Ooh, let me run in there. Fucked up parents? Ooh, let me lay myself out flat. You see where I'm going?

You're projecting your vision of how you would be and feel under the same circumstances, making dangerous assumptions that because he's shared a story or a tear that it means he feels very deeply about something – it doesn't. He may have told the story fifty, or a hundred, times and be very distanced from it, and, once it's left his mouth and you've been suitably mollified, he doesn't dwell on it – after all, he's emotionally unavailable, so avoiding uncomfortable stuff is his speciality.

It's easy to be a Fallback Girl if you're always in the mode of 'please use me in case of an emotional or sexual emergency'. We don't use our airbags in the car all the time but we know they're there – that's how he sees you. Willing, able, and ready to be defaulted to or 'fall back' on should he need to avail of the option but not in use on a permanent and extended basis.

Men that tell you One Time at Band Camp Stories are actually giving you a heads-up and a *Get Out Moment* and if you don't grab it with both hands, they become your future sob story.

WEARING YOUR HURT ON YOUR SLEEVE

Your willingness to listen to pretty much anything that comes out of his mouth and feel sympathetic or discover a loophole is why you become the repeated lamb to the slaughter. This is another way of you looking for an excuse, a justification to feel invested, and you deduce that, because you have problems in your past that you recognise on some level impact your ability to be successful at your relationships, you should not only be sympathetic and empathetic to his stories but that he will be empathetic and sympathetic to you.

A prime example of this is that every Fallback Girl has her own *'Hurt Stories'*, you know, your own tales of the various hurts that you've experienced, more than likely at the hands of other Mr Unavailables. However, often he either doesn't want to hear it or listens to it and draws the conclusion that you're just as screwed up as he is, hence you can't want a relationship either.

Privately he's often tuning out and saying, 'Here we go again.' He doesn't join the dots with his behaviour and think that it's made a contribution to the situation, or genuinely feel remorse for his actions and his inability to either commit to being with or without you.

Unfortunately, when he hears you talk about your past, *you* become the One Time in Band camp!

You're actually trying to say, 'I get you and we have a connection. It's OK to relax and love,' and he's basically saying, 'Don't expect too much of me because I'm screwed up.' This is why he's not dancing to your beat.

You have to stop telling men about your insecurities and laying yourself bare in the hope of empathy, understanding, and the reward of a relationship. Instead, deal with your insecurities so you don't have to look for empathy in the first place and can instead focus on building a relationship with someone who treats you with love, care, trust, and respect.

PLUGGING INTO PAIN

If you've been receptive to tales of woe, or felt connected by the pain of someone's past, or believed that whatever information you knew about someone's experiences gave you a legitimate reason to 'love and stay', you do it because:

It gives you a purpose. You need to be needed and, with him, you can imagine that with you at his side, he can overcome his problems.

It gives you a reason to stay. It's easy to get 'lost' in someone else's drama and decide that if you can 'support' him, it will eradicate the other issues that exist. It's a bit like assuming that the problem is exclusively his and there are no other reasons. You may also look for return on investment and fail to recognise when to 'fold'.

You believe that you and your 'love' can be the 'solution' to someone's problem. Tying into the need to be needed is the idea of being a buffer, fluffer, gap filler, human airbag, or nurse.

You believe that he'll be more receptive to what you have to offer because he's 'wounded'. Yes, it's basically like dating someone with problems because you're afraid to truly put yourself out there. Naturally, knowing that you could do better, you'll expect him to be 'grateful' and express his gratitude by sorting himself out.

You try to heal your own wounds by attempting to heal his. You want to right the wrongs of your past. It could be that your parents (or someone else of importance) were similar, or that you've had a really painful experience where someone else's pain clouds out yours and acts as a distraction. You also hope that he'll understand your pain and then be caught off guard when he doesn't.

It lets you feel in control. If you only seem to be involved with 'wounded' men, or those that you perceive as having fixer-upper potential, it's because unproblematic relationships would have you feeling out of control. Secretly, you're worried about whether these 'other' people would reject you – at least you know what to expect with your usual guys.

You make dangerous assumptions about him, almost verging on pitying him and believing that he 'needs' you to fix/heal/help him and add whatever is missing to his life. I've heard from many Fallback Girls who believe themselves to be compassionate, but most don't know what that means: **Compassion** is sympathetic pity and concern for the misfortunes of others. (Source: Oxford Dictionaries)

That deep sense of compassion that you think you have reveals a fundamental flaw in your plan – pity isn't the same as love and nor is it a reason to remain in a relationship, plus it's not the way that most people want to be regarded by another.

BREAKING THE CYCLE

You're trying to be the emotional airbag solution to Mr Unavailable's problems and you've got to stop. Empathy is a fundamental component of healthy relationships, but make sure that you're actually empathising because, often, instead of placing yourself in his shoes, you place yourself in *your* shoes and project your own stuff and what you think, feel, and do, which isn't *actually* the same as truly considering and understanding their position. You're stuck in a cycle of pity, which is not conducive to a relationship.

If you need a sob story to feel connected, this says more about you than it does about them. Don't look for pain as a common ground – look for shared values, love, care, trust, and respect. We all have a past and some of us have painful things to deal with, but it would be better to address those pain points than to look for a *pain partner*.

Stop throwing your past and the whole kit and caboodle at them in an attempt to draw empathy and to send a protection warning signal. Address any hurts and issues and learn to evaluate each of your relationships on their merits. Before you tell anyone anything deeply revealing, make sure you know what the purpose is – to draw sympathy? To say, *"Please don't hurt me!"* or *"You can't hurt me because look what happened to me?"* To manipulate him? Or are you saying it as something that, even though it has hurt, you have or are dealing with it and you're sharing it as part of your emotional honesty and have no agenda? Make sure you're comfortable with what you're sharing and never let yourself be coerced or even badgered into it. You tend to find that when you're at peace with what you have to share or you at least have a calmer perspective on it, you're less likely to experience anxiety and negative consequences.

You will learn far more about them and the possibility for a healthy relationship if you're not so busy pitying and over-sympathising. This stops you from giving them qualities, characteristics, and potential that they don't possess and seeing them in reality. You're not really listening – you're hearing what you want to hear. You're not really seeing – you're seeing what you want to see. Some of the things you're hearing and seeing are huge pieces of information that tell you about their capacity for a relationship. You've got to stop thinking that, since you have problems and believe you're ready to commit, you can see past his problems. When you see it like this, you won't be so quick to downplay his problems because you now recognise how your own issues are impacting your capacity and who you're attracted to.

Stop looking for Bingo Moments in every conversation and action because you're missing the bigger picture. Also, realise that you only have to look for Bingo Moments when the content of your relationship is *lacking*. This is like clutching at straws and going through a painful extraction process. By stopping the search, you'll lose a sense of desperation about finding any ole reason to stay and recognise who and what you're dealing with. Look at partners in their entirety, including both 'good' and 'bad' bits, and make sure you're not just focused on moments, especially those you've latched onto as a result of a painful revelation or experience.

REMEMBER!

They or you can cry but it doesn't mean that the problem is gone. It also doesn't mean that either of you should do what the other expects, because that's manipulation.

Have you got your own stories on repeat? Play a new record and ensure that *you're* not This One Time at Band Camp-ing.

You don't *know* the solution to their problems – trust me, it's not *your* love. If you did know the solution, you'd realise that it's their responsibility to address the issues that existed before you met them.

If you want to put your sympathy and compassionate urges to good use, go and do charity work. There's a wealth of people, young and old, and causes that need dedicated, sympathetic, compassionate people.

You can empathise and even sympathise without assuming all of their problems and getting 'down with them'. You also don't have to go out with everyone you pity and, in fact, it'd be good to take a holiday from dating problematic men – ideally a permanent one.

HE ONLY THINKS OF HIMSELF...YOU PUT THE FOCUS ON HIM

It's a wonderful life for Mr Unavailable. It's a me, me, me trip for him all the way and the fantastic thing is that every Fallback Girl that welcomes him with open arms, only thinks of him, too! How wonderful to never actually have to consider someone else *and* have a woman marginalise her needs, her aspirations, and her expectations so that she can stand by a man who is living on another planet. Wonderful, my arse! Who is thinking about you?

When you're not thinking about you, and he's not thinking about you, that equals serious problems. When Mr Unavailable says or does something to you, you don't stop to consider whether it's in line with your values, needs, desires, etc.; you wonder how you can position yourself to be in line with his wants. You're too caught up in the world according to him and, as a result, you're an over-giver with codependent tendencies who keeps picking the wrong teammates.

GIVING WHAT YOU WANT TO GET BACK

Remember when I explained earlier how he gives, not what you need, but what he believes that he has the ability to give? Well, you're the same, only you don't just view your contribution from what you have to give, but also what you would like to get back. In thinking about what you perceive love and relationships to be and how you'd like to feel and be treated, you determine that what you need and want is what the *relationship* needs, especially in the early stages when he may be claiming that you're both on the same page.

Fallback Girls, in losing their identity, also tend to see the relationship as an extension of themselves.

You get trapped in your feelings and stop seeing each of you as individuals and, because of what you want and need, and the intensity of what you feel, you keep assuming that he's feeling it to the same depth and wanting the same things, which is highly unrealistic and blinds you to him. When things don't go according to plan, you're bewildered.

You think that you would be happy if your needs were being met in this way and wonder why he's not happy and reciprocating and making you happy. However, his needs are not your needs and vice versa. What you're happy with isn't what he's happy with. What he's seeking or happy to get by on is different from you. The danger of treating partners and relationships like extensions of yourself is that you become *complacent* and *assumptive*.

By persisting in giving what you think you need, you're not really giving *to* him; you're giving to you. By *choosing* to give to him, you're also giving to a very inappropriate recipient. Healthy relationships require recognition of individual needs and not treating one another like mirrors to generate what we need. It's also important to recognise that you may have unrealistic expectations or be looking for stuff that's either stuff that you should be doing for yourself or just isn't appropriate for a healthy, adult relationship.

FOCUSING ON EXCUSING

You think he's scared, tired, confused, busy, hurting, needs more time, etc., when really... he's unavailable. The amount of excuses you are prepared to make and take are a barometer for how deep you will get into unavailable relationships.

Excusing is the loyal sister of denial and it's important to remind yourself of what excusing actually involves: defending or justifying what in essence is wrongdoing. It's overlooking and forgiving stuff and quite frankly, you can't afford any more excuse credits – you've run out! It's impossible to actually deal with issues or understand the impact of them if you're too busy making up excuses for why things are happening. Ever left an abusive relationship? It's because you ran out of excuses.

Don't make excuses for other people's behaviour as you're assuming you know better because you don't want to hear the truth. You really don't know better and, by accepting the truth of what he (or anyone else) has done, it means you can make the decision to stay or go under real circumstances and, ultimately, protect yourself from ending up in a dangerous relationship or clinging on for dear life in a relationship long past its sell-by date. You also know you've got major problems in the relationship if you're making excuses for his excuses because it means that the original excuses were crap. You're a person of value – you don't *need* excuses.

PICKING THE WRONG TEAMMATE

With Mr Unavailable, you're choosing the right teammate for unhealthy relationships and then being 'shocked' when he underperforms or performs exactly as you expect a poor teammate would. Fallback Girls consistently avoid choosing decent partners because they're scared of what they may learn about themselves or panic that they're not good enough – they don't believe they can forge a relationship with a healthy partner.

When your pattern is to be with Mr Unavailables, when things don't work out, deep down inside you're OK with it. You're still upset but you're unsurprised and the ending only serves to confirm your beliefs. You then lather, rinse, repeat with a new partner or, if you're a glutton for punishment, you keep going back to an ex trying to get him to be different, ensuring that you continue engaging in relationship insanity and generating the same result.

BREAKING THE CYCLE

When you change how you feel about you, which impacts how you feel about everything else, you'll opt to be a co-pilot in your relationships. For a quality journey through life that doesn't keep playing out old hurts, don't be a passenger in poor relationships.

You need to start asking yourself: 'Is this what I want?' and other such questions. Fallback Girls do what works for Mr Unavailables and assume it's what they want without genuinely considering whether it's what they actually want. Your needs and motives are different from another person's. Don't assume that you're coming from the same place.

What do you want? Trust me when I say that it's not what he wants. You're two separate entities. What do *you* want? It's back to the short, medium, and long-term goals again. Where do you see yourself? What type of relationship do you want? Do you want a committed relationship with an available partner?

What does he want? Write it down. What has he told you he wants? What has he *showed* you he wants? The 'different' is what he actually wants. If you both want different things where it really matters, you have different values, which makes you *incompatible*.

If you don't have an identity, it's time to create one independently. Start immersing yourself in creating your life and, if needed, sit down with a professional so that you ensure that you don't end up in a co-dependent relationship again. Learn to stand on your own two feet independently of whoever you are involved with.

REMEMBER!

Learn to give to yourself and meet your own needs. You'll recognise when someone detracts from you rather than adding to your life, plus you won't feel so lost if and when a relationship ends.

Don't be a Transformer, twisting, turning, morphing, and adapting to suit each relationship. Be yourself.

You cannot please everyone all of the time. If your way of making you happy is to try and make others happy by running yourself into the giving ground, you need to find another way.

You are good *enough* without having to give the crap out of yourself.

If you are going to attempt to meet someone's needs, ensure that it's within a mutually fulfilling relationship. Take the time to find out exactly what their needs are, either by paying attention to them or asking, which is better than projecting your needs.

Stop giving to people in the hope of getting back what you want and need. This is not wholehearted, generous giving – it's a secret contract and you're going to be disappointed.

THE MAKING OF A FALLBACK GIRL

Since the summer of 2005 I've been answering a question for myself that many other women have been using to answer questions in their own lives: *Why was I a Fallback Girl who pursued relationships with unavailable men?* The question of why you want an unavailable man and it feels like no other one will do is something that consumes millions of women each day and, I assure you, all of the reasons are very familiar, but you either don't recognise their importance or you've been denying them for years. There are behaviours that let him know that you're the ideal candidate for an unavailable relationship and that also reflect your mental and emotional state.

You're attracted to and 'comfortable' with Mr Unavailable because you're emotionally unavailable too. The primary reasons why you're unavailable do have elements that crossover with him –you get involved because you have low self-esteem, you have negative and unrealistic beliefs, poor emotional schooling by one or both parents, painful breakups and experiences, and fairytale ideas that have you looking to be the exception.

YOU DON'T LOVE YOURSELF ENOUGH

The first time I truly recognised and accepted that I had poor self-esteem was after my epiphany when a specialist advised that I needed to go on steroids permanently as my disease had returned. A massive wake-up call, a deep sense of shame followed when I realised it had taken eighteen months since my diagnosis to actually take an interest in my well-being and act like someone who gave a damn about what the hell happened to her instead of chasing 'love'.

Many women are actually raised to have low self-esteem and it's so ingrained that feeling how you do may seem normal, until you hit rock bottom after one involvement too many in a poor relationship and start looking for answers. You may have grown up believing that your feelings weren't important, that you had to work hard for the attention and affection of others, that men are more important than women, that without a man and a relationship something is wrong with you, or that if you actually allow yourself to be vulnerable you'll be abandoned. You may not like how you look, or have struggled with friendship or siblings, or had a terrible experience that broke your trust in yourself and others.

'Self-esteem' and 'self-love' are spoken about frequently, particularly in regards to women, but many us have little or none and it's reflected in our interactions and how we view the world.

Self-esteem is about having confidence in your worth, which comes from acting with love, care, trust, and respect towards yourself. It's about having a positive relationship with you, where you not only *value* you but recognise yourself as an individual entity of importance.

If you lack confidence in your capabilities and your value, you won't be confident having boundaries and you'll try to gain confidence and experience love via external sources. To get that love, you'll give what you believe is 'unconditional' love, which, in your eyes, means loving without limits. You'll believe that you have 'flaws' that make you unlovable or difficult to love, and will choose people who reflect your beliefs.

By loving someone unconditionally who you know is 'flawed' in ways that are familiar due to your own unavailability, you hope that he'll reciprocate. Of course, this isn't what happens.

Unconditional love is liking, loving, and staying true to you, irrespective of what's taking place around you. It's not internalising external factors and keeping a healthy sense of self and self-love so that your perception of you doesn't become distorted. This also means that you won't look for people to do and be things that you're not being and doing yourself, and you won't look for unconditional love from inappropriate sources.

This means that your way of loving unconditionally is flawed because: 1) You love with little or no boundaries, which is loving without limits, which, at best, has you taken advantage of, and 2) when you experience problems, or a relationship doesn't work out, how you feel about you is greatly impacted.

You have an attitude of: I'll love him unconditionally —> I'll be there, stick to him like glue, accept boundary-busting behaviour —> He'll love me back unconditionally and because I turn a blind eye to his behaviour, he'll turn a blind eye to my so-called flaws —> I'll be accepted and validated, I'll feel the love that's been eluding me and I'll like and love myself at last —> We can live happily ever after.

More often than not, it becomes: I'll love him unconditionally —> I'll be there, stick to him like glue, accept boundary-busting behaviour —> He'll love me back unconditionally and because I turn a blind eye to his behaviour, he'll turn a blind eye to my so-called flaws —> He doesn't love me back unconditionally —> What's wrong with me that someone so flawed, who has the option to behave as they like and *still* be loved, doesn't love me? —> I must be a very unlovable person if I can't even be loved by someone like that.

Your self-love is easily dented, yet it takes a *lot* for you to shift how you feel about someone that you're involved with. If you don't love yourself first, you'll look for people, things, and even substances, to create feelings in you and do things that you should be doing for yourself and/or who have not shown themselves capable or willing. Continuing the pattern means that even going on dates will deplete you, because you'll internalise each one not progressing as rejection and confirmation that you're not 'good enough'. If you also try to be whatever you think the relationship requires, it means that you have morphed and adapted so much that you lose sight of who you are.

I hear from so many women that don't know who they are anymore. Their passions, dreams, interests, plans and ambitions have been forgotten because Mr Unavailable became their vocation. After being so indispensable, it's very hard to leave because their identity is so entrenched in this person and the success (or failure) of the relationship.

Low self-esteem means that you find it much easier to focus on others, as you don't think that you're worthy of your own time and energy.

When your relationships 'break' you believe you're 'broken'. You may even believe you're worth *less* or *worthless*. It's like you don't exist, have no voice, and have no recollection of your identity and values. When you did consider leaving you panicked that because of being with him or your past, there's obviously *something* wrong with you and no one will want you 'like this'. You believe that the 'flaws' will be found by someone new, so you figure it's better to stay with the devil you know. When you attempt to end it or do, it feels too hard to be alone with someone that you don't like (you), so you look for someone new to give you 'life' and a sense of value and purpose again. And so the cycle continues.

When you don't see change or love from unavailable men, it cements the idea that you can't change or be loved either.

Women always ask me how they can learn to love themselves, as if having self-esteem is something 'mystical'. The key is always treating you well even when others won't, which means, at times, opting out of dubious situations. You're never going to feel confident about yourself and your value if you keep waiting for others to do what you can't even do yourself. If you keep doing the same stuff and expecting different results (relationship insanity), you'll quietly, or even openly, hate yourself for putting yourself through this. You'll lament your mistakes and then feel unlovable because you know you treat yourself so badly – vicious cycle. If loving them means that you can't love you, always choose you. You've got to stop choosing him. You've got to stop choosing pain because pain isn't love; it's pain.

Validation is about seeking confirmation of your value or that something is 'right'.

One of the biggest traps that women fall into is continuously looking for external validation from peers, the media, family, and, of course, men. We read or hear something and, if it's not reflective of the choices we've made or speaks to an insecurity of ours, we question the validity of those choices. Instead of knowing what feels good and right for us, we go around looking for others to tell us what feels right and good for us. Instead of knowing what our boundaries and values are, we allow others to determine what we'll put up with and try to fall in line with their values. This means we're not living congruently with our own values, which detracts from us. If we don't value ourselves and the good things we *do* have, when others around us 'succeed' we wonder what's wrong with us.

The media also streams out constant messaging about our bodies and beauty, as well as critiquing our choices, from how we educate ourselves, to where we fit in the workplace, breastfeeding vs. formula, whether we're doing 'enough', whether we're shit mothers, good lovers, girlfriends or wives, and basically constantly telling us who we are and what we can and can't do. Many of these messages pit us against one another and we lose confidence in ourselves that we're capable of being a 'good enough', lovable person. We may even try to be 'superwoman'.

Many women are not confident that they can live up to impossible standards that they don't acknowledge are *impossible*.

In particular, a lot of what we're taught about being confident in ourselves seems to be intrinsically tied with our success at being with men and holding down relationships, and a lot of the standards within this are tied to unrealistic and conflicting standards regarding appearance and sex. When we pick up magazines, they're suggesting 50 ways to please our men and claiming to be interested in our emotional welfare while selling distorted images of women or using language that seems to undermine us. When brands and the media speak to women, they play to insecurity. When brands sell to men, they play to confidence and their sense of 'manliness'.

Unfortunately, you gravitate towards people who reflect your unhealthy beliefs so they're validating the lack of confidence that you have in you. You keep letting others define you. Mr Unavailable *isn't* as good as it gets, but until you put the process of doing things to nurture you instead of doing things to get validation in motion, you set the bar low and limit your options in limited relationships with limited men.

Loving yourself is not about being a narcissist and having a disproportionate ego; it's about extending the same due level of care, love, and concern that you expect to receive from others to *yourself*.

We're all far more likely to fixate on the negative things that people may say about us. This means that even if you heard 100 positive validations, hearing just *one* negative from someone you truly desire validation from, means those 100 validations no longer matter. In real life, this is the equivalent of being pursued by lots of lovely available men who want a relationship, but fixating on that *one* guy you met last year, who was a bit ambiguous and never did call again after you thought you'd hit it off.

But when you learn to love yourself unconditionally and without reserve, you validate you, which means that your life doesn't come crashing down because you didn't get validation from someone that doesn't know his arse from his elbow. This is because that one validation that matters most becomes *yours*.

FEARS & BELIEFS

I could discover plenty about you and give fifty examples of what makes you such a valuable person and why you should embrace you and not hide behind these demeaning relationships, but if *you* don't believe and recognise those things *yourself*, I could give you a *million* reasons, but you'll still find it easier to stick with one negative belief.

Like him, most of what you do is motivated by fear, especially when you seek out drama and act up, because you keep placing yourself in situations that realise your fears and then fight against it. In understanding what your 'drama triggers' are (the things that set you off in the pursuit of drama), fear is often at the root of your behaviour, and when you look at one fear, you find others hiding behind it.

Everything we tell ourselves confirms a few core beliefs that we hold. It means you may overestimate your capabilities – for example, you'll think that if you love enough, all problems can be solved. It also means you may at the same time, underrate your capabilities and undermine your own efforts – for example, you'll think that you're only capable of having a relationship if you have little or no boundaries, because if you do have them, it will scare them away because you don't think you're worthy of a relationship with mutual love, care, trust, and respect, after all, if you love enough and you're loved, love can overcome the lack of boundaries. And round you go. Fallback Girls also think stuff like:

I'm not good enough. You feel undeserving. You'd feel more inadequate in a healthier relationship.

All men cheat. You assume you're moments away from being screwed over while gravitating towards men who reflect this mentality. This doesn't mean all men cheat – it means the type of guy you're attracted to cheats.

Everyone abandons me eventually. By forecasting exits, no one gets too close, plus you'll try to avoid conflict for fear of abandonment. You'll either be with flaky men or sabotage relationships.

There's something unlovable about me. Believing you're fatally flawed, you tend to try to get love from the worst of people. When they don't, it confirms your beliefs.

If someone loves me, they'll change. You feel that you can latch on to anyone, even Mr Unavailable, and prove your worthiness. When they don't change, you believe you're not good enough to be changed for.

You can't help who you love. Avoiding responsibility, you believe you're helpless with him. You persist in relationship insanity and believe that if you love enough and stay, he'll eventually match you.

You tell yourself stories about why Mr Unavailable and the types of relationships that he generates are the best for you and you use them to legitimise your position. Even though you've been validating your beliefs in your interactions, it's not because they're actually true, but they're true of the situations that you get involved in.

If you were being involved with available people and had good self-esteem, you'd see that your beliefs are very shaky, to say the least.

Judging the world through unavailable eyes puts a filter on life and cements your beliefs. Of course things look bad, but there are plenty of people who *are* available and contradict what you believe about relationships, love, life, and yourself. You cater to your self-fulfilling prophecy. You use your fears and beliefs as a benchmark to predict what you think is likely to happen.

You consciously and unconsciously act in line with your beliefs – your mentality is reflected in your actions so, for example, if you don't believe you're good enough or lovable, you act like you're not good enough or lovable and participate in situations that reflect this. As we tend to go around blindly living our lives with our beliefs, most go unchallenged.

With your fears, you'll also be scared of getting out of your comfort zone, as it holds your firmly held beliefs. As a result, your relationship insanity continues because, like a cyclical effect, you use your fears and beliefs to predict what you think is likely to happen, you act accordingly, the self-fulfilling prophecy happens, your fears and beliefs get confirmed and lather, rinse, repeat on the cycle.

Your comfort zone is Mr Unavailable.

If you didn't make choices that cater to the self-fulfilling prophecy, you'd have to realise that they weren't true and get uncomfortable. You've been trying to get love in your comfort zone from someone who cannot meet your needs. You're trying to take a shortcut by extracting a healthy relationship from an inappropriate source, instead of loving you properly.

On the occasions that you trust your decisions, gut, emotions, and opinions, you have such a skewed vision of what you think a relationship 'should' be, and your self-esteem is so 'off' that they're often the wrong choices anyway, which further erodes your ability to trust your own judgement.

Trust is about having confidence and faith in how you believe you and others will act.

You're more confident about trusting what you know will go wrong. You don't want the uncertainty that comes with a guy who's available and may actually require you to invest yourself fully. Yep, self-fulfilling prophecy. If you have incidents from your past where people you've placed your confidence disappointed, you lose not only your trust and faith in other people, but also in yourself. The only way that we can trust and have faith in people is by having boundaries and parameters to assess the reliability of them.

You show your vulnerable side to Mr Unavailable because you're hoping that you can trust him enough not to take advantage and expose you to further vulnerabilities. Unfortunately, your pattern ensures that you reaffirm your beliefs, because you're exposing yourself to more risk. But... even if you have skewed ideas about relationships that need to be healed (you do), your gut can still tell you the difference between a situation that you should or shouldn't get out of, hence if you learned how to trust yourself more, you could minimise your risk and vulnerabilities.

You behave as you do because you trust that all relationships bring tears, drama, and heartbreak, and that all relationships are about one or both of you masking your emotions, and that it's your fault because there's something wrong with you. That is your 'truth'.

Having higher self-esteem, being able to trust, and not living in the shackles of fear are all intertwined because the moment that you do one, you start to do the rest and build on it.

CHANGE THE TAPE

This isn't how relationships are supposed to be. You can't learn to trust yourself if you won't prove your own trustworthiness by having boundaries and opting out of situations that deplete you. You believe it's the job of other people to give you trust and faith, but you have to actually show up with a reasonable level of them and adjust accordingly, instead of being distrusting or trusting blindly.

When you're suspicious of a decent guy who doesn't set off your drama meter, it's because he's not making you jump through hoops and him behaving in a semi-decent manner invalidates what you think you know about yourself and relationships, and that makes you feel uncomfortable. You don't see anything of you in a man like this and you can't relate to him, because sitting in front of you is a man who's connected and you're used to being around men who have emotional force fields surrounding them.

You trust Mr Unavailable because you trust the same old messaging that you've been listening to for as long as you can remember. If you don't trust at all but you still plough on regardless chasing relationships, you draw in negativity and even around a half-decent guy, you chase it away with distrust. You can let fear have as big or as small an impact as you want it to, but the point is that the choice is yours. You *can* address your beliefs and fears, and you *can* make better choices. Believe it by *doing* it.

PARENTAL ISSUES

Often when I listen to readers tell me about their relationship experiences, I guess that they're going out with people just like one of their parents. My 'spidey senses' even pick up on the possibility of their parent cheating even before they admit this. How do I know? I'm attuned to picking up on relationship patterns and subtle, near casual things that people say that aren't actually that casual. That, and I've dated nearly every possible variation of my father and even some variations of my mother.

You may not believe you have any issues because you've spent so long denying and/or rationalising it. If you have a habit of being involved with unavailable people, it's highly likely that you have unresolved issues with one, or even both, parents. Combined with how you were emotionally schooled, what you learned about values, and how your beliefs have been shaped, you're likely following unconscious patterns and may even be inadvertently trying to right the wrongs of the past, heal old rejections, and get the validation you may be missing.

This isn't about blaming your parents but it is about tapping into your underlying beliefs, resentments, hurts, and buried feelings and taking a long hard look, because, somewhere, you have a problem in your past. By examining these things and the events that may be connected to them, you give yourself a starting point for understanding your pattern, which you can use as a springboard for either working through on your own or spending time talking through stuff with a professional. If you've been thinking that you'll wake up one day and all these issues will have melted away or that you'll get into a relationship and they'll cease to matter, it's safe to say that you have more than enough evidence to show that your expectations are unfounded.

We don't wake up as adults suddenly equipped with the tools to handle our relationships. We learn through our environment and those around us whose love and approval we naturally seek as validation of the expected relationship with them.

If your parents were emotionally unavailable, you can be pretty damn sure that you are, too.

Yes, you can intervene like you are now, on long-held beliefs and change your future, but until you get to that point where you realise that you need to understand what's been happening, you're blindly following a pattern that you don't even know exists. You didn't just wake up this year and, Bam!, you were a Fallback Girl – some of you have been cultivating this life for as long as you can remember. It could be your father, it could be your mother, it could be a divorce, or it could be all of them, like it was for me.

DADDY HUNTING

With parental relationships, it can be all about setting the tone. You may have a good relationship with your mother, but your chances of having a bad relationship with yourself and future partners seriously increases with a dubious interaction with your own father or strong male figure. The pattern of being involved with unavailable men can be deep-rooted, learned in childhood. It doesn't have to be an absentee or 'bad' father; it may be that the significant male figure in your life didn't express his emotions or made you work hard for his affection, and for all intents and purposes, he was emotionally unavailable. It's called going after what you know.

Your relationship with your father may have you believing that you've been loved conditionally.

In turn, you'll look for that unconditional love that you always wanted from your father and, coupled with unrealistic expectations, create the wrong messages about yourself with mistaken love habits. You'll then look for love in all the wrong places in a quest to be 'loved', so that you can fill up the void. You're likely to be afraid of abandonment and rejection and have been inadvertently trying to recreate aspects of your father-daughter relationship with Mr Unavailable in a doomed self-fulfilling prophecy. You may be 26, 36, 46, or whatever age, but when you're around a man, you may be 6 or 16 again, playing out the relationship that you had with him.

Typically, if you find yourself recreating patterns based around your relationship with your father, it's likely to be because:

He prioritised his needs to the detriment of you/your family.

He emotionally, sexually, or physically abused you.

He abandoned you or was fond of disappearing acts.

He may not have met his financial or family obligations.

He was unresponsive, uncommunicative, and undemonstrative.

He *was* communicative and demonstrative... but only when expressing negativity.

He was ambiguous and noncommittal.

He was very charming and a ladies' man, so there may have been cheating.

He was an addict.

He may have actually been a great provider, but didn't provide emotionally.

He may have played you off your siblings or even your mother.

He may have made you work for his attention.

He may have said something that led you to believe that you were responsible for his behaviour/him leaving.

You may have witnessed him emotionally, sexually, or physically abuse your mother or siblings.

He may have left and you assumed responsibility.

After he started a relationship with someone else, your relationship with him changed.

These things and more will mean that the prime male figure in your life will have significantly affected your beliefs, which, left unchallenged, affected:

Your values Your fundamental beliefs about what you need to live authentically, what makes you feel good, bad, happy, sad, etc.

Your boundaries Either repeatedly lacking boundaries with partners or veering in the opposite direction and having more walls than Fort Knox.

How you emotionally connect Plus what you perceive as 'connecting'.

Empathy You need it, but may look for sympathy and may also find yourself involved with people who are lacking in empathy, making them potentially cruel, distant, and unable to connect with what you're experiencing in your position. You may assume victim status and avoid accountability and responsibility.

Love, care, trust, and respect You may not be used to having these, which means you may not look for them in a relationship.

The healthy things that we should seek from our partners and relationships, are what we should ideally have had, albeit in a father-daughter dynamic. If you don't have a reasonably healthy relationship with your father to draw upon, you will be:

Afraid of men leaving or withdrawing.

Chasing similar partners.

Trying to right the wrongs of the past.

Trying to gain the validation that you failed to get from your father.

Clinging to an image of the father that you'd like but didn't get and then projecting it onto your partners and tying them and yourself up in unrealistic expectations.

In spite of my experiences with my own father, I drew a halo around it and created an image of the father I would have had in an ideal world. This was an unconscious act and it didn't reflect the real him at all, plus I knew nothing of values, boundaries, and healthy relationship behaviours.

What I did was take an already very imperfect man with not so great relationship habits and basically tag him with loving me unconditionally and making me feel all the things I didn't feel for myself and doing everything I thought that relationships were all about. I then went out in search of 'him'. This person was a figment of my imagination and I'd made a person with conflicting qualities and characteristics and expected it to give me a relationship it was incapable of giving. It's like going:

MR UNAVAILABLE DAD + MY EXPECTATION OF COMMITMENT + MY EXPECTATION OF A HEALTHY RELATIONSHIP + MY EXPECTATION OF UNCONDITIONAL LOVE = MY IDEAL MAN = MR UNAVAILABLE = ME EXPECTING COMMITMENT, A HEALTHY RELATIONSHIP AND UNCONDITIONAL LOVE FROM AN EXTREMELY UNLIKELY SOURCE

Father Image + Unrealistic Expectations = Mr Unavailable, the man fundamentally incapable of meeting your needs.

This is why we often get involved with Mr Unavailables and want them to make us the exception – they're reflections of our father with selective ideas and characteristics, that we've added on with our expectations, that have absolutely no basis and are actually incompatible, which sets your relationship up to fail and then leads to a self-fulfilling prophecy. It makes the pattern of being involved with him very familiar and 'comfortable', even though it's very *un*comfortable.

174

At the end of the day, the one man you ideally need to get a consistent message of love and care from is your father. If you don't get that message and the nurturing that comes with it, human nature, coupled with other events that may happen, will get in the way of your perception of yourself as a result.

THERE IN SPIRIT

Very often, men have to be 'strong like bull', and, as providers, they focus on providing security and fostering a good life, often stemming from the material and practical aspects of life, with very little thought given to how much emotional sustenance is being given to their children. They look around and see food on the table, a mother doing her 'motherly bit', a car in the driveway and everything provided for, plus they work long hours, and they determine that their work is done. There is an element of them thinking, "We're here, aren't we?" You then believe that all men need to do is show up, not participate.

He had good intentions and was doing the best he could, often based on his own experience of being parented, however, being raised by him may have you looking for love in all the wrong places. We do need emotional attention and, as children, when we see the world according to ourselves, it can feel very bewildering and scary to not receive it from a parent.

There's no disputing that these fathers are there but I don't support this culture of patting parents on the back for being there for children that they've created. When men boast, "I take care of my kids!", I'm thinking, "What's the big fricking deal? You're *supposed* to!" There's 'there' and there's being present and accountable. While I appreciate that sometimes very innocent things can be misconstrued when you're a child that, on reflection as an adult, aren't actually the world-crushing problem that we perceived them to be at the time, the role of a parent *is* to nurture a child and shape their world, and help them to navigate it.

Yes, men don't always find it easy to express their emotions, and, yes, our own fathers are likely to have their own issues with their own parents that govern their own behaviour, but many men do make a consistent effort to try. This isn't about blaming your father for being there but not giving you enough attention; it's about understanding that, as an adult, you keep acting out your desire for attention by taking up with emotionally vacant men that make you jump through hoops for crumbs.

ABUSIVE FATHERS

If he was violent, aggressive, nasty, demeaning and basically anything inappropriate, whether that was towards you, your mother, or your siblings, it will have left a lasting mark. In adulthood, you'll gravitate to abusive men including narcissists. They're shaping the negative perception that you have of yourself, reinforcing the idea that you're ugly, unlovable, responsible for his aggression, and this is how easy it can be to become a woman who spends her life assuming the blame for a man's bad behaviour.

How could you not? The one man who you're supposed to trust and who you may have idolised may have been telling you since you were a child that if only you'd do as you were told, he wouldn't have to hit you or your mother, or that no guy will want you.

I challenge anyone who is being abused, or at the very least subjected to a heavy level of negativity by a parent, not to be affected. As a child who isn't accepted by her parents, you'll either keep seeking acceptance, or wonder what was so wrong with you that they behaved as they did. You may also have felt hopeless to stop him abusing others and, as a result, feel guilt and the weight of failure.

It gears you up for Mr Unavailables, plus witnessing or experiencing abuse is something no child should go through and it removes an innocence you don't get back. Whether you witness aggression, violence, or nastiness, or were actually the victim of it, this trains you to gravitate towards relationships full of drama or that, at the very least, have very little chance of survival, because you either choose men who exhibit all of those traits you actually despise, or you choose men who are broken and wounded who you can right the wrongs of the past with, because the power base will be more comfortable for you. This will definitely play itself out if your father had an addiction, as you're likely to replicate his pattern of destructiveness by playing Florence. It takes time and love to heal from abuse which is all the more reason *not* to use that energy in an unavailable relationship.

ABSENT FATHERS

It's extremely difficult for most children to comprehend why their father is absent, even if they have a relatively happy home with their mother, or with her and subsequent partners. It may feel like he didn't love you enough to stick around. Whatever a father's reasons are for abandoning his child, it can never quite be explained or rationalised, regardless of whether his reason involved the child or not. Whether he's in and out of your life, or doesn't show up at all, both can lead to you growing up and finding yourself seeking out relationships that replicate that sense of abandonment and sometimes you'll also seek comfort with older men that fulfil the daddy need.

With the father who shows up from time to time, you get to learn how to seek his approval by trying to do all of the right things. The child mentality says that if you just do enough, he'll stick around and be your father full time. But then he's gone again. You'll have developed a pattern of your hopes being raised, trying to win him over, then feeling disappointed, and, even though you may not have given up trying, you learned what to expect and started to derive your value based on your interactions with him. Hence him dipping in and out of your life, blazing in on his white horse and making you the focal point of his life again, became, *"Men that are attractive aren't always physically available and, because I'm not as important or as lovable as other things or people that he may have in his life, I need to accept that this is how life is."*

You'll find it easy not to be a priority which will make you ripe for being the Other Woman.

You may, as an adult, recognise that you want to be with a man who is consistent but the elusive, inconsistent Mr Unavailable is eerily familiar, and, because of how he behaves in the beginning, you get high on the pattern that you know so well. You'll revert to being that child who wants to make her father stay for a bit longer, to put off his 'other life', to choose you over 'them' or whatever is seemingly holding him back. It's not because you're an unimportant person; you gravitate towards men who have 'other things' going on, then make it your vocation to change that.

If your father outright abandoned you or you may even still be waiting for him to turn up, you not only fear abandonment by all men, but, at the same time, you may seek a relationship where you let them have more control, in the hope of finding that intangible feeling of comfort that you've been missing all of your life. You end up being uncertain about what type of man to chase, due to the lack of shining example in your life and will struggle to engage with men in a healthy way. I know some women who are still that little girl waiting for their dad and have spent most of their lives feeling disappointed because everybody but him showed up.

A father who abandons his child is abandoning a part of himself and has no real confidence in his abilities. Just like you can't change Mr Unavailable with 'love', parenthood is too 'challenging' for some men. They may even think they're doing you a 'favour', because they 'know' they wouldn't have been up to much, but, the truth is that, much like the Mr Unavailable that doesn't know whether he could have made a relationship work because he never actually genuinely risked and *tried* and *continued*, neither does the father who bolts from responsibility and a life he's helped to create.

THE INBETWEENERS

Another pitfall of daddy hunting is seeking out what you think are opposites to your father or trying to do the impossible and find a replica. There are three classic examples of this:

Good girls, from stable homes. Both parents still together, happily married for a gazillion years, loves Mr Unavailable – why? Their marriage is the stable future you want eventually, but, for now, you need 'excitement'. Of course you get hurt which can put you into an extended spin cycle.

Women who date men who are highly educated, high achievers, but still Mr Unavailable. Some Fallback Girls prioritise the power they feel that their father didn't have or exhibit. For example, if the mother was the breadwinner and especially if your father lorded it up in spite of not contributing. You'll be blinded by the power and fail to recognise less favourable qualities.

When nobody can compare to your father. If you idolise him, you may languish with men who don't meet his approval as nobody can compare. It's the equivalent of being a mother's boy – a headache-seeking, unattainable perfection. You end up remaining 'his girl' while having no life!

THERE'S SOMETHING ABOUT MOTHER

Naturally, if we can find ourselves learning unhealthy beliefs from our fathers, we can certainly learn from our mothers, too. But not only can we end up dating reflections of them, we can also end up reflecting their own love habits and ideas that they've passed on to us, or that we've absorbed.

In recent years, I've spoken with many women who have very fraught, and sometimes abusive, relationships with their mothers. Even if it's not been at the crazy end of things, many women today have had mothers who carried their own baggage, beliefs, behaviours, and attitudes, and therefore parented and communicated, either through actions or words, messages to their daughters that affected their view of relationships and themselves.

I'll be honest – until my late twenties I carried a secret shame about my relationship with my mother as I saw it as a reflection of myself. Everyone else's seemed so 'normal', but, over the years, I've come to realise and accept that many women have stood in my shoes, and much like the issue of Mr Unavailable, it's recognising that this isn't a unique situation that frees you because you know that it's not about you.

All the reasons that create the issues with father-daughter relationships described in *Daddy Hunting* can create problematic mother-daughter relationships – just substitute her in, plus:

She abandoned you or kept disappearing.

You were taught to feel bad about loving your father, or to even be ashamed of your background.

She was/is a drama queen invalidating everyone's feelings.

She prioritised her love life, choosing men over you, and maybe even standing by as they mistreated you.

She was jealous and treated you like an enemy or a love rival.

She was near obsessed with what she thought you were and weren't doing, especially around sex.

She critiqued you constantly.

When your father was verbally or physically abusive, she stood by, encouraged it, or told you that it was because he loved you or that you deserved it.

She knows that you've been sexually abused, but denies it.

She's moody, manipulative, controlling, depressed, emotionally high strung, or may even be a narcissist.

She decided that because she believes she's had it worse than you or that materially you are provided for, that you have no right to express your feelings.

She regularly ridiculed things that you said or did, plans you made, and aspirations you had, and may still continue to do it.

She crosses boundaries under the guise of 'friendship', even though you never had a good relationship.

WORDS OF ER... 'WISDOM'

Many mothers misguidedly pass down and spoon-feed their insecurities and their own dubious relationship habits while repeating outdated, insecure, social messaging that creates uncertainty and conflict with their daughters. When they do this, two things can happen:

You believe that relationships are fraught with danger and assaults on your vulnerabilities and so avoid them.

OR

Even in knowing that what your mother said was rubbish, you'll have conflicting beliefs and seek to fill voids.

Some of the most common careless comments and statements I've experienced been told are:

You're no good, not good enough, a disappointment to her. It then feels like you not up to standard and put others on pedestals.

You won't amount to anything. You either prove her wrong and overachieve, or genuinely believe you're not good enough to amount to anything.

If you don't have a man, you're incomplete. Men then become the definition of your success.

You need a man for security. Even if you have your own security, you'll feel insec without a man and prioritise being in a relationship over quality.

You mustn't rely on men because they let you down and hurt you. You then c yourself about the threat of hurt and become guarded.

'Missed opportunities'. You're taught that children and husbands rob you opportunities, so it's best to delay them or avoid at all costs.

If you don't find a man and settle down, you'll become a spinster. Being sin becomes negative and you fear being alone.

Any man is better than no man. You learn that quality is irrelevant; it's being i relationship that counts and will focus on changing them.

The Cheater is a 'good man'. You're then too understanding of poor excuses a situations. In some cultures, being the other woman or having a husband w cheats is acceptable.

It's your fault. You then learn that anything bad that happens to you is a result something that you've done, so when you find yourself with Mr Unavailable, y blame yourself for his actions.

Mothers generally have good intentions when they bestow their 'wise' words, b much of what they say is their perceived fear of living *your* life. They believe th they're thinking about you, but they're actually thinking of how they would be an based on what it was like when they were the equivalent age or younger, you lifestyle choices can seem downright scary, even if they secretly think you're brave

And then, sometimes they don't have good intentions due to their own insecurities, and, to be honest, mothers who repeatedly drain you with outdated bullshit are walking a very fine line.

Only you know how much your mother cares about you, and, ultimately, if she said some of this stuff, but actually acted with love towards you, while you may have your frustrations with her, you're probably in an OK place. If, on the other hand, you had a lot of these 'wise' words, while at the same time experiencing neglect, hostility, or abuse, you may have very mixed feelings about her, not least because we're taught that no matter what our mothers do, it's all said and done out of love, which actually isn't always the case.

CRITICAL MAMA

No parent is born one and it means that they have to learn from their own parents and by experience. If your grandmother bestowed her with her own brand of messaging, she can unconsciously find herself repeating history with you, like my mother did, even though it may be the last thing they want to do. One of the biggest things that I had to learn in my healing process was that *parents are not infallible*; they do screw up, and, while it may feel like your mother appears to have been put on earth to make you feel bad, there are lots of other mothers out there doing it. You're not alone.

She may not recognise how hurtful her comments are but they *do* have a long-lasting, negative impact on how you perceive yourself, which affects how you interact with others. It's not the one individual comment she makes; it's the repeated need to find *something* of fault to point out in you that's damaging. You can't help but believe there's something wrong with you when she's on your case over everything.

They don't teach you how to deal with ongoing criticism from your mother when you're at school.

You'll believe that you're not 'good enough' and be very quick to seek faults within yourself, even when you may not be at fault. They think they're being helpful, or that by giving you a hard time they're making sure that you don't make the same

mistakes that they did, but something gets lost in translation along the way and, if there *isn't* enough positive affirmation going on or even some level of explanation, plus it's coupled with other dysfunctional behaviour and situations, you learn the wrong things. Next thing you're in a relationship and believing you're not 'good enough' and persistently seeking validation.

You may discover that you find it difficult to handle what you perceive to be criticism in relationships and, in fact, may even be sensitive to even the onset of criticism, feeling panicky or agitated when you think that something's about to go wrong. You may veer between assuming the responsibility for everything and apologising even when it hasn't got a damn thing to do with you, or you may get very aggressive when you perceive yourself to be critiqued, threatening to bail or leaving when you don't like what you hear. It may even be that you're very critical of others, as if balancing out your childhood experiences and, if you have children already, you may already have fallen into the habit of fault-picking.

You may try to avoid conflict by either quickly compromising when it arises or pre-empting, which compromises you anyway. That's why you end up not knowing which way is up with Mr Unavailable – you're pre-empting, dodging and compromising yourself to get a relationship with someone who's uncommitted anyway.

Criticism will feel like rejection, something you don't handle well. The more criticism or lack of acceptance you felt in childhood or even now with your mother is the more external validation you'll need. If she says stuff like, "I don't know where I went wrong", it's to keep that mental image of a perfect parent intact and deny any or all of her own contribution.

Ultimately, to move past the scars of criticism, it's not only about embracing and learning to love you, but no longer seeking the approval of people like your mother or Mr Unavailable so they don't have that kind of power over you. There are many women trying to get their mothers to see the error of their ways and it's like forcing them to see something that they just don't want to see. Oddly, when I learned to love myself, not only did I stop needing my critical mother's approval, but the volume of criticism from her has shrunk. Why? Because I'm no longer a willing and receptive ear.

ABUSIVE MOTHERS

There's a fine line between being hypercritical and being abusive. Feeling that you were rejected by your mother and experiencing abuse, or being abandoned so that others could abuse you, leaves what can be an indelible imprint.

Over the years, I've heard from many women who've literally had the self-esteem and boundaries stripped from them by the one person from whom you take being loved and wanted as a given. These women have grown up into often smart and attractive women who have *zero* self-esteem and have been abused repeatedly, or, at the very least, found themselves in emotionally depleting relationships. Whatever you've experienced, don't deny it. You don't have to pretend that your mother was a saint or feel ashamed about her behaviour and how it reflects on you.

It's the ability to take a parent's abusive behaviour as a reflection of ourselves that sets us up for the very dangerous ground of not only being involved with Mr Unavailables, but with the abusive version. We become predisposed to internalising other people's actions, changing our view of ourselves, and then often end up seeking approval from the very person who is abusing us – trying to please those who can't or don't want to be pleased.

Especially if your mother has told you that anything she was doing or that happened was out of 'love', you, in turn, will think that inappropriate and sometimes outright abusive behaviour is also out of 'love' believing you get beaten because of 'love' or that it wouldn't have happened if you were a better person or did as they asked you.

Abusive relationships will feel oddly comforting. You may also seek to attempt to right the wrongs of the past through a current abuser.

Being abused by your mother, or, as a result of her neglect abused by others, feels like a rejection of you, because mothers are *supposed* to love their children and treat them with love, care, trust, and respect. Some mothers, quite frankly, are fucked up. You can think of 1001 ways that you could have brought out a different outcome in her by being born a few minutes later, crying a bit less in the cot, never saying or doing anything wrong, being The Perfect Little Child and somehow managing to control everything around you to ensure that she was blissfully happy. The problem isn't and wasn't you; the problem is her.

It's not normal or right for a mother to abuse her child or leave her in the hands of others to abuse. That doesn't mean *you're* abnormal, hence that's why it happened; it means your mother wasn't 'normal' or 'right'. If as a result of her neglect you ended up being abused by others, that's a form of *abandonment*. Many in the same situation don't think of it this way because it seems like their mother was 'there', but if she turned a blind eye to or watched on as others abused you, that's exactly what she did.

Being rejected or abandoned by your mother through abuse is difficult to comprehend and much like when I hear from women struggling with an abuser and they're trying to understand and rationalise their behaviour, it's important to remember this: *You're not an abusive person, so you don't think and act like one, so trying to apply your type of thinking to their actions will always leave you coming up short.* You cannot rationalise the irrational... or the abusive for that matter.

ABANDONED

My friend (now in her early thirties) and her siblings were regularly abandoned by their mother every time there was a new boyfriend on the scene, until, eventually, they decided to stay with their father. Desperate for her love though, each time she swanned back into town full of charm and promises, they'd welcome her. The last time, which was ten years ago, my friend went to get milk and came back to a Post-It note saying she couldn't "do this" and had got back together with her boyfriend.

Abandonment is very painful rejection.

It can be devastating to deal with the belief that you weren't wanted, or that there was always something more important than being raised by her. You may have to grow up too fast, especially if you had to take on her responsibilities, and it will totally colour your view of healthy relationships, plus it will feel like she's nowhere to be seen when you experience difficult milestones in growing up. You'll feel deprived of what everyone else seems to have.

If you've experienced this with your mother, you may have a great relationship with your father, for example, but due to fundamentally feeling rejected, you still safeguard yourself in unavailable relationships because you fear the consequences of loving and trusting so much that you'd be vulnerable and it would hurt if they were to go. When your fear of abandonment is quite high, you'll also inadvertently end up finding yourself involved with flaky men who validate those private fears and beliefs you have about being 'rejectionable'.

Your mother putting you up for adoption, leaving, or flaking in and out is really about her, not your ability to be loved or hold on to her. Believing it's about you will replicate itself in your pattern of being with Mr Unavailable. You may find that you become the Other Woman, avoid relationships, have fantasy relationships, dig your heels in and refuse to leave, or even rush into getting married or pregnant with the idea being that you think it might be harder to be abandoned, or as a way to put yourself through a secret test.

If you have a limited relationship with Mr Unavailable, he can't 'leave leave' because there isn't a real relationship to leave and there's no real commitment. Being with him stirs up familiar feelings of abandonment. Your relationships may feel like a seesaw because when you feel afraid, it can tip into bad very quickly, plus you may also find that you set your relationships up to fail by having unrealistic expectations of partners.

It can be very tough to not only be adopted/fostered, but to also end up in a family that actually doesn't nurture and treat you well and in extreme cases, abuses you. It will feel like a double rejection. If you spend a lot of time in care waiting to be adopted or fostered it can translate into you not being good or lovable enough and like you're being rejected by the system and life, again demonstrating the far-reaching consequences of a parent's actions.

You may never fully come to terms with what you perceive as being abandoned, and it may be something that you 'walk' with throughout your life, but you learn to manage your fear of it and how you perceive yourself.

In some cases, it's direct abandonment, even though she may have felt that it was the right thing to do (and maybe in the wider sense it was), or it may be indirect abandonment, in that her choices had a knock-on effect and, by choosing herself or opting out of the family home for example, you were abandoned in the process.

It's very possible that even though you don't, and may never, understand your mother's reasons for abandoning you, in her mind, she may genuinely believe that, at the time, the issues and circumstances were overwhelming or that her reasoning was sound.   Sometimes they do regret their actions but instead of the issue taking precedence, their pride does. This means that they don't do anything to make the original abandonment and hurt right because of their own shame and what they think you might say or do. Mothers who abandon their children, whether it's temporarily or on a permanent basis, do so because it reflects serious problems in their own lives or with themselves.

D.I.V.O.R.C.E.

You'd be forgiven for believing that most marriages meet a grisly death in the divorce court. If your own parents haven't divorced or separated at some point, you can feel like you're in the minority. The media pumps out lots of statistics that say divorce is on the increase, marriage is in decline, and that the chances of success if you do get married are limited. If you're not being force-fed statistics about marriage and divorce, then you can always witness and hear messaging about marriage being for suckers, 'smug marrieds' that become not so smug divorcees, plus a plethora of celebrities that say "I do!" and "I don't!" at lightning speed.

Everywhere we look, it seems that marriage is an impermanent state and this can create a fear of committing, because you see marriages ending and the devastating effect it can have, and that scares you. This will be compounded if you witnessed your own parents' divorce and the fallout from it.

It doesn't matter whether it was amicable or downright treacherous; divorce may represent losing any number of things – trust, a sense of permanence, one or both of your parents, or a belief in love.

It's not pleasant to watch your mother disintegrate from happy mother to the miserable one that hates your father, or to have your father on a schedule, or put up with your parents dating or remarriage woes, or their new partners, or just being a child in a single parent home. Depending on how old you were when your parents divorced, it's very likely that you found their divorce difficult to comprehend, especially if they appeared to be happy. This, in itself, makes you distrusting of your own judgment.

If you were witness to a lot of arguments or even violence, aside from being traumatic, you're hardly going to be breaking your neck to get married. You may decide that this level of commitment is for other people.

I'd be foolish to suggest that divorce doesn't happen, but, while there are clearly issues in society, particularly with how people approach marriage and the resolving of issues once within it, every day people still take a chance on marriage and say their vows. There are still more people out there married and trying, than not. What you don't hear about is that divorce rates are declining. In the UK, they've been recording annual decreases in divorce since the peak year of 1993. In the US, the divorce boom actually happened in the 1980s and divorce rates have since decreased, so your deep-rooted fear of divorce is actually very much rooted in the past, like frizzy perms and bad 1980s music.

Fear of divorce is a sure-fire way to ensure that not only do you end up avoiding marriage, but you avoid commitment to anything that may lead to a possibility of it. You're hardly going to put yourself in a situation where you'll end up married, and, if you do, you find a way to stall it happening or sabotage it.

If there are still residual feelings about the chain of events that led to your parents' divorcing that are impacting you now, have an adult conversation (if they're still alive) about why they broke up or divorced because you likely still have the perception from your childhood. It was only as an adult that I realised that my parents had never explained to me what had happened, so I'd been left to read between the lines and draw my own conclusions.

This conversation is for closure and perspective though, not a family showdown, and it may be best to ask separately, although you have to prepare yourself for potentially hearing different versions. Take from it what you will and the very strong likelihood is that neither parent is going to say that you are the reason, so you can stop blaming yourself.

If a conversation isn't possible or you already know it would be futile *anyway*, writing an Unsent Letter (download this handy guide http://bit.ly/unsent) is extremely effective because, aside from writing out your feelings, it also helps organise your thoughts, process the chain of events, and move towards closure. This did far more for me than *any* conversation I've had with my parents.

I'd also assess your beliefs about marriage and your capabilities in relationships – yes, if you keep being with Mr Unavailable you're certainly right to be worried, but an emotionally healthy partner in a quality relationship yields far better marriage prospects.

ACHY BREAKY HEARTS – HAUNTED BY OUR EXES

Most of us have tales of a man who let us down, broke our trust, put us through the wringer, let us believe in him when he didn't deserve it, stomped all over our heart, and left us irrevocably (or so it seems) emotionally scarred forever.

I hear stories of experiences from women's teens and early twenties that seem to have taken their innocence and trust and given them a very distorted view of what should determine a relationship. For most people, the first time that we fall in love (or think we have) is our bravest, because we have no prior experience of heartbreak unless we have some sort of life lesson learned from experiences with a parental figure.

How we cope with it and subsequent heartbreak is very dependent on how we're emotionally nurtured. When we've been hurt, we fought pain and eventually we've moved on, or have we? For every woman who loves an emotionally unavailable man, you can be certain that there is unresolved residue from a **critical heartbreak experience**.

This is usually the one heartbreaking event that defined how you act and feel about love, relationships, and yourself. It's that person or experience that eroded your trust and stopped you believing in love coming from a good, decent, available source. You stopped believing in yourself, or the ability to overcome the experience without needing to shield yourself from future relationship experiences. You think you're protecting yourself, but it's more akin to self-rejection.

If it's the first love, you may find that you react to and treat every relationship as if you are still that age, or you have romanticised it to such an extent that nothing quite competes with it, even though it's been over for a long time. That first 'love' may also be your father.

If you were heartbroken and unable to understand why it happened, not only will you blame yourself, you'll stop trusting, and will have reservations about your own judgment, especially if you feel like you really let down your guard.

If you've been cheated on, you put up a wall of distrust where you assume that every man is going to cheat on you and let you down, and you end up with ambivalent and distant men who reinforce your existing insecurities.

If you've been emotionally or physically abused, you may become blinded to healthier relationships and may gravitate to seeking love from abusive sources – like winning over your original perpetrator.

I can tell you exactly when I experienced my first heartbreak – early summer 1983. I was five, going on six, and the first man and Mr Unavailable in my life, my father, abandoned me when I went into the hospital for four weeks for a serious operation and he only visited me once, promised to come back, but didn't. I idolised him and when my parents split a few years earlier it devastated me, but this experience broke me and I lost my trust in men. It took 22 years to recover.

> **Every time you enter into a relationship with unresolved hurt from previous relationships, you hinder your chances of success.**

One of the biggest reasons why casual relationships are so prevalent is that men *and* women keep using one another to get over previous relationships. We're not taking sufficient time out to grieve the loss of the relationship so that we can heal and move on; instead we take refuge with new partners who are basically 'rebounds' who get used as emotional airbags to soften the blow of the fall. As a result of trying to have our cake and eat it, we perpetuate the cycle of unavailability by yet again avoiding our feelings.

The golden rule of dating and having relationships is that you're only relationship ready if you're over your past relationships and have let go of the emotional attachment that you feel for a person, whether that's positive or negative. That means that whether you're sitting around waxing lyrical about how great things were before you guys broke up, for a reason that you still don't understand, or whether you're calling him a bastard and every other name under the sun, you're *still* emotionally invested in your exes, which means that even though you've technically broken up, you haven't broken the tie and gained the all-important closure.

Women, in particular, rely on closure to be something that both parties have to be involved in, when, in actual fact, you need to and can get closure without him being involved. We get caught up in pursuing them for answers, analysing and obsessing over the relationship, and decide that the only way that we can move on is if they provide us with closure and we get answers to *all* the questions that we have.

Of course, not only may he be disinterested in debriefing the crap out of the relationship, but, even if he does agree to speak with you to help you gain closure, you may have clashing viewpoints, which will only create more questions and undoubtedly more problems.

Maybe he disappeared, claimed that he just wasn't ready yet, needed time, or maybe he dangled the prospect of coming back over the years. Maybe you don't agree with his reasons for breaking up or are confused by what's since been revealed to be lies or half-truths, or maybe you've even been sleeping with him periodically. Basically, you're still holding out hope and relying on him to say and do something final for you to believe that this relationship is *closed*. You won't have closure because you're always allowing yourself to be an option or making him your only one.

The other things that you can hold on to are regret and hope, and, judging by the number of emails I've received from women who have been burned by the *Returning Childhood Sweetheart*, it demonstrates that with a lot of heartbreak, there is that residual fantasy that they'll come crawling back, apologise, sweep us off our feet, and we'll run off happily into the sunset with all of the years forgotten. Instead Mr Unavailable comes back to burn you *again*.

Being haunted by your ex (or exes) is a surefire recipe for living in the past on fantasy and anger and either not moving on at all (I hear from women who don't date for ten years after a breakup) or throwing yourself into a cycle of unavailable relationships.

When you cry in your current relationships you may not even be crying about them; it's reliving old hurts from old relationships.

191

You're essentially allowing someone, who's moved on, to have the power to shape and determine your life. You may not have been able to control what happened at the time, but you do have control over how much it affects your present and future.

You need to break up with every man who lingers in your mind, your heart, your emotions, and in your past. For every ex you have lingering in your head space, it's like you've given them a permanent space to rest inside your home. If you're holding on to various hurts, that's a lot of space in your head being taken up. Everything gets a bit muffled, you can't access your feelings so easily or feel them. You also can't move on or be receptive to anyone new, because you haven't rid yourself of your ex(es). You'll judge situations on previous experiences and insecurities, not what's happening.

The hurt from your *Critical Heartbreak Experience* and anything that's followed have become like your security blanket, because this safety net of hurt prevents you from being vulnerable. You're also holding onto anger and you either haven't expressed how angry you were about what happened or you have, but you didn't process it and move forward.

Unless you gain closure and address the hows and whys from a different, more distanced perspective, you will not be able to begin the healing that's needed to break your cycle. You'll lose touch with yourself and become reserved, distrusting, and reliant on the safe bet of a man who always performs to type, hence reinforcing the cycle and keeping you down. The comfort and familiarity you get from feeling these emotions, is from getting confirmation that all men hurt and disappoint you.

THE EXCEPTIONAL FAIRYTALE

When you have a habit of chasing the same 'type', even though it brings you very little happiness or a successful relationship, or you have unrealistic expectations and beliefs about what love can and cannot do, or you stay in relationships long past their sell-by date, it's because you believe you're living out your own fairytale. Your idea of love is that it involves getting someone to make you the exception to their normal rule of behaviour, even though that rule might be rather shady.

Why do you continue being involved with Mr Unavailable? Because you hope that, even if it's not today, even if it's not tomorrow, but soon, he'll see something in you or value your dedication enough to change. You want to be the exception to the rule so that, Shazam! – you can have your 'happy ever after'.

You're not rooted in reality. You can't be because, if you were, you'd have let go of this man a long time ago and ensured that you didn't take up with him in a different package. Whatever issues you may have, you're oddly optimistic about extracting an ending because women are programmed to believe that love... is a fairytale.

You meet a guy, a series of obstacles comes along to make life difficult for you. You might break up, then get back together, then hit an obstacle again, then, after a few years of miscommunication and watching him date different women, he suddenly wakes up one day and realises it's you. He may not come blazing in on his white horse, but maybe you'll both get drunk and you'll wake up in bed with each other and suddenly realise that you can't bear to be apart again and the years disappear and you don't remember that time when he got off with that bitch Annika behind your back because you're in love. Next thing you know, you're speeding down the aisle in an amazing wedding dress, then popping a baby, and life goes on in a wonderful hazy glow, and the time before the last ten minutes of the film, fade into the distance. Man, I reckon I could write a good romcom...

Remember in the section about *Daddy Hunting* where I explained about how we basically take elements of our father, throw in the things that we want from a relationship along with unconditional love and focus on getting that? Well, that's the fairy-tale mentality and it also demonstrates how, by blindly running around trying to make relationships with unsuitable and reluctant partners, we're relying on some sort of 'magic' to happen.

Relationship insanity is carrying the same baggage, beliefs, and behaviours; choosing the same people/different package; and continuing to expect to get a different result. It's looking to be the exception and pushing for a fairy-tale ending. Examples:

Even though I've gone back several times, I'm returning again, because surely this time he'll be different.

If I keep pushing for change and showing how dedicated I am, he'll change, even though time and again, he's either promised to change but hasn't or was this way prior to being involved with me.

Even though I've been involved with this type before and I am yet to have a successful relationship with it, I'm convinced that this type of person is what I need to make me happy, so I will try again.

Even though he makes me unhappy and doesn't treat me with love, care, trust, and respect and I even call him an 'assclown', I love him so I'm going to keep trying/going back because, hopefully, he'll make me the exception.

Even though I don't believe I'm good enough, I'm hoping he'll prove me wrong, even if I've made a choice that reflects my beliefs, or I'm sabotaging a decent relationship.

You fundamentally know the rule; after all, you can't be an exception if you don't know what you're being exceptional to.

When you acknowledge how unrealistic some of the stuff that you're trying to do is and what you're actually trying to be an exception to, you not only realise what type of damaging and compromising situations you're placing yourself in, but you also get to learn what you believe love to be – *having someone love you against the odds.*

You're setting the tone that it's not love unless it comes from an unlikely or even *unwilling* source.

There's nothing wrong with having *some* faith, *some* hope, *some* dreams, but you've gotta have a relationship based on something other than air and a damn good imagination. I appreciate that you want to be romantic but when you write your 'fairytale' write it with a strong character with values. Write it with love, truth, integrity, and care. Write it where you envision yourself at your most positive, living a life that reflects the positive you within, as opposed to the negative beliefs that are propelling you from relationship to relationship. Don't cast yourself as a 'heroine' getting love from a villain or an unresponsive, uncaring, so-called 'prince'.

Instead of thinking about relationships in terms of big fantasy speak, focus on solid foundations, so that you don't get yanked in by the smoke and mirrors of someone who can flash the gestures or the cash for a time, but can't actually cough up a committed relationship where you feel good in it.

Love isn't about having the power to change someone, especially when their rule is not something healthy.

People get different results, because they stop believing that thinking and doing the same thing is going to achieve different results. They accept the rule. Even if they subsequently take risks, they have the rule as their baseline and they opt out of danger. Many are remarkable with the rule – there are people out there who have healthy, mutually fulfilling, love-filled relationships without having to feel like shit all the time and living in drama and ambiguity – that could be you.

While there are some 'lucky' people out there (and that's really only based on what we perceive them to be, or what they've let us think they are), the great majority of people who experience exceptional results are part of creating that. They don't wait around for people to give them the perfect job, for the planets to align, for people to change, for someone else to invent it, or for their circumstances to change.

While there will always be anomalies and those urban myths you hear about – the person with no self-esteem who with no change landed on their feet with a perfect life, or the person who used to be a major assclown who became The Perfect Person when they 'fell in love' – the overwhelming majority of us experience the rule.

Your life isn't a dress rehearsal and there's no man who 'completes you'; you complete you and that elusive feeling will remain elusive as long as you put the responsibility for your happiness and your completeness in someone else's hands. Yes, you'd have a hazy glow for a while if someone swept you off your feet tomorrow, but, no matter what happens, you still have to live with you and how you feel about yourself, so you won't be getting that fairytale if you don't learn how to love yourself.

****

This chapter was likely a difficult read – hell it was difficult for me to write! The purpose of this chapter isn't to put you in pain, it's to shine a light on the path of understanding and help you make a connection between past events, beliefs you may hold, and the subsequent actions and choices that you make.

Being with Mr Unavailable isn't an 'accident', and what you can do now is address how to get out of relationship insanity so that you start not only getting different results in your relationships, but also feeling differently about *you*.

I've learned the hard way that my parents' behaviour is not a reflection of me – it's reflective of them. To make it about you is to remove your parents' accountability and responsibility, which is what many a Fallback Girl does with Mr Unavailable.

Every day that your parents, fears, beliefs, and exes dictate your life and what you think of yourself now, is another day handing over your power.

I know after reading thousands of emails and comments from women *and* men who do things they fundamentally believe are right, even though it may hurt themselves or others, that people don't give enough thought to the consequences of their actions.

Our parents are not infallible, nor are our exes, or anyone else who is in our lives. Understanding healthy relationships, whether they are parental, friendship, professional, or romantic, can go a long way to putting boundaries in place and understanding at a top level that certain types of behaviour are counterproductive or wrong full stop. In the following chapters, discover the different roles you take up and with whom, and after that, tips and tools to put you on the path to availability.

THE YO-YO GIRL

In between a couple of boyfriends, I was involved with a Mr Unavailable for almost four years. Due to him dipping out of my life, I didn't notice the time clocking up between us. He'd call, offer little or no explanation for his absence, and, to be fair, I asked no questions, and within a week we'd meet up again, have a great time, he'd promise to call, then nothing. The first couple of times it happened, I felt confused, hurt, and adrift, but I'm living proof that if you let someone keep doing something, it becomes normal. We didn't even have sex for almost two years, but I thought that he was 'respecting' me, shy, and waiting for it to be the 'right' time.

I kept falling for the potential and wondering what I was doing to scare him off – it never occurred to me to wonder what was wrong with him. Many women are just like I was: accepting lazy texts, emails, and drunk dials from exes, dates, and difficult to describe 'acquaintances' who want to keep a foothold in their lives or are trying to reignite their idea of a relationship. If you don't keep an eye on the time, *years* can go by and you suddenly realise you have little to show for it.

In possession of a 'can't break, won't break' mentality, the **Yo-Yo Girl** has unfinished business with everyone from exes to dates, and even the briefest of encounters on the likes of dating sites or with men who you chatted with briefly, believe you felt a chemistry with, but nothing materialised. You don't handle rejection of any kind well, so you avoid accepting that even the flimsiest of possibilities no longer exists and you're basically an option for most, if not all, of the men in your past. You have a lot of 'litter' on your relationship landscape and you likely have at least one relationship that no matter how often it gets chucked away and no matter how poorly you're treated, you keep being tugged in and willingly going back – a **Boomerang Relationship**.

The **Bad Penny** is the tricky to shake guy who keeps returning and leaving, creating a boomerang relationship. He fools you because his returning is read as a sign of destiny and how he can't resist the relationship/sex when it's actually to ensure that you're still in his back pocket. He likely needs to be distracted from something else, such as being rebuffed elsewhere, peers settling down, or he's feeling insecure or at a loose end. He wants the right to exercise the option of you should he change his mind, feel nostalgic, or have a 'need' for you. Whether it's days, weeks, months, years, or even *decades*, he feels free to roll up in your life, blow hot with the charm and Future Faking, and play the nostalgia/friend/sex/connection/remorse/whatever card.

Resident in an ambiguous wasteland, you prefer to make assumptions and avoid asking questions or accepting the answers. You persist in waiting for an ex to 'come good' and likely believe that any number of men from your past could possibly be The One, so you avoid cutting them off for fear of inadvertently drastically altering the fate you've projected.

Receptive to Bad Pennies, because you're desperate for the validation of finally being chosen, it's a means of avoiding the full rejection that comes with accepting that it's over or that he's not going to treat you in the way that you say you'd like to be treated. This makes you an option.

Each reconnection is based on the premise of 'Things Will Be Different
This Time'.

While he might hang around in your life making a nuisance of himself, he may equally be the type who 'plays dead', so you don't hear from him until he reappears just as you're moving on or have forgotten him. He has a perception of you and when he returns, until he meets a closed door, he assumes that perception still holds. When he flicks through his mental Rolodex of who's likely to be the most receptive and will blow smoke up his arse, he thinks of you.

Too receptive to bullshit and operating an open door policy, by having little or no boundaries and being quick to get carried away with the possibilities of what his 'boomeranging' means, you focus on his returning instead of his leaving or what the nature of his absence was. In a number of respects, you have the hallmarks of the Other Woman but instead of being a lady-in-waiting to one attached man, you're a lady-in-waiting to your past.

TYPICAL YO-YO GIRL

Remain 'friends' with your exes.

Avoid having a definitive ending.

Avoid rejection by taking him back or chasing him for attention.

Don't distinguish between your respective feelings.

Don't believe it's 'over' – think you're 'giving him space'.

Think it's normal to break up repeatedly with the same person.

Fear being alone but don't realise that you're actually alone.

Get demoted to ex to booty call or even the Other Woman.

Think you're 'unlucky in love'.

Women Who Talk and Think Too Much syndrome.

Inadvertently behave like you're in a romantic comedy.

Latch on to excuses and BS stories to justify your 'investment'.

Often feel used and discarded.

Don't trust your judgment.

Extremely assumptive, because you avoid conflict and questions.

Can be shameless in your quest to get attention from him.

Often blinded by sex or 'we have so much in common'.

TYPICAL BAD PENNY

Likes to keep a spare woman in his back pocket for rainy days.

Keeps going back to another ex that was likely in his life before you – another Yo-Yo Girl.

Knows he's not over an ex or doesn't want a relationship, but will pass time with you.

Overestimates his interest and, when out of control, overestimates his desire to start over with you.

Future Fakes and Fast Forwards – keeps pulling the same con.

Exploits your urge to have him in your life under any terms.

Presses the Reset Button. A lot. Likes disappearing.

Doesn't want you, but doesn't want anyone else to have you either.

May view you as 'two friends hanging out'.

Thinks 'friendship' includes the fringe benefits of a relationship.

Calls you to reminisce or complain about 'her'.

Works with you, or is even your boss, and tells you that you need to be on the down-low.

Texts his harem to see who will take the ego stroke bait.

THE YO-YO GIRLS

The Ex Believing you know him best, because you've probably put up with a lot, you think the least he owes you is his improved self and a committed relationship if he decides to change. Your history symbolises your 'investment'. You never accept that the relationship is truly over, so you never accept the reasons why it keeps breaking. By hanging around, sometimes meddling and acting like, 'I'm not giving up on this relationship until he says he's done', you're attempting to control his agenda. You start new relationships to make him jealous and you'll be half-hearted with the replacement, claiming that it's missing passion/laughter or whatever excuse. When he moves on, you're dismissive of the new relationship, so when he calls for a whine about 'her' or to get nostalgic, you're practically triumphant. You may feel it's your 'duty' to let her know that he's been hitting on you, etc. The biggest shock comes when he announces that he's 'done' or getting married. The pain can be overwhelming and you may slide into depression. Either that or you start pitching to be the Other Woman.

The One That Got Away If you haven't been in touch and he blazes back into your life, it seems like a fairytale, especially if your relationship history since you originally broke up has been chequered and you've always carried a torch for him, **The Returning Childhood Sweetheart**. He may have been your Critical Heartbreak Experience so even if he was an asshole then, his return will be seen as an opportunity to right all the wrongs of the past. It's likely that you've had a long period of not dating/celibacy or have come out of a long marriage/damaging relationship. In some instances, you're still in an existing relationship, but when he comes back into your life, you're happy to play Yo-Yo Girl. If you know his ex or current partner, you likely have no respect for her, think that he's been suffering, that you're a better woman for him and that you're 'soulmates'.

Accidental Screw Buddy May have started with you both dating and you being wooed during the hot phase. When he went lukewarm/cold, it either took a while to notice or you played it down. Fearing that you did something wrong or being afraid to question it, you also may have been unsure of your feelings or worried about looking like you want a committed relationship that you weren't sure that you wanted yet, so you decided to give it some 'more time'. You likely don't regard yourself as a screw buddy and spend oodles of time rationalising your involvement. When you eventually do speak to him, you either attempt to move on or, in feeling invalidated, start seeking the validation of a committed relationship with him, even though in truth you may not even like him that much – you just want him to want you.

Miss Keeping It Casual Believing you wanted something casual, possibly because you were hurting over someone else, you're not the type to heal and then start dating; instead, you use dating to feel better. Like Mr Unavailable, you want the trappings of a relationship without the commitment. This backfires as you inevitably want more or become indignant at being regarded casually, and look for validation in the form of commitment. You over-prioritise sex and then attempt to close the door after the horse has bolted. As relationship career climbs go, you embark on the uphill struggle to be promoted to 'girlfriend' and when you feel rejected, you continue accepting the crumbs of validation while he dips in and out using you between, or even during, other relationships.

The Friend Often believing the best relationships originate from friendships, you have a hidden agenda. You believe you've supported him through difficult periods and understood his lack of readiness to be in a relationship, while all the while thinking that, because you have done this, when he's ready to commit, you're first in line for the hot seat. You may have made your feelings clear, he knocked you back, and you disregarded it and decided that you knew better and continued being his 'friend', in the hope that by being so available, he'd recognise your value. Consumed by your feelings, you're refusing to back off. You may have slept together, then it became a habit and you may even believe that because neither of you want a relationship, together as friends you're perfect partners. You also assume that because you're supposed to be 'friends' that he will treat you better so are livid when he doesn't. But you still want more and quite frankly, you're not his friend.

ACHILLES HEEL: BETTING ON POTENTIAL

Potential in relationships is consistently having or showing (via actions) the capacity to become or develop into something more serious – commitment and a shared future. You determine potential by gauging both of your actions to work out what's *currently* happening between you both and where that could potentially lead. And therein lies the problem with Fallback Girls.

Betting On Potential is the relationship version of gambling in relationships and, unfortunately, you're an uneducated and unskilled gambler. You're like the newbie who shows up at the casino and figures, "It's a casino so I'll win big eventually!" with no regard for the mental and observation skills required or understanding that some games and tables are better than others. You pick a man and either latch on to behaviour that's been exhibited that subsequently disappears/becomes sporadic, or you literally treat him like a blank canvas, putting your vision of the relationship you want as the end goal and painting in the man you think he could become. With little or no regard for the lack of capacity that's been repeatedly demonstrated throughout the relationship, you don't use landmarks such as progression, commitment, intimacy, balance, and consistency to evaluate whether your 'bet' is misplaced. As a result, you don't know when to *fold*.

Symptoms

Quickly fantasising that he's The One soon after meeting.

Saying or thinking stuff like, "I wish he'd go back to being the way he used to be!" or "Why can't he be like the old Mike?"

I Can Change Him Syndrome.

Choosing men for odd reasons that they rarely live up to or that don't make a difference to the relationship.

Believing that you have *so* much in common.

Hearing but not listening and ignoring vital information.

Loving and trusting blindly, while refusing to trust your gut or any judgements you make.

Hooked on the fairy-tale ending.

Trapped in your feelings and fantasy.

Not communicating; you just charge on ahead with your ideas.

Persistently returning to the scene of the crime to see if this time you can realise your 'investment'.

Stuck in a directionless relationship that won't 'conclude'.

Any potential you forecast should be based on the promise of actions that have already consistently occurred, not your imagination. Individual potential is not tied to you, so you can't make him have a capacity that he doesn't possess anyway. No matter the intensity of your feelings or your hopes for him to change, you can't decide that you have 'capacity' for you both until he's ready. When what you want is reliant on him doing XYZ, it demonstrates that he's not currently showing or having capacity – and that you're taking an even greater gamble.

You think that he doesn't have the capacity now but he will have the capacity later.

Dangerously optimistic and speculative, in recognising the 'synergy' between you, you reason that if you see and realise potential in him, you'll realise potential in yourself.

The potential you envision is based on your feelings and unhealthy beliefs about relationships centred on you having the power to change him. This is a fantasy and you're blinded to damn near smack-in-the-face signs that he's not even participating in the actual relationship, because you're too busy avoiding the truth and your feelings. When the gap between reality and your forecasted projections becomes too wide to ignore, you attempt to rectify this and are met with obstacles, conflict, and some rather unpleasant 'surprises'.

Stop thinking that potential exists until there's absolutely no chance because he's either treated you so badly that even you recognise that it'd be sheer madness, or he's moved on and isn't lining you up as the Other Woman. Your 'limit' for folding is dangerously high and you have to learn to opt out when someone rejects the relationship. By taking him back repeatedly, you communicate it's *OK* to reject you and you waste time attempting to avoid rejection when you could be off having a better relationship.

WATCH OUT FOR...

The Ex He doesn't truly want you, but he doesn't want anyone else to have you in case he changes his mind. Keeping his options open, and often feathering his nest elsewhere, as he's still commitment resistant, he second-guesses new relationships. He then fears he won't have the option to take a parachute, jump, and land on a familiar emotional cushion. Exploiting your shared history and the Friend Card, he Future Fakes, Fast Forwards, and is a liberal presser of the Reset Button. Secure in what he perceives as your never-ending feelings, he doesn't truly respect you and doesn't feel he has to stay because he has the option to leave and return. Often he's privately decided that if he runs out of options or reaches a certain age where his behaviour will look odd, you're his 'Settling Option'.

The Returning Childhood Sweetheart Possibly the greatest example of the history between two people being exploited, he often returns after a long period of time has passed. Likely recently separated or divorced, he may also be attached in a so-called 'struggling' or 'loveless' relationship. He's likely to think of you as you remind him of a younger, adored self. He may have looked you up online through Facebook or your alumni site, or you may also have kept in touch under the guise of friendship. If it's the latter, he's likely been dropping hints or even been sexual. Crap at being alone, he'll start up something with you, even if it's long distance, while pursuing options closer to home.

The Phantom Remember the guy who vanished after a great date, then showed up weeks or months later with some flimsy excuses (if you're lucky) followed by hot, then another vanishing act or gradual fade out to cold? This is him. A master Fast Forwarder, he's likely doing this to several women and relies on distracting you with intensity. Beholden to no one, he's either a master charmer, or relies on women who have little or no standards. May travel a lot for work or be a big socialiser, he'll boomerang into your life when he has a free period. Likely a heavy texter/emailer – he'd hate to mix up names.

The Friend Enjoying your attention, you stroking his ego, and your obvious feelings, even though he doesn't reciprocate, he was probably getting over an ex when you became friends or became interested and is happy to pass time with and 'humour' you. Assuming you know it's casual or that you know what he's like, he's unlikely to feel that he needs to explain when he starts something new, so will be taken aback by your reaction, and say or imply there's a chance because he'll be afraid of losing the fruits of your attention. Watch out for becoming the Other Woman.

BOOBY TRAPS

You reside in assumption central. You rationalise his behaviour using misguided assumptions about what you believe his motivations are, which are also mixed in with your own reasons for remaining there. You assume it's 'love', when it's actually that he's ensuring that you remain an option.

Holding on is easier than letting go. As the source of both your misery and 'happiness', you'd rather have him on some terms than no terms, which, in turn, convinces you of an imperfection that's keeping him (and others) from choosing you or treating you better. Afraid your 'flaw' will follow you to a new relationship, or that he's going to marry the next woman, eventually you'll realise that what little you're holding onto is far more painful than the unknown.

Retrieving and recouping. Making a sterling effort of trying to avoid full rejection from him, while at the same time rejecting yourself, you believe you've put in too much to leave and that to 'give up' would be a 'waste', so you continue wasting your time although you call it 'love' and 'working at your relationship'.

You hand over all of your power. He learns the pattern of what he's allowed to get away with and behaves accordingly. Often based on the longest period of his absence, he'll feel safe to disappear for that long and may keep pushing those boundaries. Leaving it all in his hands to 'do the right thing', you become intoxicated by the connection and claim you can't walk away when it's that you won't.

Blinded by sex and 'common ground'. You're likely to continue sleeping with him because it's familiar and comforting, and, when it's good sex, it convinces you that there's more than sexual attraction. Some YYGs insist that they can't manage without sex, while plenty of Bad Pennies think they're literally doing you a good service by slipping you a shag. You may also believe that you 'have so much in common', but have failed to recognise that if these things were so valuable to your relationship, you'd be having one.

He keeps contacting you. Burning with curiosity about what his reasons may be, you do know how this plays out. Whatever reason he gives, he's not honest and responsible enough to know his own mind. Completely thoughtless and a short-term thinker, he's like a thief piquing a dog's interest with a piece of meat that he's thrown over the wall.

Obsession. You've got to quit this fantasy that a man that's pissed you around so much is going to become Mr Steady Relationship. Stop the ruminating, grieve the loss of the relationship and let *go*. If you have time to think about him all day, you have too much frickin' time on your hands. Make *you* the focal point of *your* life.

TIPS FOR KICKING THE YO-YO HABIT

Stop assuming you and him are on the same page and put yourself on an Assumption Diet. The only assumption you can make is that if he's done this more than twice (I know many of you believe in second chances), he's coming back for a repeat. Don't give him that chance.

Aim for a calm breakup – big, dramatic, heated exchanges create the impression that things have gone unsaid and that what's happened can be excused with an apology.

If you went on a date or a few and they disappeared, leave them to stay disappeared. There really is no great, good, or even reasonable, reason to disappear.

No late night calls/texts or being a last-minute date option. Any man who is serious about dating you should be asking you out earlier in the week and not assuming you'll drop everything.

Don't allow anyone, or yourself, to attempt to pick up where they left off or act like nothing has happened. *Something* happened. You can't just erase the past or problems.

Instead of thinking, "Wow, they must be crazy about my ass to get in touch with me after all this time!" you should be asking yourself, **"Why, after all this time, did they decide to contact me?"** Whichever answer you don't like, it's a hell of a lot closer to the truth.

If they were an asshole when you were first involved with them, they're an asshole now. Stop fantasising. They snoozed, they lost.

If you struggle to deal with the emotional consequences of sex, talking, or 'hanging out' together, do not do any of these things unless you've asked definitive questions and got definitive answers.

Accept that if it hasn't worked, it hasn't worked for a reason. Giving a relationship a second chance is one thing, but after that, it's time to accept that something's not right and stop forcing things. Unless both parties are 150% wholeheartedly willing to be honest and address the issues that broke the relationship, don't bother trying again.

If an ex comes back swearing that he's changed and is ready for a relationship, weigh it against past evidence, and ensure that there is genuine evidence of change. He needs to have changed already, not be claiming that he's going to attempt to learn how to change on your time. The best way of getting evidence of change is asking questions about what he's been doing since you were last together.

Don't get involved with anyone who's just broken up, says they're still not over their ex, or says they're not ready for a relationship. I would aim for *at least* a month's gap if the relationship was under a year and, if it was more, a minimum of three. The moment the excuses roll out, it's time to bail. This also includes not playing Armchair Therapist and listening to their problems – you're not that woman.

THE OTHER WOMAN

Let me preface this chapter and say that if you're the Other Woman and you want me to say that your situation is different, it's not gonna happen and take it from someone who's been there.

For 18 months, I slotted into his timetable and most of our snatched get-togethers ended by 8 or 9pm, just in time for me to watch Eastenders. We argued in the stairwell at work and quite a few streets in central London, hid in corners of social occasions sneaking kisses, and exchanged long emails and texts. Yet I *actually* believed that this man who used me, sold me on a wing and a prayer, and who I ultimately reduced my self-esteem to rubble for, was The One.

Affairs very rarely have a 'happy ending', yet so many women keep venturing into this territory because, while all Fallback Girls look to be the exception to the rule, Other Women take it to a whole new level. In almost six years of running Baggage Reclaim, I've yet to receive *one* 'success story' and that's simply because there's no success in 'winning' what amounts to ill-gotten gains. There are many urban myths and Chinese whispers about that man who left his wife/girlfriend and while, occasionally, this does happen and even more occasionally it continues on into a happy relationship, for the overwhelming majority, the rule if you're prepared to be the Other Woman, is pain.

As the **Other Woman** (OW), you avoid commitment by involving yourself with attached men, then seek validation by trying to get them to leave and choose you. As a lady-in-waiting who doesn't seem to recognise that you've taken the part of understudy, you're hoping something will befall 'the lead' so that you get your moment in the limelight. While there are some women who make a professional habit from being with Cheaters, the typical OW is guilty of being naïve and unable to recognise when to abandon a situation and run for the hills. No matter how it starts, you end up struggling with the rejection that comes with taking a backseat in someone's life while they have a whole other life you're not included in. You want all of him.

Cheaters play hooky on their main relationship by being sexually and often emotionally involved with you. Some have emotional affairs (everything but the physical), which is mentally 'checking out' on the relationship and can be devastating when discovered and quite complex if you're involved in it. Remember what cheating actually involves: **being dishonest in order to gain an advantage, avoiding something undesirable by luck or skill, engaging in deception and trickery, and basically being fraudulent**. There are lies, omission, manipulation, and, for ongoing affairs, an element of being a confidence trickster. The advantage gained is having two relationships and the trappings that come with each without being committed to either. They're avoiding commitment, intimacy – basically everything to do with an available relationship.

What happens at the start of an affair governs how it's likely to play out. If he prioritises having a good time, he'll say and do whatever is needed to facilitate this. If he acknowledges that his actions signify major problems, he'll likely go and sort himself out. This way, an indiscretion and a slip in integrity doesn't become a habit of dishonesty.

Equally, what you do dictates how deep you'll get into this situation and where you're at emotionally. If you remain involved, you already believe that there's something 'different' about your situation. If you discover his status belatedly but don't leave, it's you struggling with who you 'thought' he was and already feeling invested. You'll reason that the situation created the lies. If you're initially blasé during the affair, you'll overestimate how much you can handle and then start seeking the validation of him leaving 'her'.

You'll notice that most Cheaters don't say, *"Oh, OK then,"* when you try to finish it – they'll try to convince you to hold on for a while, they'll hang around or leave you alone for a bit, then get back in touch, or they'll tell you that they will leave their spouses, only you notice that they're never in a position to do it immediately.

Out of respect for any relationship, all of us should give due care and thought to breaking the bonds and exiting. You wouldn't respect or trust a man who could shag you on a Tuesday and ditch his old life on a Wednesday. That said, cheating isn't an appropriate interim solution because it invariably becomes long term.

Ideally there should be no affair, but if he still seeks to maintain it after 3-6 months, you can be pretty damn sure he's not leaving and is very comfortable with ongoing deception. Some people couldn't tolerate the deceit for a *day*. Unfortunately he expects you to magically galvanise him into leaving and he expects the 'main woman', often without her knowing it, to curtail his cheating ways. When he doesn't leave, it's not because of anything wrong with you but because the right reasons to leave and be a better man in your relationship come from him.

TYPICAL OTHER WOMAN

Painful breakup or divorce that's left you with trust issues.

Used to feeling second best (or even worse).

May have been cheated on or in an abusive relationship.

Claim you're independent and don't want commitment.

Very comfortable with secrecy, even with close friends.

Other areas of your life suffer when you're in a relationship.

Very low self-esteem and may struggle with depression.

Believe that all the good men are gone.

Ignore inappropriate behaviour and focus on the 'good' things.

Hang with a number of women who are also OWs.

Blinded by sex, chemistry, and his apparent 'need' for you.

Afraid of being alone and also of a committed relationship.

Makes ultimatums that aren't followed through on.

Little or no boundaries so you struggle to fold.

One, or even both parents, cheated.

Fairy-tale ideas: 'Love conquers all', 'All's fair in love and war', etc.

TYPICAL CHEATER

Often a work colleague or your boss, exploiting the company policy to keep you a secret as well as exploiting his power.

Plays the nostalgia and history card.

History of cheating, although he may not admit to it.

Often has a parent who used to cheat.

Compartmentalises so much he may not recognise the deception.

May believe he's invincible, especially if he's 'powerful'.

Cultivates an image and can be obsessed with how he's perceived.

Plays hooky on his commitment by 'rebelling' against the 'shackles'.

Partner may suit his image, career, or another agenda.

Suffers from Those Who Doth Protest Too Much.

Claims neglect and has unrealistic expectations of his primary partner, giving himself licence to cheat.

Too comfortable with lies and deception.

Tends to be very routine and rigid.

Knows that he's not leaving, but doesn't tell you in case you bolt or he changes his mind.

Jealous and possessive and will seek to control your agenda so that you remain an option.

Flirts with others and may even be lining up or sleeping with someone else behind your back.

THE OTHER WOMEN

Miss In For the Long Haul The mistress. You don't seek out married men to 'tempt' them away from their wives; you're having an ongoing affair and are guilty of loving the wrong man and being quite naïve. You believe circumstances have conspired to put the man who's rightfully yours with the wrong woman and have resigned yourself to waiting in an uncomfortable arrangement. You may have kids for him, share a business, or have even set up home together, so you'll feel too embedded to leave. It's not unusual for there to be OWs in your family and you may come from a culture of believing that being his main OW is OK. There are two sub-types of this role that are particularly worrying:

The OW Once Removed (The Ex Yo-Yo Girl): Frighteningly prevalent, you believe you were destined to be together and that 'technically' you had him first. When he moved on, you should have too, but, instead, you dug your heels in.

The OW Twice Removed: You waited for him to leave, but when he did, instead of being with you as expected, he began a new relationship and still expects you to be there. This also encompasses **the OW to the OW situation** where you thought you were the only OW but then discovered you were not alone.

The Cheat Likely cheating because you believe there's something 'missing' and your needs aren't being met, you don't realise that, as a Fallback Girl, you'll feel this way no matter who you're with. You cheat with a Cheater that's likely to be a friend or colleague. Unable to deal with problems in your main relationship, you rationalise that cheating is your only option. While you may seek passion, companionship, etc., you may be cheating to lessen a commitment that's making you feel vulnerable, and then feel bad (and may even treat him badly), followed by using the guilt to create an exit. If you've been cheated on, you may be spiting or rebelling, or it may be that you feel undeserving of his trust and love and prove it by cheating. Let's be real – you might be doing it just because you can and have little regard for him or believe you have a high libido to cater to. Like all Fallback Girls, breaking up isn't your forte and you worry about making a mistake. Although you might be dictating the terms in a rare power shift, it's more likely that you're pandering to his terms because you've likely chosen someone who regards you as a fallback option anyway. You'll push to be together full-time and be devastated when he won't.

Miss Keeping It Casual You don't want to get hurt or have attachments. Initially it was a bit of fun and a challenge, and you may have laughed at his interest and reasoned that his status isn't your problem to deal with. He'll be attracted because you appear to totally understand what's expected of you, which is to expect nothing. Of course, you find yourself feeling more than you should, but become very good at keeping it to yourself and playing the game, as you don't want to be vulnerable and scare him away like the other OWs that you believe get it wrong. But you're in waaaay over your head. Next role: Miss In For the Long Haul.

Miss Accidental You're just having a bit of fun, a fling, and will actually leave it at that. You'll regularly wrestle with your conscience though, as he pursues you to start up again, but you're a Fallback Girl with limits and feel that it's one thing to have a fling, but it's another to do it on an ongoing basis. You will, however, berate yourself afterwards and may wonder if he's The One That Got Away, which will blind you to new partners until you wise up.

ACHILLES HEEL: SECOND BEST SYNDROME

We have many different roles in life. Some are created by our relationships: mother, daughter, sister, manager, co-worker, friend, etc. Most are situational, but there are other roles that you assume because you gravitate to personas that keep you in a comfort zone, even if you hate it. Maybe you choose to be a deputy instead of a leader because you don't have enough confidence in your abilities or your value, so you opt for the backseat and let others take up the more prominent/vocal role, even though you may actually want it.

Second Best Syndrome is believing that there's always somebody better than you, or assuming relationship roles that place you in a starting position below number one so that you have to fight for first place. **Earlier in life, you decided that you come a poor second around those whom you seek love and validation from.** It's like trying to run a 100m dash with a ball and chain around your ankle with you holding the key – long, laborious, very uncomfortable, and totally avoidable. You ensure that you're not in a good starting position (the leading one) because you're more comfortable in the rookie, understudy role because it validates your beliefs.

Symptoms

Believe you were secondary to your father's work, sports, his other women, or even his relationship with your mother.

Fought for attention over your siblings.

Sibling needed more attention, for example, due to an illness.

Believe your sister is more popular/prettier/cleverer than you.

Spent most of your life being compared.

Think a sibling is a 'favourite'.

Believe that one or both of your parents don't like/value you.

Think your parents would have preferred to have a boy.

Middle Child – lost. Oldest Child – everyone else gets to be a child for longer.

Raised with mother's boys.

Famous or high-achieving parent.

Parent(s) abused alcohol, drugs, etc., and you felt secondary to their 'greater' loves.

Feel that you've been consistently turned down or let go of for other women who you believe are better.

Think you're unattractive, or even ugly, so you assume that you're a pity date.

I'm not worthy of someone's full-time efforts. I'm not worthy of being his main priority. I'm afraid that if he did leave someone for me, he'd discover I'm not that special.

Hiding away in deprioritised relationships helps you avoid 'proper' rejection. As the OW, this is a safe relationship because you can't be truly abandoned or rejected by someone who belongs to someone else. You'll still seek to challenge your beliefs and gain priority and believe you'll be 'good enough' if the Cheater gives you the ultimate validation of leaving 'her', which would prioritise you. However, even if you were 'chosen', you'd forever fear that he's going to leave you for someone 'worthier'.

There will always be people who will say trite or even downright stupid things to remind you of the different roles that you play, but the only way to overcome Second Best syndrome is to *make yourself the main priority*, because it's bad enough that someone else would relegate you to such a position, but for you to do that means that nobody is taking care of your best interests.

It's not an instantaneous shift in mentality, much like many things that you believe, but from the moment that you start valuing you, your contribution, and what you have to offer, and stop assuming that it is less important, less valuable, less anything than anybody else, it makes a huge difference. You have to assume that you have, at the very least, equal stature and you have to shake off old perceptions and accept the adult you who is creating her own life, her own individuality, and her own meaning that has nothing to do with any of the people who her feelings of lacking may have been tied into.

WATCH OUT FOR...

The First Timer Cheating by 'accident', you'll get tangled up in his flip-flapping and guilt and he'll be avoiding issues in his main relationship while claiming that he's neglected or that it's over in 'his mind'. Be careful because he'll pull the Friend Card. Don't 'persuade' him into the affair – he'll yo-yo back and forth between you both, and he may even blame you for his straying.

The Playa You're one of many, but he'll claim that you're his first, or that he's different with you. He's either secretive or his partner is aware but values the 'title' of the official relationship. Shady and very charming, and often flexing money, sex, fame, or power, he likes shagging around, keeping his options open, and avoiding commitment. He has narcissistic tendencies, so will actually think he's outwitting everyone. You won't tame him.

The Friend Often emotional cheating territory, he may be rationalising that it's not 'cheating', because you haven't consummated your relationship, but your involvement may have far wider reaching consequences. Very intense, you may believe you're 'soulmates'. Likely very dependent on one another and avoiding your lives and problems, this isn't a 'friendship' that either of you are honest about the nature of. He'll be difficult to shake.

The Bluffer Loves the idea of leaving but never actually does or always goes back. An attention-seeker crying wolf, he'll claim to be 'stuck' in a long-term relationship and likely has kids and other constraints. A major flip-flapper, the affair will be intense and the plans will seem real, but from the moment he makes the grand announcement, you're on an egg timer and the negotiations with 'her' begin behind your back. You then discover he's left a number of times and that this is their 'thing'.

The Long-Termer She may know about you, or he's pretty clever with the deception. Each of you serve a set of needs and together it makes him 'happy', but if he had to choose either of you, until he addresses his issues, he'd be happy with neither of you. Often with the same woman for long periods, he may 'upgrade' occasionally. He's often respected and a 'family man' who believes the affair has no impact. He will only leave under extreme pressure or when caught. If you make ultimatums, he'll freeze you out.

BOOBY TRAPS

You believe he's capable of commitment. By believing he's capable of commitment because he's currently attached, you're showing that you only need superficial commitment, which will leave you hungry and hurt. He may appear to be available in comparison to other Mr Unavailables dodging smaller forms of commitment but it's not just about titles – you need intent, action, and actual commitment behind it.

You think there's something wrong with 'her' or his relationship. Just as you tend to assume that you've 'done' something to make him act as he does, you also assume that she and/or their relationship are failing to meet his needs, which absolves his responsibility. In fact, there may be nothing wrong and even if there is, creeping around with you won't resolve it.

You think the 'risk' is indicative of his feelings and how he can't resist you. It's not. He thinks he's managing the risk and that if he *is* caught, he'll cross that bridge when he comes to it. This isn't a symbol of how irresistible you are, because when someone can't resist you, they *don't* resist you and they step up to the plate.

All the good ones are gone. This excuse seems like the perfect way to legitimise your position. I'm not saying that dating is easy, but I find that very few women that talk about not being able to find a decent man are actually looking for or *interested* in a genuinely decent **available** man.

The illicitness and drama creates a 'connection'. Between the discussions, ultimatums, tears, the make-up sex, the break-up sex, the broken deadlines, the hoping you might get pregnant, the lonely seasonal events and much more – only someone who's blinded by chemistry and a 'connection' and has a serious need for drama and inconsistency could stomach the OW role.

Holding out for a 'happy ending'. Things, feelings, people change and when *other* people feel attraction for another, they either end their current relationship or work harder to strengthen it. There's no happy ending for an affair. Often, if he's caught or he does leave, it ends because he can't keep his dick in his pants, or because you never do quite trust him.

You're afraid he will leave her after you dump him. Already immobilised by the fear of admitting that you've bet on the wrong horse, there's a nagging fear that you'll have misjudged him and then you won't be there when he does leave.

TIPS FOR KICKING THE OW HABIT

Stop thinking you're in a 'unique' situation. It's unique because you're in it, but when you strip away the rationale and excuses, every situation has the same core elements, with one cheating man; one adaptable Fallback Girl; a convenient 'obstacle' that prevents him from leaving; many promises, ultimatums, and disappointments; feeling alone even though you're supposedly in a 'relationship'; and living in limbo till you finally make the break.

'No borrowing' is a core boundary to live by. Opt out when they tell you they're married or have a girlfriend and steer clear of recently separated or long-term separated people. Basically, only mess with men who are free and single.

Go cold turkey. If you can afford it, go away for a few days or a week to somewhere nice, or go and stay with friends and family. Turn off your phone and let the important people know where you are, so that they don't worry. There should be absolutely *no* contact.

Quit being where he expects you to be and break your routine. You may experience huge 'withdrawals' and be at a sudden loose end. Create a new routine. Turn off your phone or screen calls. Keep busy. Do it consistently – new habits will take hold.

Don't rely on him to 'do the right thing'. You'll be waiting indefinitely. What's right for him isn't right for you.

Make breaking up about YOU, not HIM. If you don't, he'll make excuses and promises that he'll renege on. You're actually breaking up because you're better than 'this'.

Break up to break up, not to provoke a reaction. You're only teaching him how to play you otherwise.

Expect that it will hurt like crazy to walk away and steer clear for at *least* six months. Use the time to occupy your life instead of occupying the shadows of his life and put 100% into it.

Steer clear of dating till you're ready to date and over him. This will stop you from falling into another unavailable relationship due to craving an emotional replacement.

Feel the pain, grieve the loss. Don't pretend you've broken up and put yourself into a holding pattern like an aeroplane circling over Heathrow; accept that it's over and feel the pain.

Look ahead to a new life without the toxicity of being with him. Strip away the guilt, secrecy, fractured life, part-time living, watching him go home to someone else, and redundant discussions.

When you experience the pain of the loss, don't try to soothe it by reaching out to him or getting back together. It's like going to your pain source to feel better.

Yes, I'm sure there were happy times, but remember how you really felt as a whole. Look back at your diary and think back to specifics. Don't romanticise and keep it real.

Think of 'her', the woman you perceive to be 'robbing' you of the opportunity to be with him, as a human being with feelings, strengths, and weaknesses just like you. Put yourself in her shoes and consider how you'd feel in the same position. Whatever story he has told you about why he's with the both of you, the cold hard truth is that he chooses to be with her. Active indecision is a decision in itself – to not make a decision – and in not doing so, he's chosen her.

THE BUFFER

In 2005, both before and after I experienced my epiphany about my relationship habits that inspired this book, a number of odd things happened. I was involved with not one, but *two* men who had broken up with their long-term girlfriends but still lived with them. I also found myself staying in conversations long past their sell-by date with men who were in the process of breaking up, had recently separated, or who were here and interested one minute and gone 'dark' the next.

It isn't a coincidence if you find yourself being receptive to men who are transitioning from another relationship that is still present enough to have an impact on their ability to be fully available. I know that while my own receptiveness decreased when I stopped being the Other Woman, I was still processing my hurt and lessons, and certainly not fully aware of boundaries.

If you've found yourself being the welcome wagon for men who reside in the twilight zone of dealing with the transition from a relationship ending, you're a **Buffer**, the woman who cushions their exit and provides a soft landing. While you may not fully realise your role, you help them get over their exes and past with a view that when they're over them and recognise your support, you'll be rewarded with the relationship you want. Avoiding your own hurt, you buffer your own feelings that you're trying to avoid by buffering him. Often too compassionate and eager to be indispensable, you lessen the impact of their previous relationships, which also enables you to hide your commitment issues and indecision behind *their* flip-flapping. In trying to prove your worth and 'win' their affections, you compete with their ex and old life, and often end up being boggled as to why they can't give you what they've given to others.

Buffers get involved with **Transitionals**, people who are recently broken up, still not over their exes, separated, divorced, or widowed – they have emotional and/or legal ties to another relationship. Experiencing the natural process that arises from changing over from being in one relationship to being single, they are still grieving the loss of the relationship/person, and are struggling with their feelings about commitment and being emotionally available. They're not ready to be vulnerable yet. They may be typically emotionally available and going through a period of temporary unavailability due to the transition, or they may be habitually unavailable anyway. Either way, you don't want to get caught in the crossfire, because, if you do, you'll be their means of avoiding uncomfortable feelings about the transition and the loss, and be their *rebound*, even if both of you deny it.

You basically spend your time waiting for him to get his shit together, while also hiding your fear of putting yourself out there with a man who's genuinely available. Being a Buffer is incredibly draining, and after being understanding, giving, accommodating, and basically jiggering around your life to fit in with his agenda, it feels like you've invested too much to leave and you want to 'win'.

You don't want to believe he's on the rebound and you think you know better. You've been caught out by him overestimating his capacity for a new relationship and his fear of being alone. He's pushed down his feelings about her and uses you, albeit not always intentionally (although it doesn't matter whether he means it or not), to get him through this 'rough patch'. He's operating under the misguided notion that if you're special enough, he'll magically get over his ex and be available to you.

It's very possible that under a whole other set of circumstances, maybe you could have had a committed relationship, which, of course, would be under the proviso that, not only is he typically emotionally available, but under the new circumstances you wouldn't be a Fallback Girl either. There's an element of this situation that's down to bad timing, but to blame it mostly on timing is to miss some glaring problems. Don't get things twisted – he isn't under different circumstances and if you've found yourself involved with him, you've missed the one piece of information that deals a crushing blow to anything you have in mind. he's not over his ex. It doesn't matter whether it's that he's scared shitless of commitment or intimacy, or whether he's moping around after her, or creeping around behind your back having talks with her; he's unavailable.

TYPICAL BUFFER

Still getting over a previous relationship.

Separated, recent divorcee.

Derive worth from relationship status – single equals anxiety.

Afraid of abandonment so playing it safe in the half-life.

Absorbs blame for everything.

May still live at home with your parents or be a Daddy's or Mummy's Girl.

Never been married and afraid of putting yourself out there.

Make yourself indispensable.

Stay and Complainer. You'll talk but not take any action.

Abandon your life and may take up his hobbies and friends.

Fixing/healing/helping tendencies.

Think Transitionals are a safe bet because they have evidence of prior commitment.

Afraid of asking questions or making decisions.

Keep making plans so that your lives can be more co-joined.

Frustrated that you aren't as included in his life as you'd like.

Feel like you don't want to live if you can't have him.

TYPICAL TRANSITIONAL

Dating for the first time as spent most of his life in a relationship.

Often quick to join a dating site so he can collect attention.

May be still hoping to work things out [with his ex].

Not very good at fending for himself.

An overestimater, so rushes into things and then backtracks.

Emphatically states that he's definitely over her, it's definitely not too soon and then tells you he's not over her and that it's too soon.

Very confused, often unsure of his feelings.

Scared of making a mistake so will flip-flap between you both.

Secretly negotiates with the ex.

Strong feelings about his ex which he may play down – love, anger, hurt, anguish, disappointment, blame, etc.

Happy to pass time with you and will know you're not The One.

Views legitimate questions about his capabilities or what is happening as 'pressure'.

Can regret getting involved [with you] as he suddenly believes he has options.

Very reluctant to let go of you as it will feel like 'two failures'.

May be grieving and only want companionship but doesn't know how to be honest.

Hints a lot and hopes you get the message and then erupts.

May not sleep with you/touch you so he can say he didn't 'do anything' if he goes back.

THE BUFFERS

Transitional Yep, you can be transitioning, too. While some people will shag and date around, you're looking to get saddled up asap and, as you may have been through what you feel are similar traumas or have even lost your confidence due to, for example, a divorce, he seems an ideal companion and you may think you're buffering one another for support. If the relationship you left was long term and you're not used to dating, especially with online dating thrown in, you'll be at a loose end and far more inclined to immediately play wifey and make yourself indispensable. You're also likely to be very receptive if you're not over your ex or have left with some distorted beliefs and want someone to help you get over your hurt.

The Friend Saying you're his friend is 'safe', because it's better than saying 'girlfriend' or 'woman who expects a lot from you'. You're good at providing a shoulder to lean on when his relationships go belly up, listening to his gripes about work, family, etc., and generally being very supportive. At some point though, while you've been buffering his various emotional hiccups, you've begun to wonder when you're going to get what you feel you're owed – a committed relationship. After all, you understand him, or so you think. You've either always had feelings, but feared being vulnerable or at some point your feelings changed. His problems help you avoid your own. Unfortunately, you haven't fully communicated your agenda, so when he wants to turn you into a casual sex partner or moves onto someone else, you feel very hurt and rejected.

Florences There's a whole chapter on Florence Nightingale, the fixing, healing, helping Fallback Girl who likes relationships with a purpose. Sometimes you need a break from tending to The Walking Wounded with 'major problems' or have got your hands burnt one too many times, so a 'normal' Transitional becomes the ideal option for dealing with what you consider to be 'manageable' problems. You decide that you just need to heal the hurt from the old relationship, rid him of his fears about trying again, or bum-rush him to the solicitor's office to get the divorce underway. You like to feel needed, so being a Buffer does suit you, but you discover (again) that slotting in around someone's problematic life has too many pitfalls.

Miss Understanding If you've left an abusive relationship and are scared about putting yourself out there, being a Buffer with a Transitional is 'safer'. Unfortunately, being with someone who's avoiding being alone while enjoying the fringe benefits *isn't* an ideal role; it will erode your self-esteem further as you switch from worrying about what makes you 'abusable' to what makes you not good enough to get his shit sorted out for and choose you. You may rationalise that he's 'better' than being with an abuser.

Petra Pan Very tied to your family, you're reluctant to cut the apron strings and be fully responsible for yourself. Whether you find it difficult to live up to your parents' ideals, or they fuss around micro-managing your life, you're not very confident. You're particularly likely to be involved with the long-term separated guy who never *actually* gets divorced, especially when you believe that your choices are limited and that you need to 'settle'. Your parents may be traditional, or just downright eager for you to finally get hitched and knock out some kids, and you'll keep reassuring them that he's getting sorted. You'll struggle to admit you've made a mistake, especially because it feels like your family's on your back. Eventually, you give in and end it. Then it becomes that the reason you're not settled down is because he didn't get a divorce.

ACHILLES HEEL: INDISPENSABLE OVER-GIVER

As you've already discovered, the way to love and commitment isn't to act nicer than you feel and make yourself so indispensable you can't be distinguished in a lineup of doormats. If you've been raised to believe that it's the woman's job to 'give', or that you're not good enough, you'll believe that if you love *enough* via giving eventually you'll 'win' your man.

Most Fallback Girls suffer with *Women Who Give Too Much* syndrome, aka being an **Over-giver**. With an excessive propensity to give, because you believe it's the only way to win people over, you're desperate for love, desperate for a companion, and *co-dependent*. Bulldozed by your feelings and desire to be in a relationship, you lose sight of yourself, and tend to think you're 'giving' as it's what's best for the 'relationship'. Just as others compensate for weaker areas of the relationship with finances and sex, you make up for the excessive shortfall with excessive giving.

Symptoms

Parent(s) made you 'work' for their love.

Feel you've been loved conditionally.

See his problems as the obstacle, not him.

Generosity is often abused.

Try to control situations by using money and material goods.

Prefer being in a relationship, even if it's a bad one.

Difficulty saying *no*, setting boundaries, and knowing the line.

Feel you need medication to cope with breakups or being alone.

Don't feel that people are giving enough to you.

Don't believe that you as an individual entity are enough.

May cross boundaries and feel entitled because of your generosity.

Often hear variations of: "Well, I didn't *ask* you to do…"

You give to show love, progress things, and to generate reciprocation so you can feel validated and worthy, which is giving to receive. This goes very awry when you choose a limited man with a limited capacity to commit. You decide that, because you have dignified a man who is separated, recently divorced, etc., you're owed his love and commitment. In making an exception, you feel he should do the same and recognise how lucky he is.

Your 'giving' is your investment into the relationship and you want a return.

When he starts flip-flapping/blowing cold, you often *increase* your giving because you think it'll galvanise him into being a better man in a better relationship with you. You'll feel taken advantage of, but remember that nobody can continue to take what you don't continue to give.

I've heard from many indispensable Buffers who basically cook, clean, babysit, chauffeur, and nursemaid uncommitted men. This is excessive. In a healthy relationship, he'll prioritise having shared values and mutual love, care, trust, and respect over your housekeeping and other abilities.

Focus on getting your relationship in order and addressing issues. Being indispensable will not address your problems. Don't substitute taking an active role in your relationship and being emotionally available with doing stuff like cooking, cleaning, etc., because they're not one and the same thing. A man who has one or both feet out of the relationship *and* has emotional and/or legal ties elsewhere will lose respect for you while availing himself of the fringe benefits of a woman who just doesn't know when to step back. If you did, you'd soon see where this relationship really was, and ultimately, why do you need to run yourself into the ground?

Real people get pissed off, don't always like things, and sometimes aren't that nice. If you hear yourself saying how nice you are and how you don't get X, Y, and Z back, this is *Those Who Doth Protest Too Much syndrome* – you're acting nicer than you feel. Instead of feeling resentful or 'owed', recognise that feeling negative about the level of your efforts means you're not giving authentically.

WATCH OUT FOR...

Dazed & Confused Freshly broken up, he's either pining for his ex and avoiding getting too involved, or he's keen to move on. An overeager friend who thinks you'd help him get over her may set you up, or you get talking and he thinks you're being friendly, and you fancy him. Or he might Future Fake and Fast Forward like there's no tomorrow, because it convinces him he's moved on, but then panic at your expectations. Next thing he's saying that he's not over her or they're getting back together. Don't be surprised if they're still living/sleeping together or have a complicated 'friendship'. If he has Bad Penny inclinations, you'll be collateral damage in their boomerang dynamic.

The Separated If they're having space and it's unresolved, your role becomes convincing him to choose you. He's still married though. If he's agreed to divorce, but has been separated long-term, he isn't ready to cut the ties or commit elsewhere, and may even enjoy controlling his wife's agenda. You should only get involved if the divorce is proceeding and he's emotionally over her. If he's not 'done' or he's backing off, he'll feel pressured by your expectations or accuse you of pressuring him to divorce. At worst, he may vacillate between you and her.

The Divorcee While many divorcees go on to have great relationships, he won't if he's either fresh out of the solicitor's office or full of anger/unhealthy beliefs. He's legally but not emotionally over her and may still be adjusting and struggling with the vulnerability. Scared of another 'mistake', holding tight to his new 'freedom', or not ready to accept the reasons and his part in the marriage failing, it won't stop him from enjoying the fringe benefits with you and he'll either overestimate his capacity or be very firm about not committing, making him at times very cold towards you. He may be 'friends' with his ex or have a 'complicated' relationship.

The Widower An understandably painful situation, he may be grieving or have grieved, but avoiding intimacy and/or commitment for fear of the pain of loss, even via a breakup. Many widowers go on to love again – I'm not saying he won't, but he's not ready now. Likely desiring companionship or avoiding his feelings, your natural expectations, despite your patience, will trigger him blowing hot and cold. Also, irrespective of the loss, he may have been unavailable anyway. If he's typically available, he's likely to be honest about his position, but if he's not and he's unwilling to consider your feelings, you'll be used to serve his needs.

The Phantom Yes, he's back again. If he's the guy who disappears and reappears from time to time, he could be any of the above guys but only enjoys you for a short-term fix. He may not even reveal that he's going through a breakup or is separated, etc. He's either still undergoing negotiations, has gone back to his ex and left again, or he's keeping to himself and managing you and any other women he's involved with by keeping you at a distance.

BOOBY TRAPS

"But nobody's perfect! We all have baggage!" True, but not all baggage is conducive to a relationship. Don't continue to bullshit yourself. You overempathise and reason that you're not perfect and have baggage so it's harsh to judge him for the same thing. Deal with your feelings about your so-called 'imperfections' instead of marking yourself down and deciding that you're only deserving of a demi-relationship. This isn't a 'perfection' and 'baggage' issue; it's a *willingness* and *mentality* issue.

You're too adaptable. Some people run from unfinished business, but not you. Eager to be the next person he commits to, you adapt the crap out of yourself. To admit you've made a mistake and that it's time to 'fold' is to admit you've sold yourself short and lost sight of you. Eventually you'll recognise that you've been contorting yourself while he's maintained his position.

You only feel like an entity in a couple. You don't know how to meet your own needs and validate yourself, plus you make men your focal point and source of happiness. Personal security is pivotal and you must learn to see yourself as an individual entity instead of a sponge to soak up the hurt from his prior relationships. Until then, you'll be waiting outside the Transitionals Ward of the Emotionally Unavailable Hospital looking for someone to pair up with.

You're half-hearted. You're just not that into him. I know, you're going to deny it and swear blind that you love him and yadda yadda yadda, but, deep down, you know the truth: *While you have some interest, you're kinda passing time and avoiding being responsible for making decisions and changes in your own life.* If the only way you can get up your interest erection is for an opportunity to buffer him, your interest *isn't* really in him; it's catering to your own beliefs and seeking validation.

Get over her, validate me. You forget that you're buffering *something*. You're helping to lessen and moderate the impact of his previous relationship, a purpose that's very wrong for a relationship. You'll come to discover that two people with lazy thinking who both believe someone else should get them over a relationship equals stalemate.

Blinded and assumptive. You think stuff like, *"He wouldn't have got involved with me if there wasn't a chance and he wasn't over her. He just needs more time."* You don't do enough due diligence and think that, if you don't get in there, he'll be snapped up because he's obviously relationship material. It's like he's been 'vetted' and pre-approved by his previous relationship, only you have the skimpiest of quality assurance. Do you know what happens to assumptive people? They wake up in a relationship they didn't intend to be in with a bad glare in their eyes.

TIPS FOR KICKING THE BUFFER HABIT

Freshly separated, divorced, widowed, or broken up isn't appropriate for you. Unless they're at least 3 months clear for separations (with divorce definite and process in place) and divorces, 6 months to a year at least for being widowed, and have had at least 1-3 months out of a breakup, don't go there.

Not all relationship trauma 'impact' is created equal. Your pain isn't his pain, so don't make dangerous assumptions.

Giving with conditions and expectations isn't giving wholeheartedly, which means it's not giving – it's *control*.

Literally the moment that you find out that there are ex or transitioning issues, step back. Don't proceed unless you're 100% comfortable and have fully assessed the situation.

There *are* no guarantees, which means you need eyes and ears open. Sometimes, we don't truly know our capacity for a relationship until we're in it and realise that we've overestimated. It's disappointing, but when feelings or capacities change, our expectations must too, even if it signals opting out.

Get over your ex on your own time. The sooner you grieve the loss and the hurt, the sooner you kick the Mr Unavailable habit.

Listen to your relationship and stop deciding that you know better. When he says he needs more time, that he's not ready for a relationship, etc., accept the feedback and act accordingly by giving him all the time in the world.

There's looking for good in people and situations and then there's making shit up as you go along and not seeing them in reality. If you have to look for the good, you're trying too hard.

Hang back. Yep, you heard me. You don't have to be the Buffer – you're not an ambulance chaser.

Compassion means pity and concern for the misfortunes of others. It isn't a reason to be in a relationship and certainly shouldn't give you your purpose. You don't need to be thinking of him or yourself as unfortunate – while relationships do end and are often painful, nobody needs a buffering nurse.

RENOVATORS & FLORENCES

Right now there are millions of women dating and in relationships with men that they 1) weren't that interested in to begin with, but thought they could change, 2) were interested in, but had to turn a blind eye to some stuff and thought they could change, and 3) were mostly interested in fixing/healing/helping. What this tells you straight off the bat is that many women end up in unsatisfactory relationships because they knowingly choose partners they deem as having 'faults' or 'issues'. They believe that if they 'give' and 'love' this will give them the power to change their inadequate partners and be rewarded with their love.

Unfortunately, believing that you have superhuman powers is what has you repeatedly returning to the same relationship crime scene, going out with the same guy in a different package, and taking on fixer-upper projects that leave you hungry and hurt.

I'm a big fan of TV shows like *Property Ladder*, *Grand Designs,* and *Location, Location, Location*, which deliver an important message that you should remember throughout this chapter and the rest of this book: it's all fruitless unless you get Return On Investment (ROI). You cannot take *any* man with any and all problems and treat him like a blank canvas and magic up the relationship you want, because it's like trying to turn a pig's ear into a silk purse – a very bad bet.

What's the difference between the woman who ditches men because they don't meet her stringent criteria and the woman who, instead of ditching, focuses on fixing and healing? A slippery slope.

When you choose men who you believe need fixing and a makeover, you're a **Renovator.** Relationships where you secretly, or even openly, put yourself on a pedestal are your preference, because underneath your critical eye and controlling ways, lurks low self-esteem. You figure that he's not right for now, but that if you give and fix, that you'll be rewarded with a committed relationship. Disillusioned with dating and scared to put yourself out there with the type of men you'd prefer, you think you're playing it safe, then Mr Unavailable turns the tables on you.

With the rehab route, you're a fixing/healing/helping **Florence Nightingale** who needs to feel needed. His problems give you a purpose, and you believe that if you love enough, even 'major issues' can be overcome, for you. You make yourself the solution to problems that aren't yours to fix and that require more than love and a woman to resolve. You're often righting the wrongs of the past as a parent/caregiver tends to be very similar to your partners, and with your low self-esteem, you think a man with problems will be grateful for your love and reciprocate. Having no idea how to meet your own needs, you become frustrated at being deprioritised and your own problems go unaddressed as you're always distracted. You want to make everything better, but you're actually making things worse.

Renovators can pretty much date any Mr Unavailable or even a decent, available guy and try to fix and make him over, but you tend to be with **Opportunists,** guys who get involved because you serve the purpose of being useful. On the take, they have little or no regard for your feelings, and, because of your renovating ways, they see it as their right to exploit the situation. Florences end up with **Woundeds**, men with excess baggage in the form of emotional and behavioural problems; addictions such as sex, gambling, alcoholism and drugs; and they may even be abusive. Whatever their problems are, they completely affect their ability to be in a relationship.

Some people run in the opposite direction from relationships where it's apparent that the person isn't what they want or that they have major issues that make a relationship a no-go area, but not you. You either seem to think you can bulldoze your changes on any man or you refuse to see problems for what they are. You don't see a man that you don't really fancy, respect, value, or accept, and you don't see a man with more baggage than all five terminals at Heathrow. You see *opportunities*.

You may not be conscious of it, but there's a Bingo Moment when you first become involved with a guy where you see, hear, or perceive something that causes

234

you to 'click' into place and feel that you have a purpose and opportunity to be needed. You have your eye on the prize and the reward.

The idea is that you invest yourself into a relationship, no matter how lacking or dangerous, and in knowing that he's not actually the Catch of the Year, much less of the *century*, you expect that he'll almost bask in the glow of a woman like you and it'll be like, *"Wow, a woman like her wants me to better myself or is willing to be with me in spite of my humongous luggage. I will love and worship her!"* You're trying to live out a very fucked up princess and the frog tale.

The reality is altogether different. There's no prince hidden in your fixer-upper/pet project and Mr Unavailable never has the same agenda as you and does things on his terms. While Opportunists and Woundeds may initially be flattered by your interest and 'love', and even appear to make some changes, eventually they *do* rebel, they *do* blow hot and cold, and the bait and switch takes place where suddenly a relationship that you felt in control of, is very much out of your control. This will boggle you. You'll wonder how even *this* man with all the changes he 'needs', or glaring problems, can't love you and you'll also wonder how he's running rings around you.

These relationships go one of three ways: he moves on and someone else appears to reap the rewards of your effort, he stays but refuses to change, so you end up living in Misery City, or he leaves and remains the same anyway. What I can assure you of is that this relationship is doomed regardless, because this isn't love; it's *control* and, as you've already discovered, messing with Mr Unavailables is one big painful adventure in attempting to control the uncontrollable.

TYPICAL RENOVATORS & FLORENCES

Fix now, let the love catch up later attitude. (R)

Love now, heal later attitude. (F)

Major control issues, although may deny it.

Childhood may have felt very out of control/controlling parent.

Parent(s) were abusive, addicted, cheating, or helpless.

Abandoned and had to be responsible from an early age.

Think all men want a woman to come along and mould them.

Fairy-tale ideals.

Afraid that you're not good enough for partners more 'on your level'.

Hiding your problems behind his.

Very comfortable around pain – see potential in even the biggest of problems. (F)

May not have even been that interested but saw potential.

Very little boundaries.

Likely have more 'criteria' than you can shake a stick at. (R)

Believe the dating pool is diminishing. Fear you have to settle.

User of the: "Nobody's perfect! Everybody has baggage!" argument.

Gritting teeth, making exceptions, focused on the 'potential'. (R)

May actually pick faults that don't exist or matter. (R)

Find it difficult to relax and be happy.

May say, "Men can't handle my money/success/beauty, etc."(R)

May prefer him to be dependent on you.

Overvalue your contribution.

Talk about people in numbers, i.e. "He's a 5 but, with some help from me, he could be a 9." (R)

See yourself as benevolent and misunderstood.

May come across as having a superiority complex.

What you feel must change matters, even when superficial. (R)

Generosity is often taken advantage of.

May cross boundaries with friends, family, and even neighbours, trying to be their solution to 'everything'.

Find it difficult to tolerate him in his 'natural' state. (R)

Openly put him down or tell people that he's less than ideal. (R)

Feels like your 'child' is rebelling against your wishes and 'rules'.

Feel like their 'mother'.

Always advising and forcing your opinions on him.

Feel very hard done by and 'owed' like a bailiff.

TYPICAL OPPORTUNIST

Pursues when you're not interested – major Fast Forwarder.

Loves a challenge – proving if you're really as 'amazing' as he thinks you think you are.

"What's a woman like you doing with a guy like me?"

Puts you on a pedestal and then yanks you off it very sharply, often putting himself in the hot seat.

Responsibility and accountability dodger.

Uses blowing hot and cold to redress the power balance.

Exploits your need for control and changes by Future Faking.

Happy to exploit for whatever he can – free rent, money, etc.

Very likely to cheat.

After you've pumped him up, he'll think he can do better.

Loves disappearing.

May be pulling the same con on several women.

TYPICAL WOUNDED

Often has a number of great qualities and characteristics... there's just the 'small' matter of his 'big' problems.

A 'but' and 'if only' guy: "He'd be so great if only..."

In possession of a major issue, whether it's emotional, behavioural, mental, or addictions.

Have other baggage to add to their load.

May feel smothered by your expectations and hopes for him.

Often numbing very painful past experiences.

Makes external things the solution to his internal problems.

Thinks if you're that great, he'll overcome his issues.

Not hot on responsibility and accountability.

Highly likely to play down his problems when you first meet.

Can be very charming, sexy, disarming. Often a very good liar.

Parent(s)/caregiver(s) may have similar issues.

Dreamer, but then fears the expectations of intentions he conveys.

Many missed opportunities that are lamented.

Will often be highly thought of, or people will think there was so much potential he could have met.

May play the victim, making it very difficult to deal with basic issues.

Often quite 'creative' hence why so many women love wounded singers, artists, actors, poets, writers, etc.

May cheat or even abuse you but blame it on the problem and be very remorseful. And then do it again.

THE RENOVATORS

The Project Manager Even though you may not be interested on meeting, your curiosity is piqued by his interest. Likely to be feeling low about an ex or failed date. You think, *"With a new haircut, a few months with a personal trainer, a facial, some table manners, and some advice on his career, he could almost be right for me."* You plan to grow to love him. You don't want him to wind up being a great guy in a great relationship with someone else. Getting any superficial issues under your control creates problems, because you almost lose respect for him due to his acquiescing *plus* it doesn't resolve larger unavailability issues, which soon reveal themselves. You find yourself picking faults and critiquing him but when he starts messing you around and acting like it's *you* that needs to change, it cuts to the heart of your secret fears and you change how you feel about him because now *you* have to work for *his* 'love'.

The Bulldozer The moment you're over those initial few dates, he's 'your' man to change. Leaving no brick unturned, you do your best to erase all trace of the previous house – I mean man – then attempt to rebuild him from the ground up. The most controlling, angry, and frustrated, you may be genuinely unaware of your behaviour. Unfortunately, like all Fallback Girls, there's a currency that will level you or put him on a pedestal and that's pulling the Bait and Switch. You get left with a man you've 'created' who's suddenly treating you like you're not good enough for him *and* making you work harder, which wrong-foots you.

The Alpha Controller Often highly successful, with a bank balance to match, you struggle to meet men on your "level", because you believe that men view you as domineering, outspoken, too smart, and too successful. Used to being in control of your life, you opt for men who let you take the driving seat, but then don't respect them for doing it. The balance tips though and because you can't control his availability and have to work for his love, you end up being a highly successful *fallback* option.

The Sugar Mama Choosing men who are 'beneath' and often financially dependent on you, this makes for a bumpy ride where you often get robbed of far more than your self-esteem. Not convinced of your own worth, you love with material goods and generosity. It's not that you're rich - often quite the opposite – but the imbalance puts you in control and you think it gives you carte blanche to implement change. You secretly believe that a man that's dependent on you can't/won't leave, and that as he *needs* you, he'll love you. But he's still unavailable and will often leave, or, at the very least, stay and enjoy the hospitality at your expense.

THE FLORENCES

The Rescuer Choosing men who wear their flaws on their sleeves, in their brokenness you rationalise your 'broken' self as normal. You think you can 'handle it' and it's the perfect opportunity to heal him, which, in turn, is supposed to heal you. The more wounded, the more attracted you are, the more of a need and purpose you see, the more potential you envision, the more invested you become. You think if you love enough, that he'll spontaneously combust into a problem-free man and are actually very comfortable around major problems if it's all you've known since childhood. His problems are a distraction from you and you also initially feel in control, but when he starts being a typical Mr Unavailable and refuses to change, or keeps Future Faking, you become frustrated and it brings up old wounds. You think if you were good enough, he'd put you above his problems. That said, you're also afraid that if he does realise his potential, your purpose will be gone.

The Mama You try to strong-arm him into changing, take him to counselling, book him into rehab, tell him what he needs and what you're going to do to help him, and essentially provide him with his own personal rehab in the sanctuary of your love. A mix of Renovator and Florence, you make it clear that fixing has got to happen and sink in all your energy to distract from your own problems. Pretending to be happier than you feel, you get tired of being the 'responsible one' and wonder when he'll take care of you.

Good Girl Gone Bad A real co-dependent, you can easily throw away your values in the name of love and will actually join him in his problems. Next thing you're drinking, taking drugs, etc., because you believe that you'll have his full attention if you can share in his problems and it might just numb the pain you already feel. Often he ends up leaving you with more than a broken heart.

ACHILLES HEEL: I CAN CHANGE HIM

Many women think that it's the most natural thing in the world to meet a guy and want him to change. It's as if we believe that we need to mollycoddle and over-nurture our men and effectively build them from the ground up. You expecting them not to be themselves, actually says more about you than it does about them.

If fixing up the men in your life is a familiar habit, you're afflicted with **'I Can Change Him' syndrome** which occurs when you believe that love, or, at least, the presence of you in a relationship, is about having the power to change someone through fixing, healing, and helping. You start out with them one way and, between Betting On Potential and your ideas about how the relationship *should* be, you're like a dog with a bone. Your thought process is: "But I love him – why won't he change for me?", "If he loved me, he'd change for me!" or "If I was good enough, he'd change for me." You actually believe that you're the solution to the problem of him and his problems.

Symptoms

Don't know the meaning of empathy, sympathy, and compassion.

Mistake pity and the desire to be in control of their change as 'love'.

If they're going to be better, it *must* be with you.

Think it's totally normal and within your right to expect change.

Operate with a hidden agenda – may plan to change them later.

Very adaptable and indispensable to get reciprocation.

Suffer with Women Who Talk (and Think) Too Much.

Mistake 'critiquing' for 'helping'.

Believe you're not just *the* solution, but also the *only* solution.

One of your parents needed to change but didn't.

Won't admit you've made a mistake.

High achiever who still doesn't think they're 'good enough'.

Underachiever afraid of living up to your potential.

Quite strong opinions on others but struggle to take criticism.

Don't recognise that your 'input' isn't always welcomed.

May be hypersensitive to even the remotest hint of criticism.

Fixing can be done quite aggressively through repeated discussions and arguments, or there's the passive aggressive route where your changes sneak up on him from behind through gestures like 'gifts' (new wardrobe, haircut), putting the job pages in front of him, or dropping hints through career and life advice.

Healing and help is more an *If-You-Stick-Around-Long-Enough-Through-Thick-and-Thin-and-Show-That-There's-Pretty-Much-Nothing-He-Can-*

Do-To-Get-Rid-of-You kind of thing. You might try therapy, rehab, etc., to fast-track the healing, but you often end up turning a blind eye to his issues.

This is an inverted ego issue – you think you can change someone's fundamental emotional style, values, characteristics, etc. That's a big ask, even for God himself.

You're not the solution to anyone's problems other than your own. You cannot fix alcoholism, sex addiction, childhood problems, unavailability, and anything else you feel like putting your hand to because you didn't make these problems in the first place.

Particularly for Woundeds, you expecting them to make you the solution to their problems, would actually be to *replicate* the same addictive and co-dependent behaviour, which only further highlights how unhealthy this relationship is and also your idea of what constitutes a relationship.

You're also not *qualified* to fix anyone with your 'homegrown' solutions, plus – let's be real now – you have a *vested* interest. This is about getting him to be and do what *you* want for *your* relationship to meet *your* needs and to cater to *your* beliefs by expecting that he should change. You have far too great expectations.

By putting all of your energy into them, you're sending the message that you don't think you have issues and are putting yourself on a pedestal. I don't doubt you have your fabulousness and I'm all for bigging yourself up, but nobody's so perfect that you get to have carte blanche to change every guy you meet.

ACHILLES HEEL: CONTROLLING THE UNCONTROLLABLE

One of the damn near excruciating things about being a Fallback Girl is feeling out of control, combined with trying to control things that are far beyond your scope. All Fallback Girls are dealing with issues of control even though most will deny it because 'control' isn't a behaviour that anyone likes to associate themselves with.

Do you know what **control** is? It's having the power to influence or direct people's behaviour, or to restrict or limit something, to manage it. And when you're **controlling** it's seeking to determine the behaviour of someone or even supervise them while seeking to maintain your influence and authority over them.

Symptoms

Fear that men who are unwilling to be controlled pose more risk.

Don't believe that there's any decent men out there.

Secretly believe that there are flaws in you that will prevent you from being with someone who you perceive as being unable to control, i.e. on your level.

Afraid that if you don't control things, he'll discover things about you that might change the relationship dynamics.

Afraid of not knowing what to expect even though being controlling doesn't relieve this fear.

Divert focus from yourself and then claim helplessness.

Major distrust and fear of letting go.

Fear of having to risk your heart and take a chance on commitment places you in situations where you think you'll be firmly in control. By choosing men who give you the opportunity to 'fix' them, you get to say how he looks and acts.

Some people spend their lives in search of that soulmate feeling where they find someone who acts, thinks, speaks, and feels exactly as they do, which is another problem in itself. The Renovator doesn't search for a soulmate; she focuses instead on squeezing her square peg man into a round hole in the hopes of creating exactly the type of relationship where she'll be happy – one where she's in control, knows what to expect from him, and because she's bestowed him with her wisdom of what makes a great man and made him attractive, either physically or in characteristics and qualities, a man who's ultimately *grateful* to be with her. He'll be willing to be and do exactly what she wants and not pose any problems.

If you're a controller (relationship-wise) you tend to put excessive controls on people, assuming a superior role. You can be quite regimented about your expectations, critical, judgmental, and have very defined ideas about what you think the other person should do to 'improve'. When they inevitably fall short of your expectations, you declare them unworthy.

Florences control with expectations, both hidden and communicated. It's *"I'm loving [pitying] you in spite of your problems, now give me the relationship I want."* It can even be *"You need me and you won't survive out there in the big wide world without me"* and if you dig a little deeper, it may even be *"You're too fucked up to leave."*

You likely see yourself in a fluffier, kinder, light where you're helping these men and assume that fixing/healing/helping is all part of normal relationships. You see it as 'nice control' as opposed to 'abusive control', but control is control.

Stick to controlling your finances, diet, departmental budgets, etc., where you'll yield far better results. Even if you didn't go with Mr Unavailables, your relationships are futile because you're trying to control something that's out of your hands. However, if there was ever one type of man that will remain so unpredictable he becomes almost predictable, Mr Unavailable is it. Trying to control him or the relationship is a waste because he'll continue to jump to his own beat, but pretend that he's still jumping to yours.

WATCH OUT FOR...

Mr Bendy Pursuing when he thinks he doesn't stand a chance, he may be dazzled by your looks, success, etc. You know him – he says, *"I can't believe that a woman like you is with a man like me"*. Initially, he'll be flattered and bending to your will, but he then loses respect for you for being with him. You've also put a wrecking ball through his perceptions of you by not accepting him. Blowing cold to regain control, he'll tap into your insecurities. When the resentment kicks in, he'll believe he's justified in taking advantage. Be careful – the shift in control may convince you that you want him more than you do. After a while, he thinks, *"Hmm, maybe I can do better!"* then prances around with his new confidence sniffing around others, 'trades up' to someone he believes is more accepting, or takes on a new challenge.

The Financial Drain Future Faking and Fast Forwarding his way in, suddenly he's experiencing some issues that he needs 'help' on or will orchestrate a situation where he'll need to move in early on. Or, at some point while dating, he made a remark about your career/money to imply that you won't want him because he's 'not good enough'. You'll get sucked in to 'proving' your love and he'll exploit your generosity and desire for validation. Unfortunately, he's unavailable *and* sucking you dry. He may even resent you for being 'foolish' enough to be with him or for 'making' him feel small, and you'll find yourself tiptoeing around him and dampening your personality to let him feel like The Big Man. Don't be surprised if you find yourself being threatened with being left, or if he and the woman he's cheating on you with are caught nicking money from you.

The Addict Whether it's sex, drugs, alcohol, porn, gambling, or even gaming, he uses them to numb and fix his internal problems. He may be deceptive about the extent until you're in too deep. Chasing a feeling while also avoiding other feelings closer to home, he cannot do honesty and responsibility. Initially, he'll be very flattered by your attention, then overwhelmed, then eventually resentful. He may actually scorn you for seeing so much in him and may feel patronised and controlled. While he's often quite charming and you may even be dazzled by his intelligence/creativity when he's 'on', you'll find it difficult to cope with the uncertainty, lies, moods, omissions, and sometimes almost scary single-mindedness. He's highly likely to sabotage the relationship to force you to see him at his worst so he can be free of your hopes.

The Faux Recoverer Some guys *love* therapy, yoga, new age crystals, psychics, regular rehab visits, starting AA and then abandoning it again and claiming that they've seen the light. Often he's been in therapy for years, which is fine but you'll soon discover that he's just been 'going' to therapy, not *doing* it. Years of experience has taught me that confident avoiders are very good at saying all the right things and trying to convince professionals of their progress. The Faux Recoverer isn't engaging in application and ends up believing that showing up is enough while using these crutches as a foil to intimacy and a distraction from the things they really should be addressing. The shrewd ones know that women lap up this type of thing and assume he's sensitive, available, and trying to be a better man.

The Hauler In possession of excessive baggage, he's chock full of big obstacles. It could be behavioural/emotional problems caused by childhood, he may be struggling with mental health issues, in trouble with work/family/friends/ex – basically *something* is always wrong. Haulers drag their baggage wherever they go because everyone else is the problem, or they think it's easier to press the Reset Button than it is to actually address the issues. You may want their problems fixed more than they do. Be careful – they often leave some baggage to load you down.

The Recycled Teenager It can seem like a bit of an adventure to date the guy who seems to have the lifestyle of a 20 year old, but is pushing 40, but, after a while, it gets really tiresome, especially when you try to settle down or have a child or run a business together, etc. You may be attracted because he loosens you up. Possibly an ex-Addict, he has an allergy to responsibility, is used to other people taking care of his problems, and 'goofs off' in the relationship. He might fall off the wagon periodically and you'll have to be 'in charge', which will feel great initially, until you realise he's stuck in a teenage time warp and not growing up. He may be a mother's boy or from a well-off family where he's not had to push himself.

The Victim Everyone else is the problem. You'll never be able to be on a level footing with him because, not only is he unavailable, but he dodges responsibility and plays the victim to basically get away with never really putting himself into things. If you call him on something, he'll project and accuse you of it. He may even make things up and go on the attack, which will then cause you to feel like you're going crazy and question yourself. Natural conflicts that arise as a part of a relationship will be a nightmare, because you'll be manipulated and guilt tripped and you may have your past thrown in your face or he may accuse you of being just like a parent who abused him. Back away. Fast.

BOOBY TRAPS

You're righting the wrongs of the past. Your pity meter runs high, because there are aspects of you or your past that you pity, which you project on him. He's an opportunity to correct, to be validated, to accomplish things you or a parent couldn't – you're trying to get him to meet needs and create feelings that were the job of a parent/caregiver. The way to right the wrongs of the past is to *break*, not *repeat*, the pattern, and to build a life on your own terms.

You mistake pity for 'love' and 'empathy'. Instead of *empathising*, you *sympathise,* which is to *pity* him. You'll know you're empathising when you accept that you don't *have* to be a part of the solution or be in control of managing it and, instead, allow him to remain in control of it. He doesn't want your pity and you'll degrade him in the process if you persist.

You need to feel needed. Renovators can be guilty of trying to fix what doesn't need fixing while ignoring bigger issues (more worried about him looking right than him being unavailable). Florences latch onto something (he tells a sad story from his life) and decide that they're needed because surely someone who has these problems 'needs' them. Both may even fantasise about how other people will think they're great for fixing him. Relationships like this are unhealthy and sometimes even suffocating and co-dependent.

He's just not good enough = you're just not good enough. If the situation was reversed, you would feel alienated, unloved, and unaccepted. You send a consistent message to him that he's not good enough and that you're dissatisfied. As it is, by trying to validate yourself through him, you end up feeling worse. Nobody else makes you 'good enough' – only you, so there's no point making him the source of your worth and confidence.

He 'owes' you the reward of change. Unfortunately, there's a major monkey wrench that's been thrown in your masterplan – no matter how much you love, nobody owes you change. Any issues he has are about him – you're not the same person. If he owes change to anyone it's *himself.* If the success of your relationship is linked to the *How Much Change Can He Realise Index*, your relationship doesn't stand a chance.

Pick me! You're like the OW to problems. You're trying to be prioritised over major problems and even over him. It's too much! Imagine that you had issues that you were battling with and, despite your protestations, he refused to back off and let you figure out things of your own accord? This is you. Instead of opting for a complicated relationship in which you are deprioritised, address your issues with change, get out of your problematic comfort zone and stretch yourself in a mutual relationship.

You're comfortable on a pedestal. Dating beneath you, whether it's consciously or subconsciously, means that, on some level, you feel he should be grateful. You think he won't be as much 'work' as someone you're secretly afraid may reject you, so you prefer to attempt to build him from the ground up to feel in control, reinforcing the idea that you're fine, it's everything else that needs to change. When he turns the tables on you, you think, "Whoa! How come *he* doesn't love *me*? He's not even all that!" and this then cuts to your fear that you're not good enough even to win a man who you deem to be beneath you.

You focus on the 'good times' and 'good points'. Let's take a worst-case scenario where you were having wonderful, loving times with a Mr Unavailable, let's say, 75% of the time, but 25% of the time he was either verbally or physically abusive – does the 75% negate his despicable behaviour? No it frickin' doesn't! Stop trying to extend the good times into a full-time gig while burying your head about the true nature of the not-so-good times!

Pet project alert. While a little help where it's wanted is helpful, your desire to take the proverbial scalpel to the man you met and pretty much remove him is frightening. While you think this will make you happier, it won't *and* you'll probably lose respect for him, too. Changing character and personality are incredibly difficult and they are part of what feeds into his values. Superficial things that you can change don't matter much in the grander scheme of things, but if you actually respected him for who he was, you wouldn't feel the need to overhaul him. He may be attractive to you now, but he's also now attractive to lots of other women, too.

Passing time to get your attention fix. Trying to convince yourself into feeling more, you'll lower your standards for attention. Opportunists and Woundeds, even if you don't want them, make you feel desired, special, attractive, beautiful, loved, and appreciated, even if you're embarrassed about introducing them to others. When he turns the tables on you, suddenly you want a relationship.

Desperate to avoid being single equals desperate choices. When you can't bear your own company, or only feel happy being in a relationship regardless of quality, you're not going to rest on your laurels waiting for a man with fewer issues to show up. I can guarantee that, until you're independently happy, it'll be difficult to be happy with someone, and certainly not with a guy who you've chosen as a fixer-upper project. You've decided that it's better to settle now and fix on the go, but end up resenting him and wondering why you're still miserable, while also struggling with him being unavailable anyway.

TIPS FOR KICKING THE FLORENCE & RENOVATOR HABIT

As long as you date men who are 'beneath' you, you'll always get to be right, and always get to be 'better' – you just won't get to be happy.

Nobody's perfect and expecting perfection from others when you're not, is unfair. By relinquishing your need to control and change them, you might actually get to enjoy your relationships.

If you hear yourself saying or thinking something similar to "I can handle it", alarm bells should be ringing. You're denying, minimising, and rationalising his actions or issues. STOP!

It's not enough for him to say he's in therapy, he's changed, he's visiting support groups, etc. Focus on demonstrable progress and consistency *in* the relationship. If he's struggling, his issues take priority, not you.

If you meet him and start pulling him apart mentally and rearranging him, *halt.* Either accept and work with who he is or get out.

Asking, hoping, demanding, expecting, pushing for change is rejection and mutual relationships require a spirit of acceptance. You hate rejection, so it's no surprise that he does, too. Staying and pretending you accept him while all the time having the hidden agenda of changing him along the way is still rejection *and* manipulative.

Love isn't about having the power to change someone. You're crossing boundaries when you try to fix/heal/help or expect change, or perceive them as needing you.

Take the focus off him and bring it back to you. You are the only person that you can control so instead of investing in fixing/healing/helping others, invest in you.

If you're that eager to be the Patron Saint of Giving, Fixing, Healing and Helping, do charity work. Seriously. It's a more appropriate use of your energies where *real* people and *real* issues that need help can benefit from you. There are a shocking number of children in foster care, homeless shelters that always need help, and a wealth of other worthy causes – go and find a new purpose. This leaves you to create healthier relationships.

THE FLOGGER

One of the misconceptions about unavailability is that once you get someone to say that you're in a relationship, to move in, to get married, etc., that they're *available*, so many people believe that unavailability is really about dating or nailing down 'commitment'. The thing is, you can do all of the above and still have unavailability issues because, as anyone who has had the misfortune to be involved with the Cheater knows, it's not all about a title.

Some relationships go the distance, not because there's mutual love, care, trust, and respect, along with the landmarks of healthy relationships, but because at least one party thinks they're busting a gut trying to keep the relationship together, and the other keeps saying and doing stuff to shut the other up and buy more time. Both parties end up thinking that they're more available than they are, when what's really going on is that you have two commitment-resistant people talking the crap out of the relationship and making threats and promises that they can't deliver on.

This is that classic relationship that epitomises where it can all go so wrong, when you think 'talking' is communication and that so much time has passed, or you've put up with so much, that it would be better to continue than to let it go, trapping you in a relationship long past its sell-by date.

If you're a serial monogamist with unavailable men, you're **The Flogger,** the Fallback Girl most likely to talk about what you've invested and sacrificed. Unwilling to fold, you'll see even the worst of commitments through to the bitter end. Often regarded as loyal, kind, a good listener, and undemanding, the same people will wonder why you're not happier/settled down/or are with him. You likely met when you were young and not wise to the shenanigans of Mr Unavailables, or, after being hurt, you latched on to what you thought were more commitment ready signs. Often obsessed with things being 'right', you still don't leave when it's wrong. As the bigger talker, thinker, and 'giver', you think you work hardest in your relationships.

It's bad enough that the average Mr Unavailable is like a cockroach after a nuclear bomb that just wont get lost even when he has nothing to offer, but the **Stonewaller** is a special breed – he's the convenient one with his feet set in cement. He veers between being a squatter (won't leave, won't change) and a silent protester, passive aggressively undermining. A major Future Faker who strings it out over an extended phase in dribs and drabs (like when he has to win you back), you can find yourself engaged, or even down the aisle, and still experiencing problems. He's highly likely to have, at best, emotionally cheated/sniffed around and, at worst, cheated on you. He believes he's entitled to have a woman at his side to put up with his crap –don't be surprised if he's a mother's boy or a charming ladies' man.

The both of you *need* relationships, believing you're more able to commit than 'others'. While your desire to hold on, albeit for the wrong reasons, is mutual, neither of you are really prepared to do the emotional and action work to resolve the issues. Regardless of what you both profess, action wise, you either don't want the same things, or you do, but differ on what form this should take.

You don't share the same core *values*.

There's often conflicting schedules about when certain things should happen, conflicting ideas about living congruently with values, plus you feel that you're entitled to change him because you've stayed/are married/have children, and don't understand why he doesn't.

Sometimes you've left or threatened it to galvanise him. He's deduced that if you were really unhappy *or* leaving, you'd have *left*. You keep telling him what you expect and, in spite of the fact that it doesn't happen, or he puts out the watered-down version of it, you keep going back to flog him and the relationship.

If this eventually ends, you'll feel duped, unappreciated, and that you've sacrificed, but, most of all, you'll be angry for ignoring the feedback from the relationship and putting up with so much. And that's what being the Flogger is all about – making someone else responsible for your happiness and choices over a long-term basis, being frustrated, disappointed, and even angry, with them for 'failing', but still not leaving, then realising that you were always responsible for your own happiness and choices anyway.

TYPICAL FLOGGER

Base your life around him.

Attracted to symbols of reliability and marriage so drawn to men with good jobs, churchgoers, etc.

Think that you're an all-round great catch and don't see yourself in the same light as what you perceive as more 'difficult' women.

Indecisive and non-committal about the simple *and* difficult.

Consider yourself to be a great listener.

Mastered the art of hiding your true feelings.

Have lots of plans that you never follow through with.

Lost in his problems.

Despite doing most, or even all, of the talking, it's rarely about you.

Always trying to do the right thing.

Scared of being perceived as not trying.

Secretly wonder if your parents didn't try hard enough.

Consider relationships to be investments that you can't walk away from unless something 'really bad' happens.

Secret trust issues.

Never or rarely listen to your own judgement.

Feel weak because you 'can't' leave / keep letting him back in.

Able to see the good in just about anyone.

Rationalise that at least you've given him a big chance.

TYPICAL STONEWALLER

Hardened by a bad breakup that may be from a long time ago.

May be very immature and have a rebellious streak.

Separated for a gazillion years but hasn't sorted the divorce.

Ambiguous and disruptive relationships with friends and exes.

Been caught cheating in the past but been taken back.

May have a 'reputation' around town – you've had to shoot down allegations that he steadfastly denies.

Can be abusive when challenged or out of control.

Like a pig in shit enjoying living with his parents.

Don't be surprised if he has no bills or commitments, a stack of hoarded cash, and is chasing you for your half of the dinner bill.

Exceedingly passive aggressive.

Major Drip-feeder. You can be assured that you're never getting the whole truth and nothing but the truth.

Many obstacles (including you) are blamed for his inaction.

Proposes and then 'needs time'. Also likely to propose to woo you back and then make no mention again.

Very fond of using the word 'pressure'.

Has a secret child (or two or three...) from a cheating escapade.

THE FLOGGERS

Lifers A battle of endurance, you're not going anywhere, no way, no how, no matter what he does. Often together for a very long time. You may have watched him shag around, lie, beg, borrow, thump, and steal, and even initially believed that it was a maturity issue. Now you focus on the fact that it's you he comes home to. The queen of turning a blind eye, you're also often silently stewing, plus you're terrified that all your years of 'sacrifice' will get handed on a plate to an upstart of a woman. Afraid of whether you could cope alone, you rationalise that he's the only thing you've ever known. It doesn't help that you've lost your confidence and are afraid that you've 'missed the boat'. If and when you do break up, it's because he's done something *so* humiliating that it makes it near impossible to take him back. Or he's run off with someone else.

Title Holders Most Fallback Girls have some level of obsession with titles, but you hold yours very closely, using it as a major source of validation. No matter what he does, you focus on the fact that you're his girlfriend/wife, or that you have a title that his exes didn't, or you've had him for more years. You don't know what commitment means so you overvalue your status. If you moved in or got married, you feel disappointed as you thought you'd be happier, plus you've seen that you still can't relax and that he's not going to change. It's possible that you fought dirty to get this far and may have backed him into an ultimatum that he couldn't escape from. He's still him and now you feel trapped because 'this' is what you wanted. One or both of you are very likely to cheat.

The Lobbyist Like a dog with a bone, you've started so you'll finish. You'll be damned if this man doesn't come around to your way of thinking. A prescriber, you thought he possessed certain characteristics, qualities, and values, and you had a schedule for the relationship. When he started playing up, you went into talking and thinking overload. Rather than admit 'defeat', you're gonna flog this donkey till it collapses, even if you have to lobby for a decade. He's stopped taking you seriously. Even if you get a ring out of him, you then have to browbeat him into setting a date and then down the aisle and you never feel entirely confident about him. When it ends, it'll be agonising, especially if you feel like you've 'left things' too late.

The Best Friend Together for what feels like an eternity but, in many respects, your relationship hasn't moved much further than the early stages – you're both passing time and coasting. People have stopped asking when you're going to progress things and when you say it's over, nobody believes you, including him. You may feel like ships passing in the night, brother and sister, friends, or like you're putting on a front to friends and family… and yourself. The sex may have died and you both know it's not working, but you value your friendship, while ignoring the fact that something's very wrong. As neither of you is being emotionally honest and communicating and taking action, the emotional wall between you both is growing. You're both distracting yourselves from the white elephant in the room and one or both of you are waiting for the other to change first or to be brave enough to end it. Or one of you will cheat.

The Responsible One A tricky dynamic, you can feel like you're playing mother when it's you who always has to step up and be responsible. You struggle to get practical and even financial 'input', although you feel like you could overlook certain things if he contributed emotionally. Coming across as controlling, because you lack confidence in him, you then end up exhausted and frustrated. You vent periodically and lay it down about what he's not doing, you get a slight change and then he's back to normal. Eventually you reach breaking point, ideally before he cheats or 'trades up'.

ACHILLES HEEL: WOMEN WHO TALK AND THINK TOO MUCH SYNDROME

While you need to be able to communicate what you're thinking, expecting, etc., what happens if you spend so much time *thinking* about your relationship, then *talking* about it, then *thinking* about it some more, that your communication becomes redundant?

Women Who Talk and Think Too Much syndrome occurs when you just can't stop discussing, explaining, questioning, arguing, debating, and, yes, sometimes talking to your man and when that's done, often switching to 'overthinking' mode, where you basically try to think out your relationship to a 100% outcome. Covering up your inaction with your urge to 'communicate', it's an overload of communication except there's very little 'exchange' of anything, which is the fundamental nuts and bolts of communication. You've been struck down with Verbal Diarrhoea.

Symptoms

Long relationships that rarely progress to any major commitment.

Many 'defining the relationship talks' that lack any real intent.

You do the bulk of the talking.

Oversharing to prompt him to open up.

Forceful conversationalist on dates or over justify yourself.

Quick to declare your feelings. Fast Forwarder alert!

A 'prescriber', you have a vision of how things 'should' be.

Often regarded as a deep thinker/worrier.

Like to see all sides of the story, but tend to over empathise.

Regard yourself as a great listener.

Important to ensure that you get your point across and that they understand *exactly* where you're coming from.

Powerpoint presentations and printable guides to explain issues.

Confused between what you said and what you were thinking.

Always on the verge of 'The Next Big Discussion'.

Obsessed with things being 'right' or trying to be right.

Friends and family aren't concerned when you say it's over or that 'Things are definitely changing this time.'

Likely witnessed the failure of your parents' relationship and, as you fear replicating their mistakes, you're extremely cautious to the point of being obstructive.

Feel like you're not being listened to, but *you're* not listening to you.

Talking and thinking too much works because you fear committing to the outcome of the discussion and the possible repercussions, but still feel proactive. You then spend time ruminating to find reasons to remain invested, to analyse both your actions, to blame him for you not making a decision, then to eventually blame yourself.

The purpose of a **discussion** is to talk with a view to exchanging ideas or making a decision. **Talking** is the act of engaging in speech. **Communication** requires imparting *and* exchanging information. Talking to empty out your thoughts or assert your point is *venting*. Venting isn't positive communication. We communicate far more with what we do or don't do. Talking and thinking out your relationship is **avoidance** of action.

When you look back on a relationship history of copious explaining, discussing, thinking, and arguing, it's easy to feel drained, disillusioned, and even unheard. However, while there's nothing wrong with wanting to communicate, verbalising every feeling, mood, and annoyance, but never doing anything, or saying one thing and doing another, isn't positive, healthy communication and you undermine your credibility.

You're either not talking about the right things, or you're hearing information and deciding you know better.

Hard as this may be to hear, you're staying and complaining, and Women Who Talk and Think Too Much syndrome arises out of a position of believing that by being there and 'loving' them and talking and thinking to infinity and beyond, plus 'suffering', that your job is done. You're overvaluing your contribution, avoiding real action and decisions, and letting yourself off the hook while putting it at his door about why you're unhappy. This is why you may be accused of nagging, because all this talk and thought expenditure isn't going anywhere yet you keep doing it anyway, refuse to accept and work with what you have, or accept and leave.

WATCH OUT FOR...

Mother's Boy There's nothing wrong with a man who loves his mother, but issues arise when he remains emotionally immature, takes little or no responsibility, and is still living with her in his 30s, 40s and beyond because it's convenient for him and allows him to squirrel away his cash/get his washing done/dinners on tap, etc., and avoid *real* commitment because of problems he claims his mother has. Or because he feels like it. Even if he moves in, or you get married, it's either like there are three of you in the relationship, or he expects you to pick up where she left off. He can often seem like he genuinely thinks the sun shines out of his arse because she's made him out to be The Messiah or cleaned up all of his messes. Don't be surprised if he has a harem clucking around him, or a woman his mother would have preferred him to be with hovering somewhere.

The Coaster Mr *We're [I'm] fine as we are*, he likes the stability and you may have been together since your teens or twenties. If he could pull off an entire '5 relationship', he would. While he may love you, he's not really stretching himself and he's passing time and coasting. He's 'topped out' and may even be quietly rolling things back. Treating you like an old pair of slippers, he takes you for granted. When you feel the disconnect and try to progress things or clarify his feelings, he Future Fakes, then backtracks, or just shuts down. Ambivalent and wanting the best of both worlds, he's afraid that if he lets you go he may regret it. He's the type that will agree to have a baby, let you think you're going to get married, and then tell you that you're not.

The Hollowman Nothing much to give full stop, he squats in your life refusing to leave completely but never actually steps up. Often fulfilling a few roles, including Mother's Boy and Bad Penny, together or not, there's not much happening, but when you tell him to shag off, he comes at you. He doesn't do grand promises; he just stumbles around with feeble non-explanations. When you tell him that it's obvious that he doesn't love you and he doesn't want a relationship, he *insists* that you have it wrong, but still doesn't explain. Likely to be a workaholic or working three jobs, don't be surprised if you don't get much sex. You may think he's cheating. You'll end up believing you're undesirable or doing something wrong – he's got serious issues and just needs the semblance of a relationship to fluff his ego. Be careful –this one can drag out for years if you keep trying to change or 'understand' him.

The Loner He has urges for the fringe benefits of a relationship, but all without letting you in or changing his life in any way. Initially, he may blow hot, so you won't see his single-minded ways. He may Fast Forward, with you in turn agreeing to move in, travel, etc. Then it's the cold shoulder and you're accused of 'crowding' him. He may give more affection to an ant going across the patio than you and you'll feel excluded. He backs away the more you try plus he may withdraw doing anything he knows you like.

The Caller A mix of the Hollowman, the Loner, the Bad Penny and sometimes even the Cheater, he's a single-minded, die-hard bachelor. Like a permanent date/booty call – you're basically waiting to get The Call advising that you can hang out/hook up, that he's coming into town, etc. When you tried to 'upgrade' the 'relationship', he'll have made clear that he doesn't do ties. In response to you revisiting the subject, he's learned to withdraw, firmly remind you, or even preempt conflict by picking fights and bailing. Beware – he may have several women on the go and is likely a heavy texter.

Mr Incompatible Timebomb Likely to Fast Forward, he then drops the bomb – because you're the 'wrong' colour, religion, your mother was an alcoholic, you're 50 and not a virgin or whatever, he says, he can't commit, etc. Yet he's still there, often keeping you a secret. This doesn't explain what he's doing with you – living incongruently with the values he claims, often rebelling against parents, religion, etc., and essentially implying that his lack of commitment is beyond his control or down to a flaw that you can't control. Basically declaring you incompatible, it also seems that his attraction is so great he can't resist you and/or he's implying that if you do 'enough', that he might 'waive' his rules. Don't be surprised if he springs an engagement to a different woman on you, or even a secret wife and child.

BOOBY TRAPS

Flogging equals working at your relationship. Many of us have been raised to believe that 'love' is sticking through thick and thin... trying to love them into changing. There's a cynicism that everyone eventually ends up miserable and that 'nobody is perfect'. While the latter's true, plenty of people navigate the rough and the smooth and ultimately have mutually fulfilling relationships. It's not about forcing yourself to be happy with things that leave you hungry and hurt in the relationship.

Trying to recoup your 'investment'. You reason, *"Right, I've put in Y weeks/ months/years, so I've come too far to turn back. It would be a waste!"* We all have to invest some time and energy into our relationships and they're not all going to work out. This doesn't mean that you're a 'failure' or that it's a 'waste', but it does mean that, sometimes, even with time and effort behind you, it's not going to work. The more you focus on the wrong things or denying why it's not working, the more distorted your investment becomes.

Clutching your 'title'. You reason that whatever issues he does have, it's not as bad as it could be in the big bad world without a title. Like OWs, you don't truly recognise what commitment involves and you overvalue your title, which also acts like the deed to your 'property'. It may seem like the title is indicative of what he really wants, but it's how his intentions translate into his actions that tell you the full story. It takes more than words and labelling – that's why you're still hungry in your relationship.

Fear of making mistakes. Flogging feels like less of a mistake than admitting that it's not worked out. It may remind you too much of your parents, or feel reflective of your worth, but, whatever it is, admitting that you've got 'this' or 'him' wrong terrifies you, especially because you've stuck around for so long. Admitting that 'this one' isn't going to work either will sting, if you have unresolved hurt from prior relationships. You may even hope he does something so awful, it makes the decision for you, or you pray someone will sweep you and your problems away.

Stand by your broken man. Many women have been raised to do this for an eventual 'reward' but it doesn't take a rocket scientist to see that this just doesn't work. While you get to avoid your fear of being single, staying means you're miserable and lonely in your relationship. Being loyal is a wonderful quality, but it isn't rewarded when you're undervalued. You're both loyal to one another for the wrong reasons, such as being afraid of having to be responsible for yourselves, start over, and perhaps discover that the problem is not all the other person. You're rowing a boat with one oar.

Afraid of leaving. Between thinking that his behaviour is down to some error on your part, fearing that you haven't given it your all, fearing not having the purpose of fighting for the relationship and being left with yourself for company, and fear that if you do leave, you'll have to fix another man, or that, even worse, your current man will be a better man in a better relationship elsewhere, there's a lot of negative reasons to stay. But if you're going to stay, make it a positive decision. Remaining because you're afraid of leaving is like imprisoning yourself in a relationship that you know isn't working.

TIPS FOR KICKING THE FLOGGER HABIT

Only have discussions if you're prepared to follow through with action. This reduces flogging dramatically as the onus is on you to act.

It *is* difficult to 'just walk away" but, as the Flogger, you wouldn't be 'just' walking away as you've already been flogging that donkey till it collapses for far too long.

Stop taking him back and believing his promises. You're too receptive and hopeful and, the trouble is, he's pulling the same con numerous times. Has he said he's changed before? The more times he's said so (3+), the least likely this is.

Convincing isn't attractive. Nuff said.

Commitment conversations should be open, honest, and avoid solely originating from negative situations. This reduces negative association, but also kills the flogging habit.

Only have a 'schedule' if you're going to stick to and communicate it. There's no point saying, "I want a ring within 18 months," if you're still going to be hunting it down years later.

When you quit Mr Unavailables, you'll discover that healthy, mutual relationships do grow organically and don't require flogging. They're co-piloted with a joint agenda but if you keep being the Flogger, you'll never know this.

Flogging is akin to *guilting*. "We've been together for X years"; "I gave up everything for you"; "I'd have left if you'd been straight with me"; etc. You don't want a relationship out of guilt.

If you expect big ticket commitment items like moving in, marriage or babies, in under a year, communicate them (not demand, argue, etc.) to him. If you have and he's not working with you on a compromise and joint agenda, don't flog him for what you think you're owed for the next gazillion years; get out.

If he doesn't want the same things, listen to him and don't have a hidden agenda of making him change his mind. If you stay, he'll assume *you've* changed your mind.

With kids you have to be conscientious in your decision, but that shouldn't stop you from making a decision.

Expectations must be both relationship and partner appropriate. It's not enough to declare your time, energy, shared commitments, etc., as being a valid source of your expectations because if he's not capable, you can't expect it.

If he's not meeting your expectations, adjust them and any assumptions you've made about him and decide how that affects the relationship you want. Floggers are often guilty of ignoring the truth in favour of believing what he could be if he realised his potential.

You know that bailiff who keeps coming around looking for the money they're owed and being told the person's not in, or that they don't have the money, or they can give a little now and to come back later? This is what a Flogger is like. You deserve better.

MISS INDEPENDENT, MISS SELF-SUFFICIENT

When I graduated in the summer of 2003, following my broken engagement, I decided in the bravado that hides a lot of secret hurt, that I was an independent career woman living it up in London who didn't need a man. It was with this in mind, that I justified the affair. "It's just a bit of fun!" I smiled and embraced my 'independence' and 'freedom'. That lasted about 3-4 months by which time I was demanding commitment. What I realised, in retrospect, was that by being involved in a faux 'relationship', I had far more freedom and independence than I bargained for and I hated it.

It's become patently obvious that not all women want to settle down, many of us like sex and it doesn't have to be in a relationship, and, shiver me timbers, we can even hold down careers, businesses, buy homes, take solo holidays, not want children, solo parent, and take care of ourselves. This is our *right*, but our choices are not always positive.

What we don't often feel comfortable admitting is that we're either scared shitless and distrusting, or that we have such distorted ideas about what having it 'all' means and what a man who ticks our boxes should be like, that our options get closed off to a limited, conflicted man – yup, you guessed it – Mr Unavailable.

Characterised by short dalliances, long spells of singledom or very ambiguous 'arrangements' that can run into double-digit years, **Miss Independent/Miss Self-Sufficient** (MIMS) is resolutely single but 'open' to dating. The most 'similar' to Mr Unavailable in habits, you also often overvalue your qualities and characteristics. Although you may initially be the 'driver', you wind up being the 'passenger', which makes you very insecure. Conflicted with trust issues, you secretly hope to be loved and are still in search of that 'feeling'. Often very focused in other areas of your life, you're very stuck on 'type'. **MIMS is also a *floating* role** – when you do end up in a 'relationship', it tends to be as the Other Woman or The Buffer, and you share similarities with The Renovator.

When you do venture into dating, you often unconsciously choose the Mr Unavailable most likely to screw you over quickly, **The Chaser**. A short-term, reactive master of Fast Forwarding and Future Faking, he's at the top of the tree for ADD. Fuelled by desire, feeling out of control, the newness and the chase, he literally runs out of steam because he's all about the sprint, not the marathon. When the honeymoon period wears off (could be hours to a few months), he'll tend to bail. Turned on by the challenge of the apparently detached MIMS, if you exhibit any of his traits or his moves, or make the 'mistake' of proclaiming your independence or lack of interest, he'll focus on 'unseating' you. Often regarded as a 'playa' and pretty shameless, he's a heavy user of the Reset Button, which means that he keeps overestimating his interest and capacity.

In the first edition of this book, MIMS was described as a 'secondary Fallback Girl' as it was a precursor to other roles. However, the more I corresponded with women who haven't been on a date or had sex for ten years, or who've never had a relationship despite being in their 30s, 40s, 50s and beyond, or can only make it to 89 days or 3 dates or whenever the date limit is, the more I realised that actually, there's a hell of a lot of permanent MIMS out there.

Your friends probably think you don't give a shit, but they likely don't know just how much ruminating you've done over a Critical Heartbreak Experience, or that one guy who bailed after a few dates, or the guy you didn't fancy until he jerked you around and next thing you were crying in the toilets at work. You have false confidence, which often has false self-esteem in tow.

The Chaser exacerbates your issues by confirming that you're justified in being guarded. Stuck in a short-term time warp and inclined to big you up on a date or Future Fake, he reasons that he's giving you a 'good time' at the time with no thought for the consequences. When he's chasing he feels 'single', when the chase is over he feels committed or fears the imminent possibility of it.

Due to your wariness, you're actually a perfect target for him as you have to be heavily pursued. When you drop your guard, he slams on the brake, which can feel like an incredibly painful rejection. You, like many others, will be left wondering what you 'did'. The truth is that you breathed and when he looked at his involvement, irrespective of anything you may have said, the only direction for something that keeps moving along and has you continuing to sleep with and see the same person over an extended period of time is a relationship, which isn't where he's headed.

TYPICAL MISS INDEPENDENT/MISS SELF-SUFFICIENT

Think independence and a relationship are mutually exclusive.

Sabotage intimacy or when you sense commitment.

Highly likely to become the Other Woman.

Divorcee or been married a few times. Likely cheated on previously.

Very flattered by Fast Forwarding and also guilty of it.

Overvalue certain attributes – looks, intelligence, money, status, etc.

May be cynical and jaded.

Strings of broken engagements.

May never have said, "I love you."

Escaped an abusive relationship and had to rebuild your life.

Afraid of ending up like your mother.

Deadbeat father so fear relying on men and/or Daddy Hunting.

Many friends – can be clusters of Fallback Girls or 'settled' friends.

May spend a lot of time on dating sites.

Secretly cry a lot.

High achiever/workaholic. Financially independent.

Likely to overvalue sex or hate having casual sex.

Secretly yearn to be a mother or housewife.

Want it 'all', but don't know how.

Get caught up in fantasy relationships, especially with online guys.

Secretly never got over one guy.

TYPICAL CHASER

Intensity mixed with charm, hence prolific and purposeful use of Fast Forwarding and Future Faking.

Cool, calm, confident, and possibly cocky.

Often propping up the bar.

Tends to go from super hot to super cold – no in-between.

Woos women into competing to snare him.

Thinks the 'right' woman will magically curtail his chasing ways.

Multiple dater, although he may not admit it.

May be known as the office tramp.

Loves dating sites for attention hits.

May send penis shots or ask you for phone/Skype sex very quickly.

Sexually forward very quickly, often blaming your sexiness.

Mirrorer: whatever you like and love, he does too. For now.

Likely has Bad Penny ways and is pestering an ex periodically, too.

In previous relationships, he's likely to have cheated, or asked for 'breaks' or disappeared.

Mother's Boy – under the misguided impression he's very special.

Been engaged several times.

Workaholic.

Known as the neighbourhood 'playa'.

Secret Wounded who bails before you find out the 'real' him.

THE MIMS

The Guard Highly defensive, you're protecting your walls from being 'breached' and experiencing attraction can make you more aloof or even difficult. Waiting for the 'catch', you're very distrusting. With a tendency to be brash about your intelligence, accomplishments, or how you don't need anyone, you can be exacting and quite opinionated, which creates conflict. When this happens, you'll berate yourself, but also use the experience as a justification for why you're better off alone. Sometimes you sabotage to relieve the 'tension' and create an exit, as you fear your 'flaws' will be discovered or the other person will disappoint. If your defences are breached (more likely if you attempt online dating), the fallout may cause you to shut down and vow off sex and relationships.

Miss Keeping It Casual While the Yo-Yo Girl version keeps it casual to get over someone, you avoid attachments claiming a lack of time or interest in one. You appear to want the fringe benefits without commitment but are actually too scared to risk from the outset. While you may not voice that your feelings have changed, it's often unconsciously reflected in your behaviour, plus you experience anxiety about what's going on in his head while pretending you don't care. If he reminds you that it's 'casual', feeling upset will catch you off guard, plus you may end up erupting if he calls things off or claims he's in love with someone else. Afterwards, you'll berate yourself and be convinced you scared him off, though he was never going to stay.

The Shagger Claiming to be embracing your sexuality, sex with strangers on and offline and getting frisky quickly with dates is on the agenda. You often initiate casual arrangements, but when you start having 'relationship needs', or believing he's The One, you'll both be caught off guard. Guilty of Fast Forwarding, once the 'high' wears off you're on a 'downer'. Using faux confidence to control situations by appearing to be the 'driver' and liking how you feel during sex and the chase, your insecurities and his behaviour eventually unseat you. When you're treated casually or even rudely, you take it hard. You believe sex is what you have to 'hold' men and/or that sex *is* intimacy. Very likely to swear off dating and sex, if you don't pull yourself together, you become The Guard or find yourself getting treatment for sex addiction.

The Collector Your friends and family likely believe you're seriously searching for 'The One'. However, between your short attention span, spreading yourself thinly, and your overthinking ways, you're actually just collecting attention. You love the newness, feeling desirable, and being kept busy but you're not actually genuinely looking to commit. It seems like fun and a means of trying people out, but, in truth, you *need* the validation. By keeping up a steady stream of attention, it's a distraction from the bigger issues you're avoiding. When he acts up, this triggers your interest and next thing you're angling for a relationship you didn't know you wanted. Like him, you've always got 'one in the hand' – someone that you're not even *that* interested in that you can fall back on for a rainy day attention fix.

The Lobbyist The MIMS version of The Lobbyist has some serious resilience, which is needed when you're prepared to cling on to an ambiguous arrangement for years, or even beyond a decade. Likely meeting after a bad breakup and/or an extended period of not dating, you're under the misguided impression that you have a lot in common and that, should he ever see fit to commit, it's you he owes a relationship to. Having played it cool for a long time, you've taken to haranguing him periodically (or even ending it) about being with you 'properly', even though he's repeatedly made it clear that he doesn't want to. Likely reasoning that this must be 'all you want', he enables you to remain in your 'comfort' zone.

The Stealth Bomber All Fallback Girls consistently undermine their own relationship efforts, but you're an out-and-out saboteur. Dangerously similar to Mr Unavailable, your internal panic alarm is triggered and it consumes you until you 'relieve' the feeling by, for instance, disappearing or being incredibly difficult, or you'll cheat or flirt with others openly. You can't cope with the possibility of commitment and being liked, and when you think that you've created disdain and that they may even see your 'flaws', you almost feel relieved. When you've calmed down, the desire often returns. If you ever make it into a relationship, you'll enjoy it for a while but feel overwhelmed by their feelings and hopes for you and even lose respect for them. Until you address your feelings of low self-worth, you'll be crashing out of relationships.

The Runner By all accounts, you should have been married 20 times but you've always found a reason, no matter how flimsy, to end your engagements or stop a move. While you may display your jittery side in the run up to the exit, you may actually appear to display no outward signs, or you 'hint'. Very much a version of the Stealth Bomber, you likely don't know what you're running from, although you're often outwardly optimistic. Guilty of pressing the Reset Button, you abandon and disappoint first out of fear of being abandoned and rejected, and it's highly likely to do with your father.

ACHILLES HEEL: TOXIC TYPE

One of the most hotly debated subjects by women who haven't met the 'right' man yet is 'type'. You use your idea of what's 'right' for you to justify why you continue the insanity of repeatedly going with the same guy, different package and expecting a different result, or to justify why you won't try something different.

When your 'type' gets in the way of a mutually fulfilling relationship, it's a **_Toxic_ Type**. While you may claim many qualities, characteristics, etc., for your 'type', you're likely blinded by one or a few 'criteria' that you overvalue to the detriment of recognising other far less attractive and incompatible behaviours. When you experience a 'match', you assume that a relationship and the appropriate behaviours will fall into place. Often your type is either in conflict with what you want or is based on criteria that aren't relevant for a successful relationship. Whatever your type, if you've never had a successful, healthy relationship _with_ it, it's not because you're a special case and your 'type' is tricky to find amongst 6.8 billion people, but because your type isn't compatible for an _available_ relationship.

Symptoms

Feels so 'right' when it's so wrong.

Meet a 'match' and start planning your life together.

Insisting that you 'have so much in common' even though you don't.

Claim connections from 'random shit': "We're both only children."

Intoxicated by superficial qualities and characteristics.

Blame an inability to have success with your type on being 'too intelligent', 'too successful', 'not the right look', etc.

Overuse of words such as 'chemistry', 'passion', and 'soulmate'.

Betting On Potential, plus projecting your feelings.

Deal in extremes. If someone says, "It's not just about the intelligence /money/ looks/weight," you shoot back with, "So I should be with a stupid/poor/ugly/fat person?"

Claim to be helpless to who you're attracted to.

Insist you couldn't be happy with a non-type and that you've 'tried'.

Have dated lookalikes of your ex, or even your father.

Openly like 'Bad Boys' but feel angry when they treat you badly.

Feel attracted once you sense rejection or have been rejected.

Thrive on the thrill of the chase and being pursued.

Some of us prefer blondes, others are suckers for dark hair and a bad boy exterior, some have a penchant for black guys, others like a man with a big dick and not much in the way of conversational skills, and many love the poetic, creative types. It's very easy to get into the nitty gritties, but, if you're reading this book, your type is *unavailable*. So far, I've never heard someone say, "My type is nice guys." You may think you don't have a type; if you have a *pattern*, you have a *type*.

If you don't understand the origins of your 'type', you're blindly chasing a conflicted, unrealistic set of pipe dreams. While you may recognise The Chaser for what he is, it's some of the apparent shared interests, common characteristics such as high work ethic, driven, self-starter, confidence or *false* confidence, and a recognition of his own apparent need for independence, that can make him so attractive to you.

All type does is limit your options. The more criteria you have, the less likely you are to be *in* a relationship. Being hypercritical is a defence mechanism that caters to your commitment-resistant tendencies. Relying on type helps you avoid being a responsible, committed adult within a mutual relationship where you stretch yourself out of your comfort zone.

Ultimately, you can be attracted to people for any reason you like but you still need to ensure that, whatever you believe you 'need', they're also available. If being with your type hasn't worked, it's time to recognise that these things you value so much are not the reasons that hold a relationship together and that there are other more pertinent characteristics, qualities, and behaviours that you're not recognising the importance of.

WATCH OUT FOR...

The Shagger While he may not disclose his activities, he's had more arse than a toilet seat. Brilliant at turning on the charm, you'll feel like the centre of his universe... until he pulls out. Literally. It's highly likely that you won't hear from him again, or you may be charmed into a 'casual arrangement', or he may be The Phantom version of The Shagger and keep pulling the same con where he reappears, Fast Forwards, shags, and then leaves. He gets off on having the 'power' to charm people into bed, and has no affinity with intimacy. Like the person who enjoys how they feel on a drink or drug buzz, he enjoys the chase and the 'high' but then has to chase a new 'fix' to help avoid his issues. A major Fast Forwarder, his cycle can last for as little as a few hours. Don't be surprised if he ends up being treated for sex addiction or leaves you with a STD.

The Colleague One of the easiest ways to pull women is to work with them. The shared connection of your careers, the possible social dynamic, and the natural element of secrecy that tends to exist, make the workplace the perfect environment to be unavailable under the guise of keeping what happened between you undercover for the sake of your professionalism. He may have a reputation for working his way through most new arrivals, be in a position of power, or just very bloody charming. The less known his activities are, the easier it is for him to shag his way around but don't be surprised if he's brazen enough to appeal to the competitive nature of women.

The Dreamer Floating along with his moving goalposts and vision of perfection, he's like a Fallback Girl in search of a feeling. Deep down he knows he's not likely to feel it, which means he can dream away, because it's not his fault that he hasn't met the 'right' woman or been in the 'right' circumstances. A prime Future Faker, he overestimates his capacity and interest and once the chase is over, suddenly there are more holes than a pair of fishnet stockings in the relationship. Guilty of entrapment, he's the type who'll suggest sex on the early dates and then cross you off, reasoning that the 'right' woman would turn him down. When even he can't escape his own Groundhog Day, don't be surprised if he knee-jerks into 'settling' with some unsuspecting woman who'll have to bear the brunt of his exacting ways. Also don't be surprised if he returns, claiming how he 'dreams' about how things would be so much better with you.

BOOBY TRAPS

Conflict and confusion. It's a tricky time when you believe stuff like, *"There are no good men to date"*, *"I don't want to be alone"*, *"I want to wake up to someone I love"*, *"I'm afraid of losing myself"*, and *"I don't want to depend on anyone"*, especially if you believe some or all of these at the *same time* while also believing that you're "not good enough". And, yet, you'll often still date! This conflict makes you closed, not open, plus you still end up wanting Mr Unavailable to be available and want a relationship with you, even when you don't know what you want and are unavailable yourself. I'd be confused, too!

Dating for the wrong reasons. If you date because you think you 'should', out of fear, to 'pass time', avoid loneliness, etc., you, like many, are dating for dysfunctional reasons. You may even be treating dating like a competitive sport or collecting attention, which can make you picky, numb, or even blasé. All of this activity becomes a catch-all justification for believing that you've worked very hard at meeting someone, but you've just been 'unlucky'. Until you address your beliefs, having a relationship for the right reasons will elude you.

Want to be casual, don't like the territory it comes with. The sheer volume of emails I get from MIMS hurt or frustrated after they were 'just' looking for companionship and sex is scary. While it's very possible that someone could be available *and* a great lay and companion, casual, ambiguous relationships are the domain of the unavailable. In truth, you often opt for a casual relationship because it's like 'backdoor entry' (excuse the pun) into upgrading to a proper relationship without having to risk from the outset. However, you can't get what you want out of the relationship and control it on your terms while avoiding vulnerability *and* have him behave like he's in a relationship – Mr Unavailable doesn't play that way.

Clustering with your friends. Many women are reaping the emotional and social benefits of friendship and fostering strong female networks. However, you may further decide there's no 'need' for a relationship or may become reliant on these friends for validation. In unhealthy situations, they may sabotage your new relationships with 'advice' or negativity, plus you may fear losing them if you commit. Sometimes, with your shared dating woes, you're like the blind leading the blind and friction can arise if you change and they don't. Be careful of replicating your self-esteem habits in your friendships.

Only 'needy' girls get upset and ask for stuff. Scared of being needed or behaving like someone who 'needs' others, 'depending' is seen as a weakness, so you tend to refuse to ask for help, deny and rationalise your needs, and withhold affection from yourself. This makes you ripe for Mr Unavailable's crumbs. It's easy to be 'self-sufficient' when you deny your emotional needs but it's just 'existing' which is a half-life. Stop looking down on others and thinking they're weak. Sometimes they are, but often they're not. It's not a crime to cry, to have 'feelings', to make mistakes, to trust, to ask for help, and to even ask questions. Let your own feelings in. You may not have asked for much but, whether you admit it or not, you *have* been upset – you've just been crying on the inside. It'll never stop hurting if you keep punishing yourself and denying your needs.

That's a negatory on independence. Women's rights weren't designed to create commitment-resistant women who use their 'independence' to avoid intimacy and relationships. You're trying to have it 'all', without risking yourself. Sound familiar? You've lost sight of your values and desires and may eventually question whether you could have had independence, self-sufficiency, *and* the relationship, and may be making choices that actually have nothing to do with independence and everything to do with fear. Remember, risk in a mutual relationship is *mutual* so it's not actually as risky a prospect as you fear. You can be you *and* have a relationship, or if you're going to be single, make it a positive choice.

TIPS FOR KICKING THE MIMS HABIT

Create your life on your terms and ensure that you're living the life that you want to lead. Many MIMS are being the person who they think 'everyone' expects them to be. You may be successful or liked but if you don't like you *or* your life, it's pointless.

While I don't doubt the importance of sexual chemistry, if you don't have *other* sources of chemistry, you don't have actual intimacy – you just have sex. That said, without sexual chemistry it may feel like a friendship. On the other hand, sexual chemistry without much else is 'casual' territory. When you're both *available* it's easier to find chemistry across all areas, including shared values.

It's not weakness when you need someone. But don't get that confused; at times, you'll need people, and you'll need the man you love, and, at times, people will need you.

Don't Fast Forward to test people to see if they're worthy by having them meet your 'demands'. Stop relying on heavy pursuit. All this does is offer a red rag to The Chaser bull.

When you do meet someone, keep your life *balanced* with friends, hobbies, work, etc., but *also* ensure you make room for the relationship.

Be careful of being the over-idealistic perfectionist. Obviously flush for unhealthy relationship behaviour, but do be careful of ditching for superficial reasons or in haste.

Don't bail when things aren't going your way or you're experiencing conflict. It can't be all on your terms – mutual is the only way.

Be careful of women who suffer with Frienvy – when they can't be happy for you and undermine you. Surround yourself with people who make you feel good about yourself and avoid those who don't have your best interests at heart.

If you're going to be part of a couple and have a healthy relationship, you must trust, which means you're going to have to be vulnerable. If the thought of letting a man into your life scares you, start by letting others in and asking for help.

You can be in a relationship without being co-dependent, which is unhealthy dependency. Healthy, mutual relationships require two individual entities with their own sense of self that co-pilot the relationship together. Neither of you are losing anything.

Mutual means *interdependent*. When it's imbalanced and not mutual, *that's* where dependency issues arise.

You're never truly independent and self-sufficient without self-love and self-esteem. Provide those and however you choose to live will be very much a positive choice.

Address how you feel about you and any fears *before* you date again. Don't knee-jerk into a new relationship, or settle out of loneliness, or feel like you 'should' be dating.

Having a 'toxic type' doesn't mean that you should wallow in acceptance and leave yourself at the mercy of chance and an inherent pattern – it's a wake-up call.

Be open to different types of guys. Take a chance and talk to the guy that you normally wouldn't pay much attention to. You may just surprise yourself and find happiness with someone who you wouldn't have dreamt of being with.

Never make a lifestyle out of fear, as it's a pretty lonely and precarious existence. If you know you have that much fear, *deal* with it as opposed to being *ruled* by it.

Recognise that if you persist in trying to find someone who will allow you to never have to relinquish your 'independence' and have to be vulnerable, your *only* option is Mr Unavailable. He's only too happy to ensure that you never want, need, or expect more than he's prepared to give while having at least a foot out the door.

From now on, your 'type' is available. Nuff said.

MOVING FORWARD

The question everyone asks once they discover who and what they've been involved with is, *"So, Natalie, where do I find an available guy?"* People ask *literally* where to find them, as if they all cluster in certain places, but the key to being attracted to and *recognising* an available partner is being available yourself. I can't emphasise this enough; when you're attracted to unavailable people and stick around and attempt to change and win them, even busting your own boundaries, you need to address your *own* unavailability.

You're not going to read this book today, then *Shazam!*, Mr Available falls out of the sky tomorrow and you live happily ever after. You need to do some work and make a conscious, concerted effort to break patterns of behaviour and thinking that have propelled you into your relationships in the first place and created your own unavailability.

Fear not though, knowledge combined with consistent action is more than half the battle. Scary a prospect as it may be, you already know what results from continuing your pattern, plus you know that you're not alone. Whether you've arrived at this juncture after one unavailable relationship or many, it's imperative that you face your own emotional unavailability if you genuinely do want to find love and a relationship.

BEING AVAILABLE MEANS...

Desire, willingness, and actual need to feel your emotions.

Emotionally engaging consistently, not just in short bursts.

Having fears, but addressing and not living by them. Being emotionally honest and allowing yourself to feel means taking mini, medium, and, sometimes, big risks.

Not relying on newness, drama, or the prospect of losing the relationship to feel desire.

Removing the limitations on yourself and actively working to challenge unhealthy beliefs.

Embracing true intimacy and accepting that love and a relationship requires vulnerability.

Accepting what results from emotionally engaging with others instead of sabotaging. No creating drama, disappearing, sprinting from the scene of the relationship, and putting up walls.

Being yourself in relationships because it would feel too damn awkward for you to be anything else.

Loving yourself and avoiding negative self-talk blame and shame, while building compassion and understanding.

A low bullshit diet. No excuses because you don't lie to yourself.

Removing your walls and opening up.

Never apologising for having standards and boundaries.

No desperation.

Walking **instead of** *hanging around* **waiting for him to become available.**

It's also safe to say that even if Mr Available bit you in the bum tomorrow, until you feel better about you and relationships, you won't appreciate him. Be available, to attract available. Find you first because you have to be willing to do everything it takes to be available, not because it 'gets you the guy', but because you'll be a happier person who can recognise a healthy relationship.

If you're still afraid of being vulnerable, afraid of trusting, afraid the last chance saloon has closed down, afraid you're destined to be alone, afraid of trying again, afraid of making a mistake, afraid of admitting you were wrong, of seeing the truth, of making changes, of being uncomfortable, of stretching yourself, of bucking your own trend, you're not ready to be emotionally available in a relationship... yet. But you will be, if you keep being honest with yourself, are willing to be patient, face your fears both acknowledged and secretive, and address your beliefs.

Be patient and compassionate with yourself. Considering how overly patient and compassionate you've been with others, it's time you directed some of that at you. If you feel like time is running out, start doing whatever it takes to be available and get uncomfortable *fast*. If you're not uncomfortable, you're not changing enough.

All those times when you banked on someone else to fill your voids and chase away your fears? Yeah... you remember where that got you. Don't take shortcuts through others or expect that life should throw you an available man because you feel like you've cut your teeth on enough Mr Unavailables. There's no magic dating site, bar, or club, although staying at home or doing the same stuff day in day out won't help your cause either. You can't avoid what you need to do and be. It starts with you.

THE QUICK GUIDE TO KICKING THE MR UNAVAILABLE HABIT

Find and Break Your Pattern. Whatever your pattern is, home in on it, define it and then make the conscious decision to kick it. The biggest help to defining your pattern is sitting down with a paper and pen and writing down the characteristics of your partner. You're bound to find a consistent thread in your relationships that's holding you back. If you don't crack it, you can't define it. Take the time to do it! Use the relationship crime scene investigation exercise later in this chapter.

Put Yourself on Lockdown. Slow down with getting sexually intimate especially if you struggle with the emotional consequences of it.

Normal Waiting Time	New Waiting Time
Up to 1 week	3 weeks minimum

2 weeks	4 weeks minimum
3 weeks	5-6 weeks minimum
4 weeks	6-8 weeks minimum

Remember: Don't be involved in anything casual (booty call, ambiguous, Friends With Benefits, etc.,) for more than three occasions or a month – whichever happens first. Also remember that you won't die without sex and if you're truly serious about getting into a relationship, I'd put your vagina and libido on the back-burner.

Do have the DTR (Defining the relationship) talk. Don't be an eager beaver and do it too quickly, but by the 3-6 month mark, know where you are. Most of us are too long in the tooth and have more feeling than a stone, to be able to put up with being casual for longer than 6 months. Unless you both say you're exclusive and committed, you're not. In a healthy relationship, this happens organically. DTR talks are far more prevalent in ambiguous relationships, but I'd rather you said something at this stage than stayed silent and woke up in Yet Another Bad Relationship.

Spell out your needs. No need to be a prima donna, but you haven't got time to play guessing games. If he's calling you once a week, tell him it's not acceptable. If he's not making the appropriate effort for the relationship tell him and be straight up, not wishy-washy. Which brings me nicely to...

Be substance focused. The problem with being involved with Mr Unavailables is that it's indicative of the fact that you're overlooking substance to invest in other qualities that don't really hold up in the cold light of day. What you're focused on tends to add nothing to the relationship – it doesn't benefit you. Make sure you're action focused, because it's a lot easier to see the wood for the trees when you're not blinded by your libido or very big illusions.

One strike and you're out. Until you really have shaken the habit, stick to one strike and you're out. When he does something that clearly shows that he's a Mr Unavailable, or is just downright wrong, walk away. Remember that, eventually, most of the adult population ends up in a relationship, so walking away is not the end of life as you know it. The problem with women who love Mr Unavailables is that we don't know when to walk away. He's not the last chance saloon!

Easy on the drugs and alcohol. Severely impacting your judgement of a situation or person, if these have tended to be at the centre of your previous liaisons, make sure that you address this because they'll derail you.

Stop worrying about him, worry about you. The reality is that if he was thinking about you, not only would you not be reading this, but you also wouldn't be in a relationship with him. Be selfish and put you first. If you don't, you'll **always** be on the back foot and always be unhappy. If we don't love ourselves, how the hell do we expect to welcome love, and good love at that, into our lives? And remember, you can't blame him for the fact that you've burned up your energy being focused on him; you have to be responsible for yourself.

Listen to your gut. The problem is that you fail to listen to your gut and allow the brain to rationalise crap behaviour from a partner and justify your choices. If you don't listen to your gut, you're ignoring the core of yourself.

Do new things. Break old habits and do new things. If there are habits that have contributed to your dubious relationships, stop doing them and don't fall off the wagon. If you do fall off the wagon, get back on it – don't succumb to your own bad choices.

Change your social locations. If you always go to the same places, change the routine, as you'll tend to see the same people in the same places. New people, like a new partner, could be in a new place!

Separate code red and amber behaviour from inconsequential things that don't warrant a breakup or an argument. If you have a lot of breakups, I'd examine whether you've broken it off for trivial reasons and why.

Say goodbye. If it's not working, get out and save yourself the agony of dragging it out any further. Saying goodbye leaves you open to saying hello to someone else.

If you're unhappy with the state of your love life and you have a written or mental list of the qualities and characteristics of your ideal man, ditch it and open yourself up to new possibilities. It doesn't mean that you lose your judgment skills, but it will protect you from being rigid about things that are surplus to requirements. I tend to find that people who have 'lists' often overlook important stuff because they're too busy looking at what is either superficial or 'interests' that don't actually mean anything positive to the relationship.

Let yourself be set up. What's the worst that can happen? You might just fall in love! But don't get set up by another Fallback Girl… A big piece of advice I can give you about setups is, that while a reference is good, listen to your own gut and don't buy into the hype because matchmakers can be a bit like estate agents/realtors – they call it bijou when it's actually tiny, your friends call him shy when he's actually rude, difficult, and superior.

Acknowledge that you're in good relationship when you finally get in one. Don't persecute the guy because you've had a dubious relationship history. Let him know that you do love and appreciate him and that you see him as him, not as 'all the other guys'.

Get happy. If your self-esteem is low, the addition of a guy will only be a temporary fix. You owe it to yourself to have good self-esteem, so that you attract positive relationships and interactions into your life, otherwise it's difficult to operate from a positive place.

If you're not being yourself, start now. You don't want to wake up one day and discover that, not only do you not know who you are, but that you don't like yourself either. If you have to compromise the fundamental you in order to have a love life, something is very wrong.

BE YOUR BEST YOU

While the drama stems from your fears, much of it centres around having his attention focused on you and getting him to do what you want.

When I was the Other Woman, I obsessed about getting him to be with me full time, while also wrestling with the fact that I knew he wouldn't. When I stopped fighting this, I was finally able to focus on loving me and being true to myself.

Of course he still persisted; the ones who tell the most lies and can't hack being out of control always do. He'd tell me I was amazing, how much he loved me and blah blah blah. Of course he was still with her and I realised that his actions were about *his* drama seeking.

You could spend a lot of time wondering whether he'll call, whether it was all your fault, or what he's doing with someone else but, eventually, you need to get back to you.

GOOD THINGS DON'T FEEL BAD

One of the things that's significantly different in me now from before is that I'm very aware of how I feel about everything – not just men, but people with whom I come into contact, how I react to stress, and how I generally feel about myself. Looking back, I think everything must have been very cluttered, cloudy, and fuzzy back then, but, as a result of shaking off baggage and negative feelings about myself, it left me with room to *feel* and to use my gut and common sense to judge my interactions.

The primary thing that I learned after my life seemed to nosedive and I had to pick myself back up again was that **good things don't feel bad.** From the moment that I was feeling bad – negative, uneasy, wary, scared, distrusting, etc., I knew that it was time for me to sit down and have a calm, rational, self-discussion and evaluate the situation.

Feeling bad in itself became its own early warning system.

So now, instead of feeling bad, and then giving into feeling bad, and creating drama through Drama Seeking, and then feeling even worse as a result of it, and then continuing the cycle, using Good Things Don't Feel Bad as your basis, this means that you now have:

- A back away warning.

- A get the hell out and abort the mission warning.

- A signal to evaluate the situation and decide how to proceed.

- A signal to watch that person closer to see if your initial feelings were well placed or misguided, then take action.

It's important that you realise that, while you do feel bad because you're in poor relationships with inappropriate men, you'll still feel bad outside of these relationships if you don't start finding reasons to love you.

LEARN TO TRUST YOU AND YOUR GUT

Drama had a friend in your own Bad Cop or the Voice of Unreason, but the more you start to feel good, the less room 'the bad voice', or the Voice of Unreason, has to enter into your life and when it does, the gut with the Voice of Reason kicks in.

The Voice of Unreason is powered by insecurity. The Voice of Reason is powered by higher self-esteem, intuition, self-awareness, and the ability to judge a situation without lust, libido, or insecurity getting in the way.

The only way that you're going to learn how to trust yourself is to start liking and loving you, and the only way you can start doing that is by withdrawing out of situations that contribute to making you feel bad about you, or serve as a great big glaring reminder that your gut and judgment radar must have been turned off.

I realised that it was better to be alone than to be in a relationship and feel worse. I know people who feel alone in a room full of people and I can reassure you that if you think that the species with a penis and a whole load of baggage on his back is going to make you feel at one with the universe, it's just not gonna happen.

"But I love him!" you may say. You love the drama, the dependence, the emotional rollercoaster, and placing everything on him, rather than having to trust in you, because, if the shit hits the proverbial fan, you can say, *"Well, I loved him unconditionally and he didn't appreciate it and give me what I want."*

Sometimes when our gut is telling us something, we choose not to hear it because the truth is uncomfortable. Some of us actually hear the gut loud and clear but go ahead and do the opposite anyway because it gives us the self-fulfilling prophecy, which is sabotaging your own chances.

This is like the house of cards. You remove one Drama Seeker out of the situation and everything else falls down around it. Likewise, your progress and route to a happier you has a positive knock on effect.

You start liking you... you start loving you... things look different... you feel different... YOUR GUT RESONATES... you move with positivity instead of negativity... you vibrate differently to those around you... you radiate a better you... you draw in better people around you and those who know you and love you feel a positive benefit, and those who know you and take advantage find themselves having to buck up their ideas or get out... even when you get some knocks you realise that YOUR GUT reminds you that, irrespective of what is taking place around you, you love you unconditionally and that makes it easier to overcome difficulties rather than writing yourself off as soon as something bad happens...

Your self-esteem and gut go hand in hand.

You always have the choice to listen to what might be the incy wincy Voice of Reason, your gut, trying to make itself heard over the louder booming voice of insecurity. Listen to your gut and if it's possible that it's asking you to opt out of the familiar into an uncomfortable territory that will yield you better medium, long-term, and even short-term results, listen, hear it, and act upon it. Your gut is your friend; drama is not!

HOW TO BE AVAILABLE

This entire book has been a crash course in unavailable relationships and what happens when there's a lack of self-love. Use what you've learned to open new doors in your life and firmly close others. This is a springboard to better things. Kick-start your move towards being available by addressing some key areas and consistently working at them while increasing your self-awareness.

1. Understand code red and amber behaviour.

2. End unavailable relationships and cut ties.

3. Define and maintain boundaries.

4. Break your pattern.

5. Address your beliefs.

6. Discover your values.

7. Own and use your power instead of being helpless.

8. Use dating as a discovery phase.

9. Ask questions and make decisions.

10. Be accountable and responsible – no absorbing the blame for others and shaming yourself.

11. Get on the Bullshit Diet.

12. Get a life.

All of these actions feed into you treating yourself like a person of value with love, care, trust, and respect *always*.

1. CODE AMBER & RED BEHAVIOUR

To know the line, it's important that you first of all familiarise yourself with code amber and red behaviour: undisputedly unhealthy issues that communicate that you need to stop, look, listen, address, and don't proceed until you're 100%

comfortable (code amber); or that signal that you need to *opt out* (code red). There are two codes because many people think that *all* issues can be solved with a discussion and 'love', but some *can't* and are actually dangerous. You're now going to be a conscious, self-aware person who listens to herself and processes feedback from her relationships. There are some markers that differentiate between the two or even change the status based on context:

If you've previously been involved with similar partners, or their behaviour is similar to a parent or authority figure from your childhood, or you share the same issue, it's *code red*.

If you've not habitually been involved with someone similar, there's no family history with whatever the issue is, plus the person states and can show that they have been dealing with it for at *least* 3-6 months prior to your arrival on the scene, it's *code amber*.

If you've previously been in unhealthy relationships and experience a sensation of familiarity, it's code amber.

If you're acting without self-love, care, trust, or respect during your involvement, or would need to in order to continue, it's *code red*.

	AMBER	RED
Mistreating yourself	Immediately take steps to address this.	If by treating yourself better they rebel/the relationship flounders.
Unavailable	If initially appear available but start to roll back, address immediately.	Persists in not committing, reducing expectations.
Married/attached		OPT OUT
Separated	If very recent.	If long-term.
Current addictions		OPT OUT

In recovery	Must be at least 3-6 months before meeting.	They stop working on recovery or it becomes difficult to recover AND have a relationship.
Not over ex		OPT OUT
Anger and aggression		OPT OUT
Controlling	If unsure & been involved 3 months +.	0-3 months especially if shown within days or weeks.
Playing the victim		OPT OUT
Problems with past/ childhood (not an issue if it's been dealt with)	If currently affects but are aware of issue & are dealing with it via therapy.	Currently affects but not dealing with it AND it affects the relationship.
Dodgy attitude towards sex	If they're into shady stuff.	Different sexual values, coercion, etc.
Irresponsible	Depends on level of discomfort.	Borrowing money quickly, trying to move in, reckless, etc.
Sleeping with others	If it's a casual relationship that you agreed to & expect nothing further.	If emotionally invested/ think you're in a relationship/want more commitment.
Nasty and spiteful		OPT OUT
Primarily communicating by text/email, etc.	If it's early in the relationship 0-3 months.	If they dodge calls & intimate discussions.

Jealousy and possessiveness. It's not 'love'; it's control.

Manipulation, aka Mind Fuckery. Feeling confused? Denying stuff, mind games, coerced into assuming blame or that you're worthless, pressing the Reset Button, name calling, accusing you of what he's doing, embarrassing and humiliating you, insisting he's right, denying *provable* stuff and claiming you're crazy, withdrawing to create anxiety, etc.

Using isolation as a control device.

Control Freak.

Disproportionate feelings far too early into the relationship.

Verbal or physical abuse, plus the threat of violence.

Blaming drugs & alcohol for abuse.

He likes to be the decision maker and won't entertain anything that you suggest.

Sneaky invalidation.

Lies.

Forcing you to perform sexual acts that can be combined with any of the above to coerce you.

2. BREAK UP & CUT TIES

In the chapter *He Keeps a Foothold in Your Life... You Keep Leaving the Door Ajar*, I explained No Contact, which is by far the most effective way of ending ambiguous relationships, as well as dealing with those with guys who don't want to break up, but keep overpromising and underdelivering. There is, of course, your bog standard breakup as well as the Get Out Plan, plus you need to declutter.

HAVE A GET OUT PLAN

For some, if you break up or cut contact now, you'll jerk back. The Get Out Plan is a watered down version of No Contact, that enables you to plan your escape route with a carefully coordinated effort of easing out of the relationship in preparation for breaking up and cutting contact. It gives you an opportunity to reconcile your illusions with reality and prepare yourself, emotionally and figuratively, making it less of a shock to the system.

If you keep going back because you don't handle the short-term pain and sense of rejection plus you make no real preparations to help you, the Get Out Plan helps to validate your decision to end things and make you accountable for making your life better.

You should only do this if you 1) keep falling off the wagon with the same person, 2) are in a casual arrangement, or 3) are in an abusive relationship.

There are two glaring questions that you need to ask of yourself before starting:

1) Do I want to break up or am I buying time to remain invested?

2) How much worse do I need to be treated or how much more drama do I want to engage in before it's *enough*?

If you're not sure if you want to break up, this may not be for you. If you're sure, but you know it's not going to be easy to do, whether it's because you know you'll be suckered in, there are things to sort out (could be financial, for instance), or because he's a persistent bugger who will up the ante when you cut him off, the Get Out Plan *can* help you. But be careful of being sucked into more drama or being mistreated even more. There *has* to be a cut-off point.

Set a deadline. Not a faux one. Make it challenging but obtainable – not so short you panic and reschedule, not so long it's a joke. No longer than 6 months away though and preferably 1-3

Or, choose The Next Big Thing. Setting a date may be tricky so go with The Next Big (Shitty) Thing that happens. Only thing is that it could happen tomorrow.

Tell someone trustworthy. Secrecy is isolating; sharing sanity checks your decisions and helps your accountability.

Begin slowly breaking habits – this is the key. Gradually change things to help you withdraw and gain objectivity that lets you see him and your situation in a more realistic light. By the time you end it, the cold turkey is not going to be as bad as combined with wrenching yourself out of habits. What does this involve?

- **Stop responding to every contact.** Gradually reduce, don't respond to contact after 10pm – leave it till the following day. *Don't* tell him that you're reducing contact! Line him up for the reduced contact by feeding him a story about your increased workload. Also make him wait a bit longer for replies to texts or emails.

- **Stop engaging, stop explaining.** He may pick fights if he senses a shift. Note this could speed up the breakup. Anything you'd normally get upset about – don't. Sit on your hands, tape your mouth, whatever, but bite your tongue and play nice.

- **Stop agreeing to every meeting he suggests**. Make plans when he's likely to expect you to be available. It's liberating to decline to get together. Don't agree to every invitation. Basically reduce the amount of time you spend with him.

Don't let sex blind you. By seeing him less, there's less opportunity to be seduced.

Be careful of alcohol. If getting tipsy or drunk fuels some of your drama or passion, cut back so that you don't get derailed.

Pay more attention to his actions. Also listen attentively, and observe the changes in your own behaviour around him that are resulting from the change in dynamics. If it helps, keep a *Feelings Diary,* which is basically noting your moods and the shifts in them and what triggers them. It's great for identifying your triggers and also what he's doing to impact you emotionally.

Seek professional help. If you're concerned about how you or he will cope, especially if he's abusive, get external support to help you make the transition and keep you safe.

Get a life. Create your own life with meaning and embrace family and friends, or take part in activities that help you to meet new people. When you end things, you'll feel like an entity as opposed to feeling empty because he's not with you anymore.

You may find that you break up or start NC before reaching your deadline because the great thing about withdrawing is that you see them as they are, but you also recognise how much better you feel by not being drawn into the cycle.

'TRADITIONAL' BREAKUP

Unless he's dangerous, everyone deserves a 'traditional' breakup (obviously on the proviso that you have a relationship to break up from) which is where you say that you want to end things, you very likely tell them why, you agree to go your separate ways, and in theory, beyond the first few weeks where there may be some sorting out of the de-merging of one another's lives, you both respect and accept the decision to end. Some tips though:

Casual relationships make breakups very ambiguous. It may simply mean ending contact. Especially if he was tapping you up for a shag, an ego stroke, etc., don't lose any sleep over it.

It's important to word the breakup carefully. Anything that's code amber and red behaviour, you can simply say that it doesn't work for you. Don't imply or state that things would be different if only he'd changed XYZ, because it invites him to claim he can change.

Don't play games. Only break up to end things.

Do set a period of time where you won't contact each other initially – note that if he doesn't respect this, it's not because he's crazy about you, but that he doesn't respect basic boundaries.

Do it calmly – breaking up in hot temper gives way to one or both of you thinking you can apologise later.

Don't take responsibility for stuff that you don't need to.

Don't guilt with "You made me..." and "If it weren't for you..."

Avoid assassinating his character and telling him all about himself.

Avoid re-entering into an old discussion and basically revisiting the past – it implies there's room for negotiation. You've had the whole relationship to discuss the issues.

Be decisive and firm, especially because Mr Unavailable relies on your indecision and chases when out of control.

DECLUTTERING TIPS

It's imperative that you release a lot of the negativity hanging around and stop providing access to those who, quite frankly, don't deserve it. You need to face forwards not backwards.

Either delete all exes' numbers or replace with better names such as 'Do not answer', 'Looking for a shag', 'Dipstick', 'Assclown', etc.

Do delete exes you haven't heard from in more than 6 months.

De-friend from Facebook (and other social media) any exes who you're not actually friends with, brief encounters, and dates.

If you have feelings for more than one ex, choose *one* to stay in touch with and cut off the rest.

Box up anything of genuine sentimental value and return the rest by post (if recent) or give away to charity.

Rearrange your furniture if the layout reminds you too much of him.

Block email of any and all guys who randomly get in touch to collect attention or to tap you up for a shag.

If you're being pestered by an ex, change your number or put it on voicemail and get a cheap pay as you go for friends and family.

If you have any mutual friends, do ask that they not share personal information about you to him and try to avoid asking about him.

Loosen the ties with your ex's family – it's great that his mother liked you but the relationship is over now.

If the friendships aren't genuine with your mutual ties, cut 'em loose.

3. KNOW YOUR LIMITS!

Boundaries are awareness of what you will and won't accept. Acting as self-protection and warning system combined, you use the knowledge of what you're uncomfortable with and standard norms of unhealthy behaviour to prevent you from living outside of your values and doing things that cause you pain. Teaching people how to treat you and what to expect, boundaries also impose *limits*, not just on others but also upon you. They communicate that you're uncomfortable; that you need to stop, look, and listen; or that you're in danger and need to take measures that may include distancing yourself or opting out. When they're crossed, you're receiving feedback that affects your perception of them and/or a situation, plus it's also telling you something important about yourself.

If you imagine that every single one of us on this planet has our own invisible electric fence – these are our boundaries.

It may seem confrontational, scary, arrogant, or whatever spin you want to put on it, to have boundaries, but they're a fundamental part of human interaction, which is based on communicating acceptance and rejection of what is and isn't acceptable. Silence, saying one thing and doing another, giving them another chance in the hope that they'll see it as an opportunity to prove themselves – all *communicate* that you've accepted the boundary-crossing behaviour, even if you *haven't*. Not accepting it and setting limits communicates that you have standards and value yourself.

DEFINE AND ESTABLISH BOUNDARIES

It's imperative if you want to experience real change and be available for a healthy relationship that you define and stick to your boundaries. Without them, any 'ole Mr Unavailable can come into your life, show you a good time, say all the right things, and then treat you in a 'less than' manner.

Think about the various experiences you've had and compare them with your vision of a healthier relationship. What *aren't* you prepared to accept? What do you dislike and find disturbing when they're present in a relationship? What makes you uncomfortable and causes you to feel disrespected. **Be specific, because vagueness makes for very easy letting up on the maintaining of boundaries.** Example: Must not be attached to anyone, mustn't shut down my needs and feelings. **Write out a list of major NO-NOs** – you should be able to come up with at *least* 5-10 (number them). Anything less is like a free-for-all. Be careful of excessively long lists – you're looking to identify your limits, not everything that irritates.

As a hint, anything code amber and red should be automatic boundaries, but aside from these, you need to listen to yourself and register what makes you truly uncomfortable and has you living outside of your values. What you've listed are now your boundary zones – if he tests or busts these boundaries, take it as a code red to parachute and jump the hell out. These things are *unacceptable* and experiencing them signals that you need to take action – not a long-winded discussion or trying to change them; walk away.

The true test of your boundaries is what you do with them. By accepting, you set a tone that makes it incredibly difficult to come back at a later date and reject it. Vetoing the behaviour, he has two choices – respect your wishes or walk away. You'll soon discover if you're with a disrespectful person – if they stay, they'll test it again or try something else. You haven't got time or energy to be repeatedly swatting off a boundary buster – a decent person in knowing that you find something unacceptable *doesn't* keep doing it.

He's not irreplaceable so don't act like he is. Anyone who will bust or test your boundaries just isn't that special.

Boundaries are for you, not for others. If you're fighting them, it's like fighting the right to have some self-respect. Make boundaries part of your natural habitat so they become second nature. Recognise that *everyone* has boundaries, even *Mr Unavailable*, hence why he blows hot and cold. And remember, if you allow someone to cross boundaries that are code amber and/or red on your list, it's a green light to cross others. You're not access all areas. You're just not that desperate.

LISTEN TO YOURSELF

One of the biggest lessons that I've learned is that we are more than capable of working out whether the relationship we're in is a good one or a bad one. In our quest for answers, we put the focus on the guy in the scenario as if his answer solves everything, but we need to turn things back to ourselves. When we're in unhealthy relationships with Mr Unavailables, our own mind and body are telling us that things aren't right, we just don't pay any attention! We really need to not only heed the warning signs such as red flags, but we also need to heed our own warning signs where our body, mind and senses scream, "ABORT, ABORT, ABORT Mission!"

Do you feel agitated a lot of the time?

Do you feel uneasy or anxious? If you're the paranoid sort then this may be a difficult thing to figure out...

Do you get a nagging sensation in your stomach which is often mistaken for the flutters of love, but is your body's way of saying stop messing with this fool?

Do you go so far as to have stomach or headaches that seem to mysteriously materialise when you're with him or after he's left? (This could be a medical condition although obviously look out for stress aggravating things...)

What about sudden onset of headaches straight after sex each time? (This is a possible indicator, but it may actually be that you have a medical condition!)

Do you feel listless or fatigued since you've taken up with this guy?

Has your self-esteem taken a knock?

Do you find yourself constantly trying to please, even though you're never rewarded with a proper relationship for your efforts?

Do you spend your time feeling constantly worried?

Are you crying a lot? Secret tears on your own? Constantly telling yourself not to cry and fighting back the tears and the feeling?

Even though you think you're happy and in love, when you're with him do you feel underlying sadness, which can often be caused by the ambiguity?

Are you suddenly a lot more stressed at work, even though your workload hasn't changed?

Do you either stop talking about yourself and him under the pretext of wanting to keep things private, or find yourself having to justify your own interest in him or his behaviour constantly?

Do you have conversations with yourself where you make excuses for him and explain away his behaviour?

Do you find yourself hearing what he's said and then searching relentlessly for something in what he's said to reassure your position in The Justifying Zone?

There are lots of things that can happen when you're in a situation that just isn't right for you and it's up to you to listen to your gut, not what a little cajoling voice or many orgasms are telling you. Often we always knew what the outcome would be; we just failed to listen to our gut, our intuition. The key is to learn to trust yourself, believe in your gut and what your body is telling you. Enough experience with Mr Unavailables should give us some judgement skills. Being in a good, healthy relationship doesn't feel bad.

4. UNDERSTAND YOUR PATTERN

Now that you have your boundaries outlined, it's time to explore what's been making you tick in your relationships by looking at your past. Unless you have an exceptionally good memory, I suggest you start with significant boyfriends and then move on to the memorable dates. The more you can remember the better, and make sure you go right back to the very beginning. Either photocopy the questions or grab the PDF online where you can then print it out.

This is a big exercise and requires time and effort. I suggest you make it a priority if you really want to do the important groundwork of getting in tune with yourself. Start the exercise and do a bit each day – it only requires short answers so you can certainly spend 20-30 minutes a day to work through it. While some unpleasant memories may get dragged up, remember that this is about gaining understanding, eventually getting closure, and moving on. You won't know how to go forward if you don't understand why you're here in the first place and how to avoid falling into the same trap.

See your past laid out in front of you.

Put a rational view on relationships that you may not have examined for a lengthy period of time.

Acknowledge your different experiences, including the part you had to play in them.

Be real and confront your truths.

Begin tracing the origins of your relationship habits.

Tips: Use a highlighter to mark anything that repeats itself across partners. A number of the things you discover here will help you in other parts of this chapter.

For significant relationships:

How did you meet? If there are similarities among the first-time meetings, it will highlight where you need to be self-aware and/or broaden your horizons.

_____

_____

_____

Who pursued who? Were you interested? You might identify passive interest, or that you like to be chased a lot, or that you chase when you know they're not interested.

_____

_____

_____

How long was it since you had broken up from your previous relationship? Were you over your ex? Also note how long he'd been out of his previous relationship. Identify if you have a pattern of starting relationships too quickly or when you're not over an ex.

_____

_____

_____

How did you feel when you first met? (Disinterested, excited, horny, etc.). You may pick up on a pattern of Fast Forwarding, ignoring your own feelings, or attraction being based on illusions.

_____

_____

_____

_____

_____

When did he start blowing hot and cold? How did you react? Note if it reminds you of a previous incident.

_____

_____

_____

Any excess baggage (i.e. girlfriend, wife, separated, ex lurking)**?**

_____

_____

_____

What were the 3 most positive things about him? This identifies whether you value superficial aspects of him, or whether you even have shared values, or even value things that don't exist.

_____

_____

_____

_____

What were the 3 most negative things about him? These will be strong indicators of where you don't share similar values and where your relationship wasn't working.

._____

_____

_____

_____

Choose up to 10 words to describe how you felt during the relationship. Try to choose the most consistent feelings. *This* is how you truly felt.

_____

_____

_____

Choose up to 10 words to describe the relationship. Comparing to your other relationships will help you identify what you regard as 'normal' or 'attractive'.

_____

_____

_____

When did you break up? Who initiated it? If you didn't stay broken up, who initiated the contact?

_____

_____

_____

_____

If you could explain in one sentence why the relationship didn't work and why you broke up, what would you say?

_____

_____

_____

_____

Now, bearing in mind that you compiled a list of boundaries, note the numbers of the boundaries that he broke (e.g. 2, 4, 8)

_____

_____

_____

For significant dates:

How and where did you meet?

_____

_____

_____

Who pursued who? Were you interested?

_____

_____

_____

What was your first impression? This gives some insight into what you tend to focus on initially and what attracts you.

_____

_____

_____

How many dates did you have?

_____

_____

If you slept together or had some sort of sexual contact beyond kissing, how many dates did you go on before this happened?

_____

_____

_____

Why did you stop dating?

_____

_____

_____

What danger signals (if any) do you recognise now that you may have missed at the time?

_____

_____

_____

If you could sum up why you both stopped in one sentence, what would you say?

_____

_____

_____
_____
_____
_____

Now, bearing in mind that you compiled a list of boundaries, note any boundaries that he broke.

_____
_____
_____

Miscellaneous

Do you have a One Great Love?

_____
_____
_____

How many times have you believed you've found 'The One'?

_____
_____

In hindsight, now that you're out of the relationships, how many of your 'The Ones' do you still think were 'The One'?

_____
_____
_____

When was the first instance of having your heart broken? Are you over them?

_____
_____

Do you remember who you lost your virginity to? Do you feel positively or negatively about the experience?

_____

_____

_____

5. ADDRESS YOUR BELIEFS

Many of us are going through life unconscious of what we believe and why, and we're not challenging these beliefs to see if they're valid. We're assuming that if we're being dealt crappy cards by life, in line with what we believe, then what we believe is true, even though we're actually inadvertently helping to create those circumstances ourselves. It's time for you to uncover how you _really_ feel because whatever you do believe, you can address it and transform it.

Remember that a **belief** is something that you hold to be true. You may be treating beliefs that you hold as if they're 'true', but they're not actually true in the wider sense. Whatever it is you do believe, you act in line with this so if you want the self-fulfilling prophecy to stop, you've got to believe something different and _act_ like it. What you believe is very much rooted in what you feel your capabilities are in that context so:

Negative beliefs are about not having any confidence in your capabilities so you'll underrate yourself.

Unrealistic beliefs are about overestimating your capabilities. Prime example: believing that you can love and fix someone into changing.

Thinking that you can't, won't, mustn't, shouldn't, couldn't, wouldn't, etc., be or do something is based on what you perceive your capabilities to be in that context – all this does is create limiting beliefs.

Your beliefs all feed into the **sticking point** – not believing you're capable or good enough means you become afraid of truly being vulnerable and genuinely risking being different for long enough for it to make an actual difference. You often give up too easily on the changing and feel *stuck*.

Example: *I don't believe that relationships work out* **can equal** *I don't believe that I'm capable of having a relationship that can work out,* **which can stem from** *My own parents were not capable of having a healthy relationship* **and** *I don't believe that I'm capable* **can lead into** *My father left us so there must have been something wrong with me if he didn't stay* **can lead to** *Men are unreliable and leave* **can lead to** *I'm afraid of being left and afraid of relying on somebody* **can stem from** *He didn't love us enough to stay* **can lead to** *I'm not lovable enough* **can lead to** *I don't think I'm worthy of a healthy relationship* **and can keep leading and leading until you get back to square one, which is** *relationships don't work.*

There are a few beliefs that you hold that allow you to keep telling the same story to yourself over and over – what are they? I have a free detailed workbook called *Get Out Of Stuck* available from **www.getoutofstuck.com**. For a quick exercise that can be very revealing:

Write down 3-5 positive (if you have them) and negative/unrealistic beliefs about 'you', 'relationships', and 'life'. If you have a lot of casual relationships, I suggest doing a separate list for 'sex'. Take each one and ask:

1. Is this true? Is it true some of the time or all of the time? Under what circumstances is it true?

2. Is the belief false for *other* people? If so, it's only true of your circumstance, which can change.

3. Are you trying to be responsible for other people's actions? Are you trying to control others with your beliefs?

4. Most importantly, has holding on to your belief and living it yielded *positive* medium to long-term results? If not, why are you holding on to the belief?

Example: *I believe that love is about having the power to change someone.*

1. Not really. I've heard stories about people changing for others, leaving their wives, etc., but, equally, I've heard plenty of stories where they haven't. I just want to be the exception. I think it is true when someone truly loves someone but then again I think it's actually only true when they really want that change for themselves *anyway* and would do it regardless.

2. Yes.

3. Yes – I'm making his failure to not do what he needs to be a better person a reflection of me, but they're his changes to make.

4. NO. He changes for a short time and then reverts. In fact I've never been able to change any of the men I'm with so I don't know why I continue. I thought it was because I'm not good enough.

TRANSFORM YOUR BELIEFS

There are more detailed instructions in the Get Out of Stuck workbook, but this quick exercise helps you turn unhealthy and unrealistic beliefs on their head into positive, healthier beliefs.

1) Take a belief. 2) Write out in plain English what it means. Basically make it plain speaking. If it's a general statement, add your accountability by attributing the meaning to you. 3) Write down the opposite meaning. 4) Is the opposite more realistic or negative? If not, translate it again, this time to something more positive and realistic. 5) Sanity check the positive belief against the original negative belief. A good way of sanity checking is to ask yourself: Has experiencing the negative belief in effect, yielded positive results? 6) Affirm the more positive belief by expanding it. 7) What can you do to help you make your belief a reality?

1) If I have sex it's because we have an emotional connection. 2) Having sex with someone means an emotional connection. I assume that an emotional connection exists if I choose to have sex because I think that one begets the other. 3) Having sex is not an automatic result of an existing sexual connection nor does it automatically create one. 4) More realistic. 5) I've assumed that I have an emotional connection with men I've slept with and then assumed a greater relationship than

actually existed. 6) I recognise that there's a difference between the two connections. 7) I'm going to go slower and either sleep with someone with a large degree of certainty that a relationship actually does exist or be prepared to deal with the emotional consequences if it doesn't. What I won't do is assume I'm entitled to a relationship because of sex.

The only reason to hold on to a belief is because you experience positive medium and long-term results, *or* it helps you to have healthy boundaries so that you can treat you well. It's of no benefit for me to believe that the world is an unsafe place full of people who seek to abuse but it *is* of benefit for me to believe that while there are plenty of decent people, there are also some shady folk, which means I should be street smart, self-aware, and not *knowingly* put myself in situations that could cause me harm. I don't leave money hanging out of my back pocket, or walk the streets alone late at night in the dark.

Likewise, it's of no benefit to you to believe that the world is full of assholes who break your heart – it's not, but there are men (and women) that do this. The answer isn't to close yourself off to love; it's to have boundaries and walk away from anything that's unhealthy and get a more positive view of relationships. People from all sorts of backgrounds find love every day – so can you! I certainly did! I've had people say to me, "Natalie, how can I ever believe I can have a healthy relationship when my parents split up when I was young, my dad drank too much, my mother and I had a terrible relationship, one partner cheated on me, I've treated myself poorly and I just have one bad relationship after another?" If I can move past all of that, so can you...

6. DISCOVER YOUR VALUES

Values are your firmly held beliefs about what makes you a person of value and also what you see as valuable in others. As they're based on your experiences in life, they'll impact everything, from who you're attracted to, your political leanings, your tastes, things you do in your spare time or have interests in, your religious and social interactions, where you want to live, what you're passionate about, and more. They work in tandem with your *boundaries,* so if you have one, you have the other. Where you have little or no boundaries, your values will still exist, but are likely to be focused on more superficial, insubstantial things that don't make a positive impact on your life. You'll find that you're not living congruently with who you profess to be and what you profess to want.

Values (and boundaries) allow you to know what's good and bad, and right and wrong, about life, both in terms of morals and how you feel about everything around you. You have two types of values, much like businesses have two types of costs (fixed and variable).

Your **core (primary) values** stay in place for very long periods of time and tend to endure even when other aspects of your life change. These represent what you cannot do without and will make you absolutely uncomfortable and acting out of step with yourself if you don't respect them. Very important and tied to your belief system, if you improve your self-esteem, your values may shift to accommodate your new beliefs; likewise, if your self-esteem takes a knock, your belief system can change as a result.

'Variable' (secondary) values change as you go through life. These grow with you and reflect where your position is at a particular time. They include hobbies, interests, some personality traits and qualities, and for the most part, superficial stuff that are nice to have, but not absolutely necessary. If you value something that doesn't actually help the relationship prosper it's a secondary value that's overshadowing a primary value that isn't being met in the relationship. Primary values come *first* and secondary values only take on any real meaning *after*.

Everything in relationships is contextual, so you've got to see the big picture and ensure that those things that you're focusing on and praising to high heaven are actually in context – if what you value in him doesn't do anything *for you*, it doesn't mean jack.

TEST YOUR VALUES

A great way of discovering whether something is a primary or secondary value is to take something that you value and believe exists in your relationship and put it with something that's missing.

Example: If you believe in monogamy and commitment, and he doesn't, it doesn't matter that he's successful, attractive, shares your hobbies and interests, makes you laugh, and is respected by his peers.

Also compare your values with his: If you value intimacy and companionship, and he values his solitude, doing things his way, and consistently doing things that exclude you and make you feel anything but intimate or a companion, you're *incompatible*. The closer you get, the further he'll move away. Even if he likes a 'little' intimacy, he only wants it when he wants it, which may be infrequently. If you cannot manage on this (and why should you), it's not going to work. If he sabotages closeness, it won't work.

And compare the values you say that you have with the things that you look for in a relationship:

If you say that you value love, care, trust, and respect, but you chase guys for passion, attraction, chemistry, sex, and excitement, you'll likely end up with a fun-loving, great lay who looks good and makes your heart skip, but treats you like a casual partner and has no desire to be in a committed relationship. Fact.

You should also ask yourself: **What secondary values will be clouded out if my primary values are being met?**

If they're not being clouded out and reduced in importance, you should be worried, because you're ignoring things that are fundamentally important to you being happy in your relationships and with yourself. Either that... or it's time to have an honest conversation with yourself and question whether your primary values are actually what you say they are. I come across many people who don't realise that they've made their secondary values their *primaries*. Doing this will put you in insubstantial relationships with conflicts of interest.

Think about what you value and ask yourself why you value it. Look at the values you expect a partner to have – do you embody them? If not, why not? You can get a list of values from the website (see resources section), including *marriage, health, ambition, success, loyalty, monogamy, spontaneity, family, and sex.*

Interesting questions to ask: Why do I value money? Why do I value appearance? Why do I value success? Why do I value passion?

What do you believe these things will do for the relationship or for you? What's the flipside to the value?

Classic examples: The flipside to valuing appearance is that you're highly likely to be involved with superficial partners who don't value more substantial things about you. The flipside of valuing success is that if someone prioritises it, they may be totally focused on work and uninterested in a relationship or having a family.

Dig deep and get honest – it will open your eyes because you may be still trying to justify his unavailability to yourself (some of you just love flogging that donkey till it collapses) and if you've moved on and met a 'nice guy' who you claim you have nothing in common with and are busting his balls for not being like your ex, you may actually be completely missing the good things by being too busy worrying about inconsequential stuff. Use the knowledge to focus your energies in the right direction – on you and moving on.

7. OWN YOUR POWER

There's no faster way to lose your power than to pander to someone who only does things on their terms, adapt to suit every partner, bust up your boundaries, and put it all on them to 'do the right thing'. Nobody can steal power that you don't hand over so you've got to arrive into your relationships personally secure and remain an equal. The moment that you start feeling helpless, out of control, like you can't do anything to change and improve a situation, feel valuable, or make a positive contribution, is the time for you to re-evaluate your position and, likely, get the hell out. You and *only* you are responsible for you. Waiting around for the 'right guy', for everything else to change, for validation, and the whole kit and caboodle erodes your personal power. Your life can, and should, be good without everyone and everything else having to chip in and do it for you.

You've spent too much time trying to influence others by trying to control the uncontrollable and *believing* you've had greater influence than you've had by believing that you're responsible for what others are and do. You've also delegated authority to others to determine your value and 'make' you – that's like screwing yourself over repeatedly. Your **personal power** arises from the ability to influence your own life by being a person of action, believing in your capabilities, trusting yourself (self-esteem), and ultimately being the authority on you. Loving yourself unconditionally, having boundaries, and acting upon them is you *owning your power*. Fallback Girls are either **being helpless** or **thinking (obsessing) about being helpless.**

Being helpless is about resigning yourself to him and whatever's on offer because he's charmed his way back in. Rather than be forced to acknowledge, make a decision and take action, it seems infinitely easier to be helpless and leave it in his hands.

Thinking (obsessing) about being helpless is about expending lots of mental energy envisioning situations and imagining what you will (or won't) say or do, with the fantasy normally resulting in you falling into his arms, or into the sack with him. This tends to take place after a breakup or argument, and is particularly prevalent with Fallback Girls who have instigated the No Contact Rule and cut contact.

Whether you recognise it or not, you have power. The problem is that you're not utilising it, either because you're afraid of how much responsibility being in charge of your own life means – a responsibility, I might add, that you have whether you choose to use it or not – or because you've never had good self-esteem, so believing that you have power is a foreign concept. Fact is, even if you don't think you have any emotional backbone left, you can grow it. Every action you take that serves your welfare, living in line with your values, having boundaries and standards, and being personally secure enough to not sell yourself short, ultimately builds up your emotional backbone.

PAINTING YOURSELF INTO A CORNER?

If it feels like you have no options, you're putting all your power elsewhere by using negative beliefs to paint yourself into a corner.

You create a situation where it doesn't matter whether it's a truth or a lie, they're still telling you the same thing.

Example: You believe you're not good enough. He says that he has problems that he needs to attend to before he can focus on a relationship. This may be true and, ultimately, he's telling you that he doesn't believe that he's capable of being available to you and building a new relationship *and* dealing with these issues. If you believe him you'll think, "If I were good enough, he'd hold on to me *and* sort out his problems," and if you *don't*, you'll think, "He doesn't want to be with me and he lied because I'm not good enough."

Whether it's the truth or a lie, the one thing that remains constant is the negative belief.

Remember, making yourself responsible for someone else's actions is attempting to control the uncontrollable and blaming yourself unnecessarily. It also removes trust. What matters is what you *do* with information. What you should hear is, "He's not available, time for me to hit the road." Take it as truth – at least he's being honest because there are plenty who would try to throw you crumbs and distance themselves – yep, Mr Unavailable.

314

WHAT CAN YOU DO?

If the answer to this is nothing, or basically there *is* something, but you don't want to, it means that you've rendered yourself helpless and your relationship's not going to work anyway. If you've already explored other options such as twisting yourself into a pretzel trying to accommodate him and talking till you're blue in the face, you must focus on *action*. Insanity would be to do anything you've already done, so, if the option that's left is opting out, take it and regain your power. If you're focusing on changes that he can make, focus on changes that you're avoiding making in your own life and put your energy there first. When you've done that, he won't be so attractive any longer.

SHIFTING YOUR MENTALITY: GET OUT OF YOUR COMFORT ZONE

AND GET UNCOMFORTABLE

Remember that being a Fallback Girl is comfortable, which means that if you genuinely want to have positive change in your life, you're going to have to get *un*comfortable. People prefer being in their comfort zone, even when they're struggling and unhappy, because it's what they know. This is why, when we start No Contact, we can often end up falling off the wagon because we hate the unknown and the insecurity of not being surrounded by a heap of drama.

Accept that it's not going to be easy, it's uncomfortable, but that you're about to learn to love you more than you love drama or him. You have to drum it into yourself that sometimes you're going to have to feel some short-term pain for some medium and long-term gain.

Breakups hurt, not necessarily because it's a signal that you're destined to be together forever in Care Bears Land, but because it's a breakup! Don't get it confused!

Something broke and it hurts but that doesn't make it right to go back! Some of us are conditioned to think that if we love someone and the relationship is right, the breakup will hurt. Breakups hurt because something bad happened, your feelings are hurt, you're vulnerable, you're insecure, you're feeling low and you're sometimes heavily emotionally invested and dependent in inappropriate relationships! But the pain of breaking up does pass... if you make a concerted effort to pick up the pieces, get on with your life, and move forward. If you spend a lot of time thinking about and imagining scenarios, you've basically cut contact or decided to change your habits, but are effectively continuing the relationship...in your imagination.

YOU'VE GOT TO STOP REACTING

You have a choice. Jump in the hot seat and take charge of your life. The more you do this, the more your self-confidence builds and, as you see positive results and realise that you aren't miserable and embroiled in drama, the more your happiness increases. You can now make the choice between *reacting* and *stepping back*.

CUT BACK ON YOUR GIVING QUOTA

People take advantage of those who do not know how to give. I'm not asking you to turn into Scrooge, but giving to people doesn't feel bad and there is no need to hurl yourself on the altar as a sacrificial lamb for your friends, family, and love interests.

ADD 'NO' TO YOUR VOCABULARY

Many of you are afraid of saying no in case there are repercussions and you find yourself alone or unloved. So, instead, you run around saying yes to everything and hating yourself and resenting them. If you're a YES Girl, it's good to say NO sometimes. It's as simple as, for every three things you say yes to, say no to one thing. Most of the time, people who are afraid of saying NO actually have no idea how people will react, because they never had a chance to find out.

DON'T SECOND-GUESS PEOPLE

Sometimes you're saying YES because you're imagining a result of saying NO that you don't want to deal with. What you're imagining may actually be incorrect, but you wouldn't know this unless you actually ventured to use a word that billions of people use every day.

You'll also find that when you start saying NO, people will be forced to adjust how they behave around you, or get lost. If a person can only be around you if they're receiving 'goods' that originate from taking advantage or even abusing you, they need to *step*. Don't train people to expect excessively from you as they come to expect it as the bare basics.

8. USE DATING AS A DISCOVERY PHASE

If you've wound up in a relationship where you've felt 'surprised', 'frustrated', or even 'duped' by their true character, it's because you completely missed the opportunity to do the due diligence to ascertain whether he was an appropriate partner for a relationship. In fact, you may have assumed that you were in a relationship *because* you were dating, sleeping together, etc. It's time for you to look at dating completely differently.

Dating is a discovery phase. You're finding out the facts about dates and seeing how much you 'click' and whether you have enough going on to forge a relationship. This period is for you to learn about one another... even if what you learn is bad news.

The facts about people are the truth of their actions, what you discover about their values, how you're treated, and how you feel. A relationship is the next step after dating and is increased commitment, so, as a result, before you commit you need to ensure that you have something healthy to commit to and that who you're broaching a relationship with is who they actually are. If you spend too much time naked, playing ping-pong, and chatting shit, rather than getting to know one another and making a link between what you hear, what you perceive, and what you actually see, you don't get to really *know* someone.

Never, ever, ever, ever, *ever* pass 3 dates or have sexual contact without asking and having a definitive answer to "Do you have a girlfriend/ wife/separated wife?"

Note that it's likely that asking this question will yield further important information, such as, *"No, I broke up with my ex a little while ago,"* or *"No, but I'm separated..."* Don't listen to bullshit excuses as to why he's concealed this information or barefaced lied. *"I really liked you and I couldn't bear the thought of not being around you!"* is pathetic, not flattering!

You shouldn't feel that you're in a position to make a commitment off the back of physical and sexual chemistry, or common interests. People date for all sorts of reasons, as you've discovered, and while you can *ask* or read it on a dating profile, the proof is in how both of you conduct yourselves, because there's no point in expecting a relationship if you're both behaving *casually* and *ambiguously*. It's also important to note that if one or both of you are sleeping with or dating other people, the discovery phase is far trickier, as it's difficult to be genuinely focused on ascertaining what's important for you to proceed.

DUE DILIGENCE

Open your eyes on the first meeting/date:

Is all his attention focused on you? Never trust a man who's skittish or whose eyes wander around the room. If he doesn't have the time to focus on chatting you up, how will he have time for the relationship?

Is he being too forward? Is he too intense? This is Fast Forwarding, not flattering.

Does he answer questions directly? Steer clear of shifty people. Unless you're asking something highly personal or inappropriate, stonewalling at this stage screams *walls*.

Does he seem nervous when his phone rings? Most honest people I know aren't edgy about their phone ringing unless they're skiving from work or trying to avoid someone.

How does he give you his details? Is he very specific about when to call? If yes, it's likely an early indicator of unavailability. Unless he's somewhere like a conference, or a workplace that's difficult to take calls, most people aren't *that* specific.

Does he mention a recent breakup or an ever-present ex? Back away right now! Also – steer clear of deep talk about exes and be cautious if he's slagging her off.

Before you so much as think about saying "I love you", picturing you both being married, or assume that you have a right to a relationship, ensure you can answer the following:

Do we share core (primary) values? If you don't know, it means you need to redirect some of your energy in this direction.

Am I able to have boundaries? If you've dismissed discomfort, or have been making excuses, this is a strong indicator of issues.

Have I experienced any code amber or red behaviour?

Do they behave with basic care, trust, and respect? You may not be at the 'love' stage, but that should never stop someone from behaving like a decent human being with integrity.

Have I learned information about them that has me hoping they'll change? This is code amber for you to address the issue instead of being a Florence – nothing is so great about a person that it warrants you investing in a pet project during the dating phase.

Am I struggling to feel good about myself and treat me with love, care, trust, and respect? If YES, this is at best code amber for you to address your own behaviour and anything else affecting it.

Do I like how they treat others? Ultimately what matters most is how they treat you, but, equally, if they treat others poorly beware.

Is what I believe I want from this relationship based on who they are, not who I'd like them to be or thought they were?

Do we share common sexual values? If you've had sex, it should be because it's what you want, not what you thought you *had* to do to keep 'the game in play'.

Do you feel safe with them? If you're afraid or even sense danger, don't proceed.

Essentials to know by the end of date 3:

This is to get some early indications of his motivations. Find out by asking stuff like:

How long have you been dating?

How do you find this dating stuff? When did you start dating? (Likely to be able to find out when he came out of his last relationship). What's the funniest or scariest date you've been on?

Find out how 'busy' he is. Do you work long hours? What type of stuff do you do in your free time? Have you been single for long?

You need to find out if he's dating several people. If he is, you need to find out if it's something that he plans to continue and for how long. Have you been going on many dates? Are you dating other people? Have you got a lot on this week? (Could also be used for finding out how busy he is.)

Make sure you know if he lives in the same town or city as you. You'd be surprised how many women find themselves dating a guy who actually lives miles away and is inadvertently drawing them into a long-distance relationship!

Where do you live? Where are you based most of the time? Do you travel a lot? (For some guys, they travel so much with work that it might as well be long distance!)

You need to know: is there any 'baggage' that could impact the success and viability of the relationship.

Is he separated? If yes, when did the separation start? Have divorce proceedings started? Are they actually getting a divorce? Are they "having a break"? What's the purpose of the separation? Some people separate to divorce and some people separate to get some head space, or they have intentions to divorce but it doesn't happen for one reason or another because they don't want the finality. Get a sense of what the separation is like. "Gosh, that must be difficult. How have you been coping so far?" It's not about interrogation. Empathise and he'll open up.

Does he have kids? Not a problem for someone to have kids, but what is his relationship with them and their mother like? When he tells you, does he display anger, aggression, or become tense?

Does he have an ex-girlfriend who's pregnant? You just never know! I wouldn't ask, but it's the type of thing that he should mention if you ask him whether he has kids…

A QUICK GUIDE TO THE FIRST 3 MONTHS

By the end of 3 months you should be speaking most days.

The bulk of the communication needs to be face to face or on the phone. Text messages, email, Post-Its, Instant Messenger are gap fillers, not staples.

You should be able to see each other more than once a week.

You've seen each other's homes.

You're exclusive and it's not because you've decided it on your own, but because you have both said so –- never assume commitment or a relationship unless it's explicitly stated and you're in agreement about what that means.

No girlfriends, very visible exes, wives, or booty calls allowed.

You talk about the future, whether it's one week or one month away.

You don't just see each other for a shag.

You should have met at least one his friends and not just the one you met him with the first time.

He's not afraid to invite you anywhere.

You've met up during daylight hours.

Acknowledge any and all code amber and reds alerts – when you don't is when they're at their most dangerous.

Your boundaries are intact. Note that having a disagreement isn't busting boundaries. Having a disagreement and excessive temper, name-calling, etc., is.

9. ASK QUESTIONS & MAKE DECISIONS

During the discovery phase of dating you've seen that you'll be gleaning information through conversations and direct questions, but there are other times that you need to ask questions in your relationship and *process* the feedback so that you can *act* upon it. It's critical to your wellbeing and success of future relationships that you're assertive about finding out what you need to know before you get too heavily invested or querying anything that causes discomfort.

Questioning techniques are often talked about in sales but some of the principles are applicable to dating.

Open questions are more indirect, but pave the way to them opening up. If in doubt, as a general rule of thumb, open questions start with Who, What, When, Where, How, and Why.

Closed questions are direct and can sometimes appear to be confrontational, and too many is akin to a job interview or interrogation. They're ideal for nailing down information and gaining clarification as they tend to require a yes, no, or more definitive response. Example: *Do you have a girlfriend?*

Tone is key and it's important that you relax and ask the question in an open, friendly, conversational manner. General conversation will enable you to glean information but it's important for you to be listening. Don't get hijacked by potential and your overactive imagination!

THE DEBIT AND CREDIT TRUST SYSTEM

The ability to trust yourself and trust others actually comes from having your eyes and ears open and processing feedback. When you're honest with yourself, you'll feel and acknowledge the impact and what it means in relation to you and your relationship. You'll experience your feelings, acknowledge any discomfort or what new information you have learned as a result of the impact, and take a view on it, and, ultimately, do something, whether that means proactively addressing any code amber concerns, or inflating your opt out parachute and jumping from a code red concern.

To work the feedback into your trust system and use it, you need to use the positive and negative 'impacts' to adjust your levels of trust. To make dating into a positive experience, regardless of whether you go on one date, several, or progress into a relationship, **you need to start out with a reasonable level of trust.** As you don't know them, trust starts with *you,* which means you need to have confidence and faith in yourself and in others and, ultimately, be capable of acting in your best interests.

Using your basic level of trust that you walk around with (let's call it 70%) and using your relationship smarts (boundaries, self-awareness, etc.), you increase or decrease (credit or debit) your level of trust based on actual feedback from your relationship – i.e. their actions, how you feel, etc. If you have *less* trust than when you started out, it means it's time to take a parachute and jump. If you keep experiencing positive, healthy relationship behaviour, increase.

MAKE DECISIONS!

A critical part of commitment is being able to *make* decisions and part of the problem as a Fallback Girl is that you've been *thinking* you're making decisions or avoiding them. But if you make decisions and then quickly start second-guessing, ruminating, and even backtracking, it means you haven't made a decision.

A decision has three key parts – a resolution or conclusion, consideration, and answering questions. If you're experiencing problems with making decisions and commitment within your relationships it's because you make decisions, either without consideration, or without consideration of the appropriate things. Or you don't reach a conclusion or make a resolution, but you still go ahead with the decision.

As part of your commitment to you and learning how to commit in relationships, you must learn to make decisions, which means considering information, processing it (instead of ruminating till the end of time), and drawing a conclusion or deciding on a resolution. A decision faces you with a choice between making changes or taking the path of least resistance. I suggest you opt for the former and whatever you do, be 100% behind it, instead of on the fence or backtracking, because, you know what? You hated Mr Unavailable doing it to you.

Questions to ask yourself:

Have you considered all important factors?

Is there code amber or red behaviour?

Are you both being genuinely honest about the reasons that your relationship floundered or broke? What have you both agreed is the way to move forward and resolve? What have you both individually done to address your own parts? If you haven't got a concrete plan of resolution and think you can love away the problems, think again.

What is your gut telling you?

What are you ignoring? Bring it out into the open and acknowledge it. Remember, a decision based on denial is a BS decision.

Is your decision based on short-term factors or have you considered medium and long-term implications? Unless your decision is about something that's only for a short time, you must weight the decision with the medium and long-term factors.

Have you been here before? Is your decision rooted in insanity – doing the same thing and expecting different results?

List the reasons (in full) why you're going back (or leaving), so you can validate your decision.

What are you afraid of? Make sure you differentiate between internal fears from within and external fears exacerbated by real external factors that you should be considering.

10. BE ACCOUNTABLE & RESPONSIBLE

Even if you were available, he wouldn't be. It takes two people with both feet in for a relationship to work. You can't make all of the contribution, hence you can't assume all of the blame and responsibility, not least because it invalidates any healthy basis for a relationship. You're just not that powerful, so stop wondering what you could have done differently for him to behave better. The only thing you could have done is not be with him in the first place.

Accountability is looking at a situation with clearer, more distanced, eyes and being able to evaluate what's happened and why so that you can be objective enough to recognise your part.

Take the focus off him and bring it back to you. If you've been in a relationship with clear signs that he wasn't available, what about this relationship was *working* for you?

Blame is looking at the situation and either placing yourself at the eye of the storm and deciding that everything is your fault, or blaming the other person and refusing to recognise your part in things.

Accountability is positive. Blame is very negative.

In unavailable relationships, you take the blame for the wrong things and avoid accountability for what you should. Having healthier self-esteem plus changing your perceptions and expectations of relationships stops this unnecessary 'work' and let's you be involved with men who actually want to contribute as opposed to work against a committed relationship. It's time to look at the bigger picture.

In **Blaming Mode,** you might say, "We broke up because I was angry with him for letting me down and not turning up. Maybe if I hadn't been so upset, we'd still be together."

In **Accountability Mode,** you'd instead say, "We did break up when I expressed how upset I was about him disappointing me by failing to turn up, however, it was a culmination of repeated poor behaviour. The truth is, if I'm willing to be with someone who hasn't actually properly left his wife, is inconsistent, disappears, calls

325

me 'needy', and continuously devalues me with his behaviour, I'm contributing by setting the status quo and *accepting* it. I need to look at why I'm willing to accept this behaviour and the first thing I recognise is that I end up in relationships like this because I don't believe I'm good enough." *That,* ladies, is acknowledgement and accountability.

Instead of blaming yourself and wondering what you can be and do to be good enough for someone who's clearly not good for you, address the real issue of why you don't believe you're good enough and work on that first. You're not responsible for his actions and shouldn't absorb the blame, but you must be accountable for persisting in the relationship and persisting in your relationship choices. You are the only person responsible for why you're enabling someone else's poor behaviour.

GET LOGICAL

Every time you go into blame mode you need to take that reason (write it down) and rationally turn it on its head.

1. Isolate the incident that you're blaming yourself for. Did you have a part to play in that?

2. Put the incident in the context of the bigger picture. Can you acknowledge what the wider issues in the relationship were?

3. Be accountable for what that means about you and your behaviour. What does the bigger picture mean to your contribution and choices? What were the choices that you made? List them and use them as a foundation for recognising what *doesn't* work for you.

This is a positive use for the energy spent thinking about these guys, because, ultimately, blaming yourself and imagining different relationship scenarios achieves nothing.

ELEVATOR PITCH YOUR RELATIONSHIP

The more layers of self-blame and the more you focus on his issues, the further away you get from the real issues. While there's the granular detail of your relationship, it's vital to summarise why your relationship isn't working/didn't work out in 30 seconds to a minute. You may even find it beneficial to also shrink it to a one-liner – like a business tagline. Cut through the fluff and get to the truth, so that you can identify issues as well as validate the true reasons why it cannot or didn't work so you can begin to heal and move forward. It's also less dramatic because the truth is, we get used to telling 'our story'. Remember if you're excusing and justifying, you're denying.

Example: My name's Natalie and I used to have a Mr Unavailable habit. Pretty much all of my relationships didn't work out because I specialised in trying to have relationships and get commitment from reluctant or pain in the arse sources. I broke up with a cheating control freak, another controlling drunk, another with a truth allergy, another with mama issues who tried tapping my friends up for threesomes, another controller with a girlfriend he wouldn't break up with, and the list goes on. They were all unavailable. I was the common denominator to all of my relationships so I had to address my own availability.

11. GET ON THE BULLSHIT DIET

The purpose of the **Bullshit Diet** is to cleanse yourself of a habit of denying, rationalising, and minimising so that you can be authentic. No more deceiving yourself on an ongoing basis – you're going to keep dishonesty to an absolute minimum in your life. No living in La La Land, no fur coat of denial and rose-tinted glasses, no pretending to be and feel things that you don't and certainly no normalising of poor behaviour. This allows you to have more self-control and to actually be in control of a life that you actually already have control over. This means:

Not being a short-term thinker.

Being conscious in your actions and feelings instead of just floating around, or acting like you're helpless and someone else is in control of your wheel.

Not allowing your mind to ramble, stew, and fester in negativity.

Arresting negative thoughts and self talk – instead of letting the 'noise' continue, interrupt, and either focus your mind on a new task or rationally talk through your thought process.

No making excuses for others and certainly no making excuses for their excuses.

Keep assumptions to an absolute minimum. Sanity check and crosscheck them against real behaviour and readjust.

No blind expectations.

No claiming you're doing things that cause pain out of 'love'.

Feet firmly in reality – no getting hijacked by your imagination.

Quit Betting On Potential and living in the past.

Focus your mind and efforts on the present so that you can work out if what's happening _now_ actually works for you.

When you let your 'story' take hold in your head or even verbally – you know that stuff you tell yourself to legitimise your beliefs, your actions, and your self-fulfilling prophecy – **follow up with 'Is that/ this actually true?'**

SPEAK YOUR TRUTH

At the core of any emotional, mental, physical, or spiritual energy you spend burning up about a relationship that's not working in the way that you want to and may be causing you to be, at best, taken advantage of, and at worst abused, you must have this as your central question:

Why, if someone is behaving in this manner, are you still there putting up with it or claiming that you'll never get over them?

If it's about a general situation: why, if this situation is not working for me, am I still complaining instead of doing something about it?

Basically – what's in it for you? If you're honest about your choices, why you do something, etc., you're a hell of a lot closer to finding a solution that you can live with, whether that's opting out, taking measures to distance and protect yourself, or doing something to improve the situation and get your power back. Until you eliminate or minimise the BS, it'll feel like you're 'helpless' or that it's the fault of someone else. Take the focus off your distractions and bring it back to you.

12. GET A LIFE & FEEL GOOD

Let me say it for you loud and clear – men aren't the centre of the universe and a relationship is *one* aspect of your life but not *all* of it and, even when you do meet someone, they're not there to fill up your life for you and give it meaning. When you have a life, and by that I mean a balanced, rounded life where you derive 'nourishment' from a variety of sources, primarily *yourself*, no jackass can come along and put a crater-sized hole in it. It's time to value you, your life, and your time.

You've spent a hell of a lot more time being unavailable and catering to poor relationship habits than you've been available. Until you exceed the amount of time you were unavailable with time spent genuinely busting a gut at being truly available, loving yourself, and getting on with your own life, you haven't tried hard enough.

I've read *thousands* of emails and comments from Fallback Girls – you've put an exceptional amount of energy into limited relationships and limited men. Now, admittedly, it was what you felt was less 'risky' energy because you weren't as 'vulnerable', but you've been doing hard time in an orange jumpsuit in the fields outside Unavailable Prison. *Enough.*

You know where you've been, so for you to continue the insanity and go back there would be deluding yourself and laziness. There's life beyond Mr Unavailable. Pick yourself up and start taking care of you.

Shake up your routine. Before you email me and tell me how you've done 'everything' to meet a man, what have you been doing with your time? The overwhelming majority of emails I receive from women claiming they've tried really hard are from those who literally go to work, supermarket, gym, home and those who do all that and surf dating sites and frequent the same bars.

What did you enjoy *before* **you took up a vocation in winning Mr Unavailable?** Often your hopes, dreams, and interests are forgotten. I frequently hear from women who've started painting again, gone travelling for 6 months, joined **Meetup.com**, started new businesses, or are clocking up a serious number of marathons.

Put your misguided energy into something worthwhile. So many readers do stuff like volunteering or have become active members of their community where their fixing ways are put to good use.

Go to networking events and use sites like Meetup.com to find like-minded people or discover new places and interests.

Learn to do things on your own. I've been to many cafes, museums, and even the cinema on my own. It's liberating.

Holiday on your own. In 2003, I went to Antigua for a week because no one else was in a position to go with me. Right up there as one of the best things I ever did.

Reconnect with your friends. If you've neglected your friends, apologise and resolve to make more of an effort.

Join a support group or go to therapy.

Challenge yourself to do something new once a week or fortnight.

Take a confidence course or any other course that will help you build personal skills.

Attend work events. While I do caution about peeing on your own doorstep, I know a hell of a lot of people who have met at work events. Stay away from the playas and office tarts.

Take a short course or get those additional qualifications you've been talking about.

Start applying for new jobs instead of complaining about work and staying in a job you hate.

Go for a run or join the gym and pound the treadmill. It's great for focusing the mind.

Be friendly and approachable – talk to people just for the hell of it. New friendships can be forged – it's how I met two of my best friends outside my ex-fiancés old building. Every cloud…

Go to markets, or what my friends calls 'antiquing'. Aside from being great fun and a boon for your home, you can meet all sorts of people.

Accept invitations from friends, even if you're feeling lazy or you think it'll be shite – that's how I met 'the boyf'!

Don't speak negatively about yourself. When you think or speak a negative thought about yourself, cut it off, change it and replace it with something positive.

Remind yourself of the good that you do. You're doing good, positive things all the time – you just fail to look at them.

Prayer can be a great source of peace and an opportunity to be more spiritually connected to yourself.

Define your goals. Establishing what you want in the short, medium and long term not only gives you something to aspire to, but also lets you know if you're living the life that reflects these goals and values. Tackle anything that can be done immediately as you'll feel a sense of achievement that will spur you on. Don't try to do everything all at once as you'll become overwhelmed, and make sure you've clearly defined what falls into 'short term' (0-6 months), 'medium term' (6-36 months), and 'long term' (3 years+). You can adjust the time periods to suit but make sure that you have a timeline.

Jot down every negative belief about yourself and counteract each one with the positive reality or what you can do to change it.

Affirmations. This isn't everyone's cup of tea, but they're great for reminding you of your worth. Write on a Post-It and stick it on the mirror (or even write in lipstick): "I am a woman of great value and deserve only the best" and say it out loud, with meaning, when you're in front of the mirror at least ten times. If you want to stop calling a guy, use that same Post-It and tape it to the phone with a message: "I know my worth and I'm not calling him." Whatever it is, find something positive and empowering to say about you. Another favourite: "I'm not that woman anymore!"

You should be able to do the things you do regardless of your relationship status. Many people treat being single as the tedious time that they pass between relationships, rather than a fabulous 'Me Time' opportunity. Never make the responsibility of your happiness or the ability to do what you want to do, somebody else's. Get on with enjoying your life now! If you've been stalling plans because you're holding out for Mr Unavailable, take action! Many of my readers have gone off travelling or moved on and lo and behold, their exes are still the same!

Place pictures and possessions around you that remind you of happier times and get rid of negative clutter. If you're clinging to things, that were given to you by exes for instance, which keep you thinking about the past, give them to charity.

Remove yourself from negative situations that may reinforce bad perceptions of yourself. Focus on allowing yourself to be happy.

Focus on the good things about you. None of us like everything about our bodies and selves, but get to know you and your attributes. If you don't like and love you, how do you expect to be around people that will? Stand naked in front of the mirror and look at yourself objectively and find something that you're happy with, because, trust me, if you can stand there in front of the mirror and hate what you see, you and your relationships will continue to flounder.

Dress happier than you feel. Often when we feel down, we stop making an effort, which subconsciously sends more messages that we're not worthy. Treat yourself well.

Put on a happy song. A bit of MJ, Proud Mary by Tina Turner, Just Fine by Mary J Blige, Beyoncé, and Basement Jaxx give me an instant happiness boost. Create a CD or playlist. Much as I love Adele, hers are like albums of a Fallback Girl!

Even when you begin dating, *don't* be one of those people who ditches everything and everyone. Keep doing the things you enjoy!

MAKE THIS EXPERIENCE COUNT

Throughout your relationship history, you've had breakups and no doubt felt that whatever happened had galvanised change, only for you to find yourself in a similar or worse situation all over again. However, when you truly experience self-defining, life-galvanising change as a result of a relationship, you've experienced an *Epiphany Relationship*. The sudden clarity and insight into that particular relationship, yourself, your actions, and potentially all of your experiences, creates a defining moment where you can't escape the truth and it becomes life-changing.

You may have had a series of *Epiphany Moments*, which, while they didn't immediately change your actions, left enough of an imprint that, when combined with others, ultimately helped galvanise the change when you were 'ready'.

I could've saved myself a whole lot of headache if my Epiphany Moments had crystallised into something more solid, but they didn't have enough self-esteem behind them to power real change. However, when I was ready to pay attention to myself and walk back through my past, the Epiphany Moments were the evidence that backed up the certainty that my judgement of my Epiphany Relationship was correct.

I'm lucky that I had my Epiphany Relationship, but not everybody gets the trigger. The key with Epiphany Relationships is that it makes it difficult for you to return back to your old behaviours and patterns because, from then on, you're doing it consciously and that means that the responsibility for your outcome lands squarely with you.

This book is supposed to give you many Epiphany Moments to connect with and help you have your Epiphany Relationship because there really is no escaping the truth of these relationships.

This is the beginning of a better relationship with you. The payoff is that a great deal of positivity can come from something that could otherwise be perceived as negative. I may not give a monkey's about the Mr Unavailable who gave me my epiphany, but, thanks to his inability to connect, I've been set free from the constraints that I had put myself in and I am definitely far happier now... without him!

Relationships serve to teach us about ourselves and until we sit up, pay attention, and heed the lessons, the same relationship will still keep coming back like Michael Myers in Halloween. Take your lessons, cry your tears, rage, howl, feel sad, but take your truths and *learn* from your past experiences, so that you can make a difference to your present and future and quit the insanity.

Make this experience count. Exceed your own expectations and don't sell yourself short anymore. *Believe* that you deserve better and, even if you're feeling a little bruised or even battered by your experiences right now, *act* like you deserve better by closing the door on that part of your life (firmly) and looking forward. When it rains at Unavailable Towers in the future and he flicks through his mental Rolodex and thinks of you, when he acts upon his short-term instinct, he'll discover that you're not that woman *any more*.

YOU HAVE TO FORGIVE

Forgiveness is not about them; it is about you. This is about freeing up some of your emotional baggage quota and making peace with you and your experiences. You don't even need to involve a third party; you just need to commit to accepting what's happened, letting go, and moving on rather than keeping yourself in shackles. This is beyond your most recent relationship; this is about forgiving yourself for the past and not being so hard on yourself for making a few (or a lot of) mistakes. You are human!

You cannot put your hand into your past and change it. Sitting there thinking about things that you could have said or done differently doesn't change anything. Attempting to control the uncontrollable will only leave you feeling deflated and powerless.

By holding onto the anger, the hurt, the frustration, the obsessing, and the chastising of yourself, the only person it's affecting is you. The scary thing is that all the tears you've been shedding, the obsessing about if and when he'll return, if and when he'll leave her, and if and when he'll change, plus the obsessing over everything he said and did, and anything else that's fuelling your misery – he's *not* affected by it.

All of the giving yourself a hard time and not forgiving yourself is doing the damage to you and it effectively means that this negative energy is wasted.

You're never going to have all the answers about the hows and whys of what has happened and where you are at. You can't think or rationalise out a situation to 100%.

This is the time to take a leap of faith on YOU.

Forgiveness is much like closure – sometimes it helps if the person in question is around, or even asks for it, but, most of the time, they make no difference and you can get there on your own. If you don't forgive, you'll just be struggling with you and it will permeate other areas of your life including future relationships.

When I felt angry and ill at ease, there I was thinking that I just felt irritated by the breakup, but, in actual fact, I had to work through forgiving my parents, ex-boyfriends, and all sorts! It was great to offload the burden.

In the end it wasn't really about forgiving them; by not making all of their actions about me, being rational, and strictly owning my own stuff, I forgave *myself*.

I realised that I couldn't change what had happened in the past, and with people who were still in my life, I could work on having a different relationship free of resentment, but it also gave me an opportunity to redefine what my life and relationships meant to me.

The odd thing is that as soon as I realised that I had been holding in some hurt, I started to feel free. It's acknowledging that you've been hurt... and letting them go. They have no power then. Some things you'll have to accept that it is what it is. You don't get all the answers and all you can do is commit to remembering what *your* part in things was, and avoid repeating the same behaviour.

DON'T PRIORITISE THEIR 'SORRY'

When people badger you to accept their apology or to forgive them, they're trying to force you to move forward on their beat. What they're really saying is, "Hurry the fuck up and accept my apology/forgive me so that I can stop feeling bad about myself." Fact is, when you forgive yourself, the rest takes care of itself. If they're that sorry, let it reflect in their actions elsewhere.

FORGIVENESS CREEPS UP ON YOU

If you focus on trying to forgive right now, it becomes this stressful experience. Focus on treating yourself well, grieving any losses and addressing any habits that have held you back and that is forgiveness in itself because you give you another shot.

REMEMBER WHAT FORGIVENESS ISN'T

You can accept what's happened without agreeing with or condoning someone's behaviour.

STOP BERATING YOURSELF

Keep telling yourself that you forgive and love you. Unfortunately... shit happens... and you have to remember that unconditional love is about loving you irrespective of external things taking place around you. Say it in the mirror and recognise that you're human, you love, you want to be loved, and sometimes you make mistakes.

SAYING IT OUT LOUD SOMETIMES HELPS

A lot of the time we are having an internal dialogue with ourselves that goes round and round. Say your stuff out loud while you're on your own and then say, "I forgive you." You may surprise yourself by meaning it or you'll quickly identify what your sticking point of anger or hurt is.

COMMIT TO LETTING GO

Don't just say you forgive, *act* like you forgive. Get up and start living. At some point, it's got to be 'bygones'. Give yourself a period of time to grieve, rage, feel anger, be down in the dumps, but ensure you commit to a date where you say 'bygones' and make that your time to focus on pushing forward instead of holding onto pain and anger, living in hurt.

USE THE UNSENT LETTER

This is pivotal to working through your feelings and organising your thoughts so that you can free yourself. http://bit.ly/unsent

DON'T FORGET WHAT'S HAPPENED, BUT DON'T CLING TO THE HURT

This is the key. Remember your lessons learned and your contribution and use those to empower yourself. Don't hold on to the negative feelings and cling to the breakup.

SOME FINAL WORDS...

If you're still wondering if he'll change, I purposefully didn't write about it. Mr Unavailable won't change with you, a Fallback Girl, at his side. You won't change either. If you change and truly love yourself, I'd question whether you really want him now that you're being the best that you can be and loving yourself.

Don't look to be the solution to his problem; that's what got you here in the first place! At the end of the day, you're learning a lot about yourself and what *you* can do to make *your* life better and change your relationship habits, but it would serve you well to learn from those mistakes now and in future relationships instead of seeking the path of least resistance and trying to go back to an old relationship to try out your new knowledge.

I'm going to validate you because even though I know that I could tell you a thousand things to try to bolster you and make you feel good (I hope you've found a lot in this book), in being a Fallback Girl, you're likely to have found me because you were looking for a solution to solve the problem – him. I want you to validate you; in fact you have to validate you, but I want to reinforce why it's important that you got to this point.

What I want to validate in you is the niggling signals that you've been having for a long time. You were not wrong to be concerned, you were not wrong to feel wary, and you have got to stop wondering what you did to cause him to be this way.

Mr Unavailable was Mr Unavailable before you met him, when you were with him, and he's highly likely to stay that way long after you've gone. You didn't 'do' something to trigger his distance; you can't win! If you'd played it cool and been uninterested, he'd have chased you down. If you'd thrown yourself at him, he'd have run away. You can't change him and I want you to stop blaming yourself for crap behaviour from the waifs and strays of the dating world and I want you to start living like someone who deserves to be here, who loves herself, and has positive love to give that is reflected from the great person within.

You're not wrong for wanting to love or to be loved, it's just that, in not giving it to yourself, you've made mistakes en route and drawn in inappropriate people. Take comfort in the fact that you know more now than you've ever known, and do something with your knowledge. Live the best you that you can be. Stop making excuses for these men. Stop sticking at their side pushing your love on them and hoping they'll finally give in and love you, and take a chance on you. Love you.

Love, Natalie (NML)

RESOURCES

Download all of the resources I refer to in the book, including the Unsent Letter Guide, Get Out of Stuck beliefs guide and worksheets, and the list of core values.

www.baggagereclaim.co.uk/mrunavailableresources

Baggage Reclaim

Packed full of dating, relationship and self-esteem commentary, advice, tips and tools, including my podcast, The Baggage Reclaim Sessions

www.baggagereclaim.com

www.baggagereclaim.co.uk/podcast

Find me:

instagram.com/natlue

facebook.com/baggagereclaim

twitter.com/baggagereclaim

twitter.com/nataliemlue

ACKNOWLEDGEMENTS

When I found myself unable to sleep on a Sunday morning in early June 2004, little did I realise that having a flash of inspiration, booting up my laptop and 'dial-up' internet, and then starting a blog, would change my life forever. I am eternally grateful for every single person who has laughed, cried, raged, and shared with me ever since then and I feel very blessed to have an enormous extended family online who have literally watched me grow into myself and championed me.

While I write the posts on Baggage Reclaim, thousands of women, *and* some men, take it to a new level, growing the conversation, spreading the word, and inspiring me to keep translating interpersonal relationships and cutting through the fluff. Thanks to everyone who comments, tweets, is fiercely loyal on my Facebook page, emails, and of course, buys my books. I love that I've bumped into readers randomly in the street in New York who hugged me and cried, that Becky in Orlando opened her home to me and stuffed me full of wine and hummus, that my girl Laura and Cosmo her cute dog had me stay for a week in New York, and that even though so many of you are in pain from your dodgy experiences, you share your stories and we often end up falling around laughing at the madness of it all.

To all the exes and the first Mr Unavailable in my life, my father, thanks for the experiences and the inspiration. You taught me that I needed to love myself, and that, actually, I could do it all on my own.

Thanks to my first daughter's godmother Nicki Nac, who egged me on to write this more than three years ago, Kate, my brilliant, patient assistant, Louise, aka Lulabird, my super-stylish designer, lovely Dee my proofreader, fabulous friends like Cate 'Bitchbuzz' Sevilla and Gigi 'Mums Rock' Eligoloff for teas, dirty laughing and support sessions, Kat and Lu for staying ever cool and easing my workload, Becks, Lulu (also godmothers), Twanna 'Funkybrownchick' Hines and

Karen for helping out at workshops, and the many friends, ex-colleagues and random people who have shared their dating and breakup stories with me. I'd also like to give a special thanks to reader 'Runnergirl', who when I was in the deepest depths of rewrite hell inadvertently reignited my mojo twice. To Cathy, Tara, Irene, Pam, Balu, Mich, Becks, Brenda, and Nicki, thanks for letting me cry and laugh on you through various breakups between 1995 and 2005!

To my family, I love you, I am truly blessed. While we're in no danger of being the Brady Bunch, we've come a long way! To my brother, Richie, thank you for 32 years of being able to laugh at the craziness with me! To 'the boyf' – thanks for having the patience of a saint, for your unwavering love and support, and for being the best travel companion I could ever hope to journey through life with along with our two beautiful daughters. Life is good.